Heroku Cloud Application Development

A comprehensive guide to help you build, deploy, and troubleshoot cloud applications seamlessly using Heroku

Anubhav Hanjura

[PACKT]
PUBLISHING

BIRMINGHAM - MUMBAI

Heroku Cloud Application Development

First published: April 2014

Production Reference: 1170414

Published by Packt Publishing Ltd.
Livery Place
35 Livery Street
Birmingham B3 2PB, UK

ISBN 978-1-78355-097-5

www.packtpub.com

Cover Image by Sagar Shiriskar (shiriskar.sagar@gmail.com)

Credits

About the Author

Anubhav Hanjura is a cloud technology enthusiast and a software architect. He specializes in server-side development (C++, C, and Java) for distributed software platforms, and is an avid blog reader. When he is not designing software systems, you can find him collecting books, pondering over puzzles, or bookmarking general trivia. He is a passionate mentor, has authored several white papers, and has also served as a project guide for students on many occasions. He holds a Bachelor's degree in Computer Engineering from NIT, Surat.

I would like to thank my parents, Roshan and Usha, for constantly reminding me of the value of sharing. I would like to thank my teachers and friends for inspiring and believing in me. Last but not the least, I would like to thank my daughter, Edha and my wife, Sheetal for letting me steal their time to write this book.

About the Reviewers

Aki Iskandar is an entrepreneur and software architect. He owns and operates two small software companies—one is a consultancy, specializing in Ruby on Rails and native iOS development, and the other provides an online marketing platform for small companies. This online service has been completely built using Ruby on Rails, and is hosted on the Heroku infrastructure. Aki has launched other subscription-based online services, before the days of cloud computing, claiming that he was spending more time administering the servers (load balancing, databases, replication, web servers, e-mail servers, monitoring, file syncs, and so on) than writing code for the applications. Today, he recommends that his clients take the cloud computing route over self-hosting, with very few exceptions. His favorite cloud provider is Heroku.

Prior to starting his companies, he spent 14 years as a consultant. During that time, he was a consultant for various large companies, including Microsoft, Compuware, Progressive Insurance, Allstate Insurance, KeyBank, Ernst & Young, and Charles Schwab. In his last full-time position, which was almost three years ago, he served as an enterprise architect at PNC Bank (as a core member of PNC's Enterprise Architecture team, and he also co-chaired their Architecture Review Board). You can read Aki's blog and learn more about his companies on his personal website www.iskandar.us. He lives with his son, Justin, in the suburbs of Cleveland, Ohio.

Andrea Mostosi is a passionate software developer. In 2003, he started at high school with a single-node LAMP stack and he grew up by adding more languages, components, and nodes. He graduated from Milan and worked for several web-related projects. He is currently working with data, trying to discover information hidden behind huge datasets.

I would like to thank my girlfriend, Khadija, who lovingly supports me in everything I do. I would also like to thank the people I collaborated with, for fun or for work, for everything they taught me. Finally, I'd also like to thank Packt Publishing and its staff for this opportunity to contribute to this project.

www.PacktPub.com

Support files, eBooks, discount offers and more

You might want to visit www.PacktPub.com for support files and downloads related to your book.

Did you know that Packt offers eBook versions of every book published, with PDF and ePub files available? You can upgrade to the eBook version at www.PacktPub.com and as a print book customer, you are entitled to a discount on the eBook copy. Get in touch with us at service@packtpub.com for more details.

At www.PacktPub.com, you can also read a collection of free technical articles, sign up for a range of free newsletters and receive exclusive discounts and offers on Packt books and eBooks.

http://PacktLib.PacktPub.com

Do you need instant solutions to your IT questions? PacktLib is Packt's online digital book library. Here, you can access, read and search across Packt's entire library of books.

Why Subscribe?

- Fully searchable across every book published by Packt
- Copy and paste, print and bookmark content
- On demand and accessible via web browser

Free Access for Packt account holders

If you have an account with Packt at www.PacktPub.com, you can use this to access PacktLib today and view nine entirely free books. Simply use your login credentials for immediate access.

Table of Contents

Preface

Cloud application development is "the new black". With the advent of server virtualization, hardware resources have become cheaper. You can buy hardware on demand and pay only for the time you use it. The next wave of virtualization is that of software virtualization, that is, having the ability to use available software on demand and build your own apps on top of it. Here too, you pay only for what you use and how long you use it. The Heroku **Platform as a Service** (**PaaS**) is a software platform that provides a combination of the underlying operation system resources, language runtime, and supporting software to help you build your own web apps on demand.

This book on Heroku cloud application development is intended to introduce you to the fundamentals of the Heroku Platform as a Service, and help you to understand the rich feature set of the Heroku platform that enables building powerful and scalable web apps. In addition, this book also showcases techniques to deploy and troubleshoot the web apps deployed on Heroku and helps you understand the nuances of the choices you have to make while building apps for the Heroku environment. And that isn't all. You will also be presented with the best practices of using Heroku for developing web apps as well as getting a feel for the advanced aspects of the platform. The book also educates the user on how to securely use the Heroku platform for developing production-ready and high-performance web apps.

In essence, Heroku cloud application development is all about rapid application development for the cloud, (re)using available software add-ons and underlying platform infrastructure to build, deploy, and manage really powerful and scalable web apps.

What this book covers

Chapter 1, Hello Heroku, introduces you to the world of Heroku. It also provides a historical background on how Heroku evolved to what it is today followed by a basic understanding of Heroku's architecture. Finally, it takes you on a test drive to get a firsthand experience with the Heroku cloud platform.

Chapter 2, Inside Heroku, covers the foundational aspects of the Heroku platform. It covers the details of various components of the Heroku architecture, including the Heroku platform stack, the request routing system, the Logplex logging framework, the add-ons, the dyno (process), and the platform API.

Chapter 3, Building Heroku Applications, covers the principles governing building web apps on the Heroku platform. It also illustrates the process of building and configuring web apps besides covering the steps involved in preparing a production-ready app from your code using language-specific buildpacks.

Chapter 4, Deploying Heroku Applications, describes the application deployment process on the Heroku platform. It covers the basics of the Git distributed version control system and illustrates the most common source management operations. It also covers the concept of forking and cloning apps besides ways to optimize your app deployment. It also showcases various aspects of Heroku app release management process through illustrative examples.

Chapter 5, Running Heroku Applications, illustrates the process of running a Heroku cloud app in detail. It covers the Heroku **command-line interface (CLI)** used to perform Heroku operations such as creating or updating apps. It also explains how to use the Foreman tool to troubleshoot the apps locally before deploying them to the Heroku cloud. Additionally, it describes the key features of the Heroku dashboard related to running Heroku apps.

Chapter 6, Putting It All Together, sums up the learning about the foundations of the Heroku platform and illustrates the whole process of building, deploying, and managing Heroku apps using Java on the Eclipse app development platform.

Chapter 7, Heroku Best Practices, covers the details of best practices that developers can use not only to deploy but also to write apps on the cloud using the Cloud 9 cloud-based integrated development environment. This chapter also provides detailed coverage of best practices such as setting up the Heroku PostgreSQL database, configuring DNS for your web app, and optimizing applications to use higher end services provided by the Heroku platform.

Chapter 8, *Heroku Security*, covers two parts of the Heroku security puzzle—the developer communication with the Heroku platform and securing the Heroku platform from malicious attacks from the external world.

Chapter 9, *Troubleshooting Heroku Applications*, describes the techniques developers can employ to fix problems encountered while developing apps for the Heroku platform. It covers how to troubleshoot application downtimes, isolates HTTP request issues, debugs database problems, and runs production checks to warn you about potential issues. It also shows how you can use the maintenance windows to gracefully handle app upgrades.

Chapter 10, *Advanced Heroku Usage*, introduces the advanced features of Heroku. It covers the Heroku Labs feature, including Websockets, illustrates the Heroku Platform API through practical examples, and shows how developers can do social coding using the collaborative features of the Heroku dashboard.

What you need for this book

The software needed for this book includes the Heroku toolbelt (client) (`https://toolbelt.heroku.com`), Eclipse IDE for EE, the Mozilla Firefox web browser, and the curl tool.

Who this book is for

This book is for application developers who are looking to learn cloud application development using the Heroku platform. Knowledge of Ruby and Java is desirable. Previous knowledge of the Ubuntu OS is helpful though not mandatory.

Conventions

In this book, you will find a number of styles of text that distinguish between different kinds of information. Here are some examples of these styles, and an explanation of their meaning.

Code words in text, database table names, folder names, filenames, file extensions, pathnames, dummy URLs, user input, and Twitter handles are shown as follows: "Use the `ps:scale` command to scale up the web processes."

A block of code is set as follows:

```
#!/bin/sh

cat << EOF
---
addons:
  - heroku-postgresql:dev
default_process_types:
  web: bin/node server.js
EOF
```

Any command-line input or output is written as follows:

```
$ heroku create myapp --buildpack https://github.com/heroku/heroku-
buildpack-mylang
```

New terms and **important words** are shown in bold. Words that you see on the screen, in menus or dialog boxes for example, appear in the text like this: "You can also restart a web application using the **Restart** button on the **Processes** tab of your web app."

> Warnings or important notes appear in a box like this.

> Tips and tricks appear like this.

Reader feedback

Feedback from our readers is always welcome. Let us know what you think about this book—what you liked or may have disliked. Reader feedback is important for us to develop titles that you really get the most out of.

To send us general feedback, simply send an e-mail to feedback@packtpub.com, and mention the book title via the subject of your message.

If there is a topic that you have expertise in and you are interested in either writing or contributing to a book, see our author guide on www.packtpub.com/authors.

Customer support

Now that you are the proud owner of a Packt book, we have a number of things to help you to get the most from your purchase.

Errata

Although we have taken every care to ensure the accuracy of our content, mistakes do happen. If you find a mistake in one of our books—maybe a mistake in the text or the code—we would be grateful if you would report this to us. By doing so, you can save other readers from frustration and help us improve subsequent versions of this book. If you find any errata, please report them by visiting http://www.packtpub.com/submit-errata, selecting your book, clicking on the **errata submission form** link, and entering the details of your errata. Once your errata are verified, your submission will be accepted and the errata will be uploaded on our website, or added to any list of existing errata, under the Errata section of that title. Any existing errata can be viewed by selecting your title from http://www.packtpub.com/support.

Piracy

Piracy of copyright material on the Internet is an ongoing problem across all media. At Packt, we take the protection of our copyright and licenses very seriously. If you come across any illegal copies of our works, in any form, on the Internet, please provide us with the location address or website name immediately so that we can pursue a remedy.

Please contact us at copyright@packtpub.com with a link to the suspected pirated material.

We appreciate your help in protecting our authors, and our ability to bring you valuable content.

Questions

You can contact us at questions@packtpub.com if you are having a problem with any aspect of the book, and we will do our best to address it.

1
Hello Heroku

The recent advances in technology coupled with a demand for cost efficient computing have led to an enormous growth of cloud computing usage in modern day businesses. Users want to optimize their resource usage of the CPU, network, and the memory and pay for only what they use. Virtualization, faster/larger computing power, and high speed network backbones have led to an explosion in the deployment of cloud infrastructure across the world. Along with the underlying infrastructure, many platforms have evolved to support the ability to develop real apps for the cloud environment virtually from anywhere. Additionally, new cloud-based software apps have proliferated so fast that they have replaced the notion of installed software for good.

Today, no developer is untouched by the cloud. In their day to day lives, developers use one or the other form of a cloud service—whether it is an Amazon-hosted virtual machine to do testing or a cloud-based development environment to write code for their business apps. Cloud is everywhere.

In this book, we will undertake the journey to explore a very significant and specific aspect of cloud computing, that is, how to develop web apps on the cloud. We will use the Heroku platform to build robust and scalable web apps and in the process understand different aspects of the Heroku platform.

All aboard? Let us begin the journey. In this chapter, we will:

- Define cloud computing and understand its various components
- Understand what cloud application development is and what its advantages are
- Introduce you to Heroku and trace its history
- Review high level Heroku architecture
- Get acquainted with Heroku's features
- Learn how to install Heroku
- Test drive Heroku

What is cloud computing?

Simply put, cloud computing is a form of computing in which the user accesses any computing resource remotely through a simple client, which in most cases is a web browser. This resource could be a software application or an operating system or remotely located hardware. Cloud computing is a manifestation of the desire to optimize the use of shared computing resources by creating an infrastructure that lets you use the computing power, storage, and network optimally and pay for only what you use.

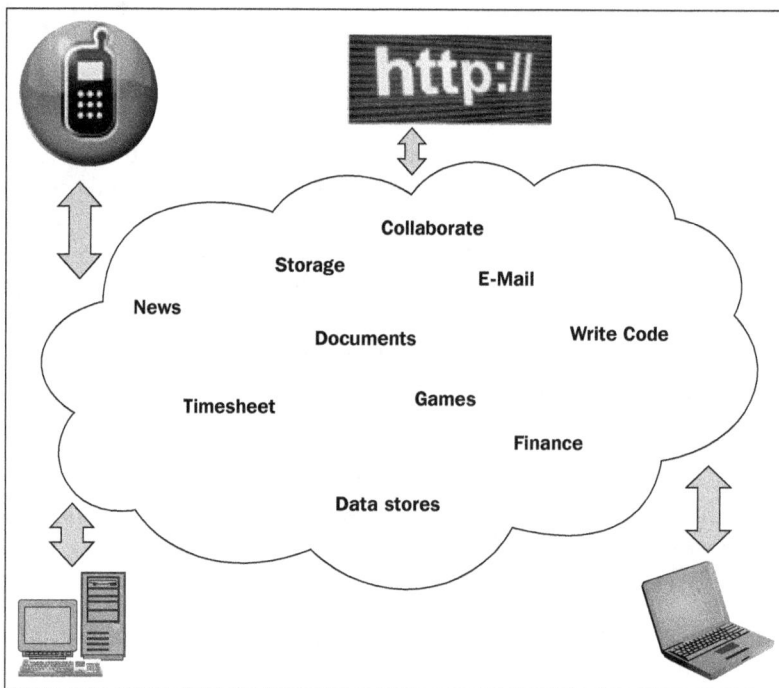

Cloud service models

The services offered by cloud computing are further divided into different service models—**infrastructure as a service (IaaS)**, **platform as a service (PaaS)**, and **software as a service (SaaS)**. This classification is done to segregate the different types of services a user can purchase to meet their business needs in a cloud computing environment.

IaaS is the cloud service model that enables the user provision virtualized hardware resources on demand. Physically, these resources could be spread across multiple data centers, which the service provider maintains. These resources include the virtual storage, network connections, and load balancers for the provisioned hardware resource. The user can use the resource on demand and pay per use. If the user needs more resources, the provider has the ability to automatically scale up the hardware according to the need and vice versa. A good example of an IaaS provider is the **Amazon Web Services** (**AWS**—http://aws.amazon.com). It is the most popular IaaS provider in the cloud. Rackspace (http://www.rackspace.com) is another such example.

PaaS is the cloud service model that provides the tools to build software applications on the cloud. A close analogy would be to look at PaaS as an operating system and middleware of the cloud environment. PaaS provides developers with the underlying platform to use to develop their apps. It takes care to support a specific language or technology that the stack developers want to use. Many PaaS providers also enable on-demand scaling of the underlying computer and storage resources, automatically, to free the cloud user from the job of allocating resources manually. In PaaS, the consumer of the service controls deployment and configuration. The PaaS provider provisions the servers, network, and the computational needs of the software application. The PaaS model also enables a multitenant architecture so that multiple users could use the web application in a secure, scalable, concurrent, and fail-safe manner. Sophisticated PaaS solutions also provide an integrated web application development environment, which facilitates collaborative coding, source control, and deployment. Heroku (http://www.heroku.com) and Google App Engine (http://cloud.google.com/AppEngine) are two examples of successful PaaS platforms.

The SaaS model of the cloud provides software you can consume from the purview of your web browser. There is no need for complex and time consuming installations. Open a browser, point to a URL, and use the app pointed to by the URL. What happens behind the scenes is all hidden from the user. SaaS has evolved considerably in the last decade. Many SaaS providers have made desktop or locally-hosted software obsolete. All you need is a browser and you are all set to use any app to do anything. No headaches of software upgrades, version incompatibility, or software portability. Google's Gmail (http://gmail.com) service is one of the most successful and widely known SaaS implementations. The SaaS component has grown exponentially with companies leveraging the underlying infrastructure and platform to build cloud versions of most of their software product offerings. By 2013, almost every company worth its salt has had a SaaS version of its popular software apps available to online customers.

While PaaS is inherently more stable compared to the SaaS component, PaaS has evolved tremendously in the last few years and provided the developer community with amazing tools to work with and deploy distributed apps in virtually no time. The Heroku PaaS is the subject of this book.

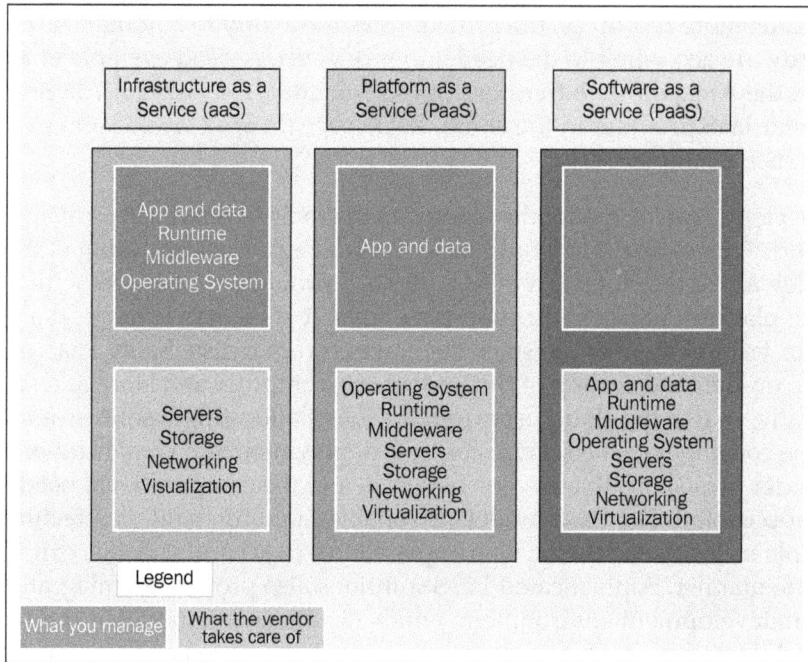

What is cloud application development?

One way of describing cloud application development is the ability to create, build, and deploy your software applications from the web browser. You don't need to install anything on your local machine. All you need is a web browser, Internet connection, and the ability to code. The Cloud9 IDE platform is one such example of a web browser-based cloud application development environment. The Cloud9 IDE development platform lets developers write, build, test, and instantly deploy their web apps from the browser. Once deployed, the developer can access the web app using a web URL.

There is another approach albeit a hybrid one to do cloud application development. In this approach, developers write code on their own machine, use locally installed development tools, build their code locally first, and once tested, they deploy those web apps to the platform service on the cloud. The platform as a service on the cloud builds the code again using a supported build tool and deploys the web app to the relevant server. Later, it returns a web URL to the developer to access the web app.

Key advantages of cloud application development

Developing web apps using the cloud application development model is a boon for all developers. It is the magic wand that developers couldn't have imagined before the advent of cloud computing and cloud-based development platforms. There are several advantages of using cloud application development:

- One of the key advantages of cloud application development is the *no software installation required on local machine* paradigm. An Internet connection, a web browser, and the ability to code are all you need to write web apps. As a developer, you can focus on building your web app functionality in the best way possible without worrying about the code editors, debuggers, or build/deploy tools to use. All these things are not your business anymore. You can just write your code and the rest gets taken care of for you. Even in the hybrid approach, several cloud application development enabling platforms provide you with compatible tools (compatible with tools in the cloud environment) that you can use to build, test, and deploy your apps.

- Another practical advantage of using cloud application development is the fact that you don't need to manage the software, storage, or hardware infrastructure being used. Supporting software (operating systems, development tools, and so on) gets automatically upgraded and new hardware gets provisioned transparently for you; you don't need to worry about compiler versions or third-party libraries you use.

- Cloud application development also means reduced the cost of building and maintaining your web apps. You pay as you go and get billed for only what you use. Developers can optimize their investment by using the right toolset and leveraging the available open source tools to build robust, scalable, and well performing web apps.

- Mobility is a reason, which by itself gives tremendous advantage to developers who want to build apps on the go. When you can develop, change, or deploy web apps from the web browser of your mobile device, it is a powerful notion. You could be sipping coffee in a local coffee shop, responding to a customer request through your mobile device, bringing your servers up/down, adding a new developer to your app, or increasing the memory required for your web app. The possibilities are unlimited.

Introducing Heroku

Heroku (http://www.heroku.com), pronounced her-oh-koo, is one of the leading PaaS providers in the cloud software business, proving itself to be the leading PaaS solution for small and big enterprises alike. With consistent improvement and the philosophy of "convenience" over "configuration", Heroku has become the leading cloud app development platform for developers, having been used by over 40,000 websites till date. The Heroku philosophy is to let developers focus solely on writing web applications and forget about servers. Heroku magically takes care of building, deploying, running, and scaling the application for the developer on demand.

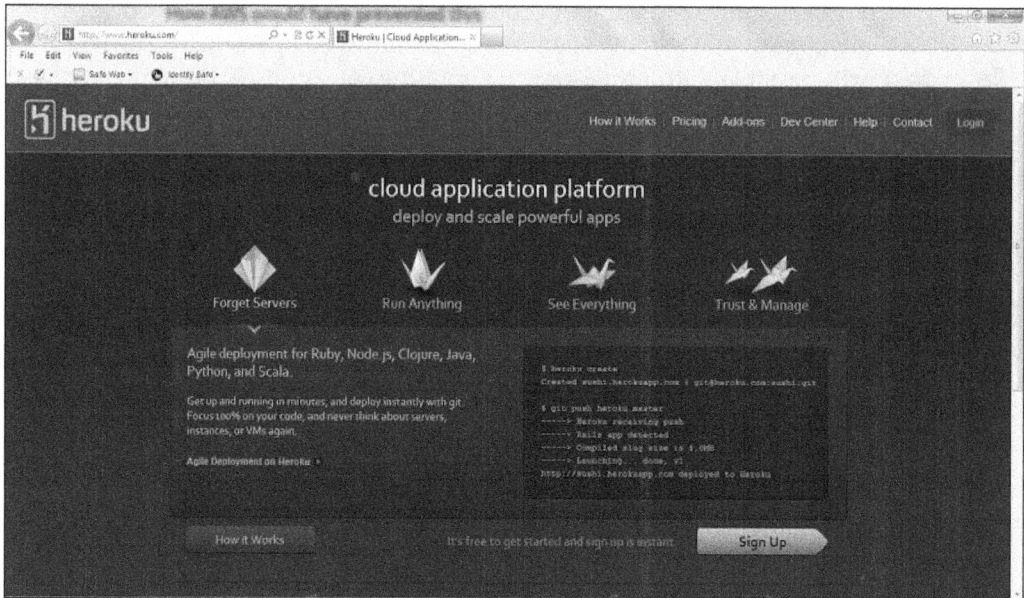

Heroku is a *polyglot* cloud application platform that provides tremendous flexibility in choosing an appropriate programming language to develop web apps. Heroku provides platform support for Ruby, Ruby on Rails, Java, Node.js, Clojure, Scala, Python, and PHP as of early 2013.

Heroku's add-on architecture allows the developers to customize the use of various third-party packages based on the need. You have the flexibility to choose a basic or a premium plan based on the requirement of your website. The developer can supercharge the apps with add-on resources, such as Memcached for caching data or a NoSQL database and create really powerful, feature-rich web apps.

Heroku provides a lot of flexibility in managing your app once you have deployed it. With Heroku, a developer can manage the app using the Heroku command-line tool running on the client machine or the dashboard running on the Heroku infrastructure.

Heroku is highly scalable. It scales transparently as your traffic spikes and it can serve applications with over 10^3 sustained requests per second today.

Heroku Git's focused workflow makes it easy to share code, collaborate with other developers, and deploy code frequently, thereby cutting down on the time it takes the app to reach its users.

Walking down the memory lane

It is very important to understand the history of something to understand how it evolved to its current state. Over the years, the designers of Heroku have made several choices to make Heroku what we see it as today. Heroku has undergone many iterations of evolution. It all started when a few web engineers got together and built a platform as a service that looked very similar to the Unix platform. Developers could build their apps on Ruby and push them to the platform for hosting. All the value added services such as monitoring, logging, or databases were pluggable and easy to use. It was a web developer's dream come true.

The following is a short summary of Heroku's history that walks you through Heroku's evolution over the last several years:

- Heroku was launched in 2007 by James Lindenbaum, Adam Wiggins, and Orion Henry.

- Heroku was a Y-combinator start up and its base increased to over 2,000 apps and users in just the first six months.

- Heroku started with addressing two common issues for web developers: deployment of applications and developer productivity.

- By the end of 2007, Heroku came up with interesting features such as "instantly live" (deployment), "create and edit online" (online source code editing), and "share and collaborate" (code sharing).

- Sometime later in 2008, Heroku was projected as a Rails-based web development framework and lot more focus was put on deployment and scaling of web applications.

- Collaborative code sharing and development through Git paved way for increased interest in Heroku by the developer community. Soon a unified API was part of the Heroku offering.

- During 2009, Heroku came up with Herokugarden — an application bed where the developer could create, deploy, and manage web applications. The API (Heroku commands) to manage web applications was part of this suite. This feature was phased out soon though.

- Heroku also added the concept of "add-ons" — pieces of software (libraries) you could magically add to your web application and use almost on the fly. By the end of 2009, Heroku had almost 20,000 apps running on various platforms including mobiles.

- Heroku was acquired by Salesforce in December 2010.

- In the last few years, among others Heroku has done several important changes to the platform, including bringing in the new Celadon Cedar stack and supporting Java, Clojure, Python, Node.js, and Scala languages. It has also added an advanced support for the Postgres database.

An overview of Heroku's architecture

The Heroku architecture consists of a platform stack comprising of the language runtime, various libraries, the operating system, and the underlying infrastructure to support development of scalable web apps.

The high-level architecture of the Heroku platform is shown as follows:

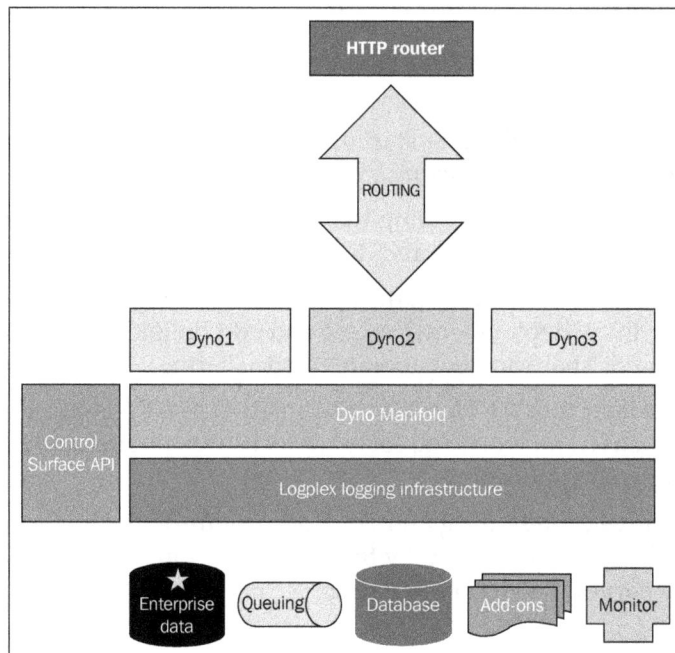

Process management

The **dyno manifold (DM)** is the foundational block for the execution environment on the Heroku platform. It is a distributed, fault-tolerant, and horizontally scalable execution environment for application dynos. It manages the entire diversity of process type instances via the process model in an automated way with zero maintenance cost.

The unit of work in the Heroku platform is called a **dyno**. Dynos are fully-isolated, highly available (virtual) containers running on the dyno manifold.

Dynos receive web requests from routing mesh, connect to application resources such as a database, for example, using environment variables, and write an output to the log message sink called Heroku **Logplex**.

A **process type** defines the template to be used to instantiate a particular process. It is a declaration of a command. The command is executed when a dyno of that process type is started. There are at least two process types available on Heroku — web and worker. An instance of web process type typically handles HTTP client requests. The router directs all the requests to the web process type. The instance of the worker process type is used to execute other tasks such as custom jobs of long running background jobs and queuing tasks. Heroku also provides the flexibility to create additional process type based on specific needs.

A **process** is an instance of a particular process type. The **Procfile** specifies the various process types and how to run them on the Heroku platform.

Logging

Logplex routes log streams originating from various sources, such as application tasks, system components, and backend services into a single output pool. Additional filters can be used to search specific log messages, hence providing flexible logging facilities.

HTTP routing

The requests (dashed vertical lines) for a web resource (for example, web page) are routed to the appropriate web process dyno using the **Routing mesh**. Incoming requests are received by a load balancer that automatically routes HTTP requests to specific dynos through this mesh. The Routing mesh is responsible for determining the location of the application's web dynos within the dyno manifold and forwarding the HTTP request to one of these dynos.

Heroku interfaces

Heroku provides various control surfaces such as process management, routing, logging, scaling, configuration, and deployment for building and operating an application. These are available as a **command-line interface** (CLI), a web-based console, as well as a full REST API. These control surfaces provide the application developer with the flexibility to control various aspects of the application through multiple touch points.

The Heroku feature set

Heroku is a fully featured PaaS that provides a complete stack of "true" PaaS features. The following are some of the core features available in Heroku:

- Heroku runtime features:
    - It enables flexible process control; scalable web and worker (type) processes (called dynos) run from a Procfile.
    - It allows a new process type to be defined such as web or worker type.
    - Process isolation—anything you store on your web process will be isolated from all other web processes.
    - Heroku even lets you run processes during the maintenance mode while serving the application users static page(s).
    - It provides fully functional multiple language support.

- Configuration:
    - Heroku does not use property files or hardcoded configuration variables to read system or application-specific global parameters; instead, it uses configuration variables or environment variables.
    - Heroku prefers convenience over configuration, hence the configuration architecture is intentionally simplistic to use.

- Effective releases:
    - Whenever new code, add-ons, or a configuration is in place, Heroku creates a new release automatically.
    - Heroku provides a rich set of capabilities to manage app releases from creating a release and listing available releases to rolling back to previous releases.

- Logging:
  - ° Heroku's Logplex facility provides you with an aggregated view of your application runtime behavior.
  - ° Heroku also has provisions to filter log records based on a certain source, process, or both.

- Security:
  - ° Heroku provides the ability to set up an SSL endpoint for your application to enable secure communication to your deployed application.
  - ° Heroku also supports SSH keys to enable a secure transfer of developer code to/from the platform.

- Real-time status:
  - ° Through a web URL, Heroku provides its users with an ability to verify the running status of the application(s) on a time-range basis. You can go back in time to check for failures and steps undertaken for their resolution.

- Git-based deployment:
  - ° Heroku uses Git as the primary method to deploy apps. Git is a popular open source code revision control system that enables shared access to a managed source code environment.
  - ° While managing apps for the Heroku platform using Git, a developer can do the following:
    - ° Build and track the app
    - ° Create remote repositories of code
    - ° Deploy the application in multiple environments (development, staging)
    - ° Use other version control systems side by side and Git only for deployment

- Polyglot platform:
  - ° Though Heroku started off being a Ruby-only web application platform, it has evolved over the years and started supporting many other popular programming languages including Java, Node.js, Scala, Clojure, Python, and the Play framework including the latest releases.

- Buildpacks:
    - Heroku's support for a language is enabled by creating a buildpack for that language. A buildpack is a set of scripts required to identify the source code language and provide instructions to build it into executable code. For example, the Ruby (`https://github.com/heroku/heroku-buildpack-ruby`) buildpack is one of the most commonly used buildpacks on Heroku.

- Add-ons:
    - Heroku offers a growing number of add-ons via its add-on provider program. Additional services, such as error tracking, reporting, e-mail services, hosted NoSQL databases, and full-text search among others are available instantly via a few clicks or commands on the Heroku CLI prompt.
    - There is a provision to add and remove add-ons using the Heroku API.

- The Heroku command-line tool (CLI):
    - The Heroku command-line tool is an interface to the Heroku web API. The tools provide an easy to use command-line interface to do things such as creating/renaming apps, running one-off processes, taking backups, and configuring add-ons.
    - This tool is usually installed with the toolbelt program. It also has a plugin architecture that allows developers to extend the functionality of the command as needed.
    - It is purposely kept similar to UNIX shell commands to reduce the learning curve for system administrators or users of the Heroku API.

- A fully featured Platform API
    - The Heroku Platform API is a standard list of functions that allow you to programmatically call the Heroku backend and perform various operations such as creating an app or deleting it. It helps the developer gain complete control of the app.

- Managed, multitenant architecture:
    - Heroku's platform architecture provides a managed process execution environment and a high degree of isolation between running apps, all of which are transparent to the application client.

Let's play Heroku

Now that we have a basic understanding of what Heroku is and what it has to offer for developers planning to build and deploy cloud-based apps, let us take Heroku for a quick test drive. You are going to love it.

Getting ready for the ride – the prerequisites

There are a few prerequisites before you start using Heroku. You need to perform the following steps:

1. Get a Heroku account (`https://www.heroku.com`).

2. Install Heroku toolbelt client (`https://toolbelt.heroku.com/`).

3. Set up SSH for your user account.

   An SSH key is an encrypted token that your machine and your Heroku account share to validate the authenticity of the user invoking a command on the Heroku platform.

In the next part, we will learn the actions required to set up a Heroku client on your local machine.

Signing up

To start using Heroku, you will need to sign up for a Heroku account. The following screenshot shows the sign up page to create a new Heroku account:

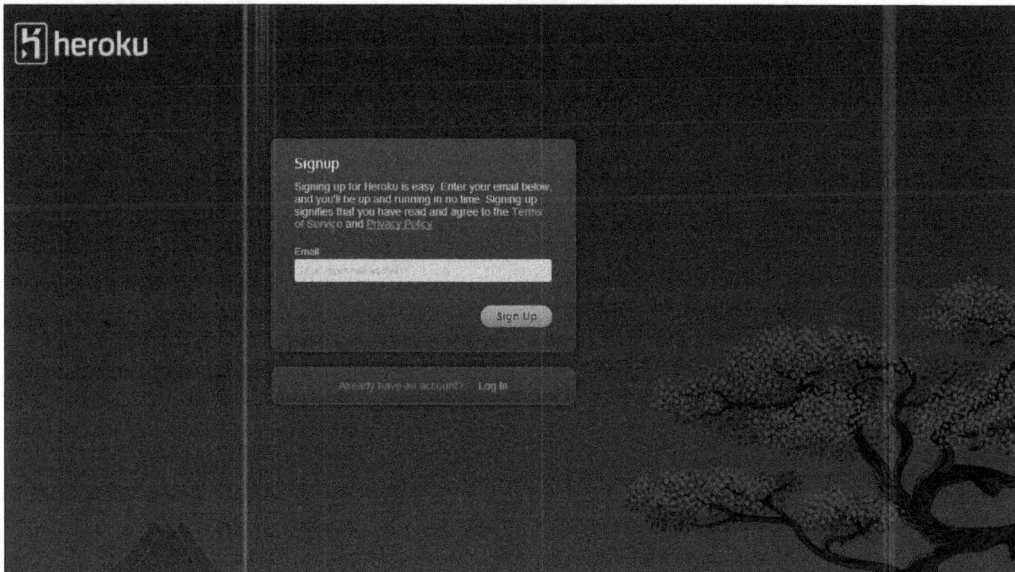

Once you have entered an e-mail address, you need to validate your credentials by logging in to your e-mail account and verifying your account credentials for Heroku. Consider the following screenshot:

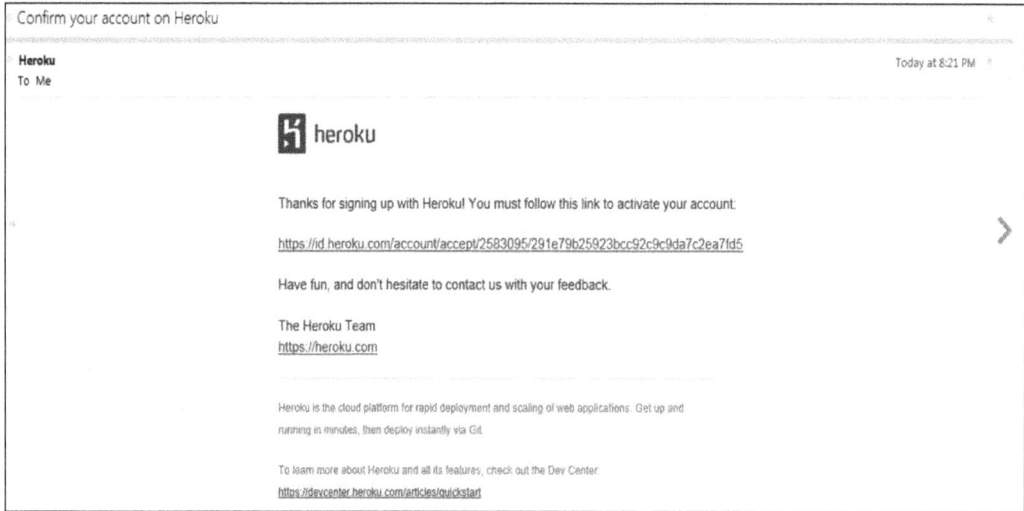

Once you validate your account credentials, you will be redirected to the Heroku password-setting page, where you need to enter a valid password and confirm it, as shown in the following screenshot:

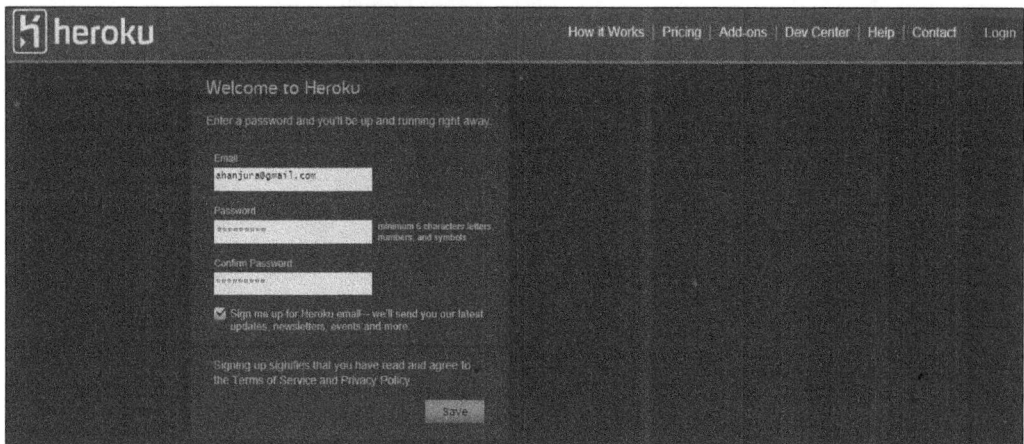

After successful password confirmation, you will be redirected to the Heroku dashboard. Since you are a new user, it will not contain any deployed applications yet. Consider the following screenshot:

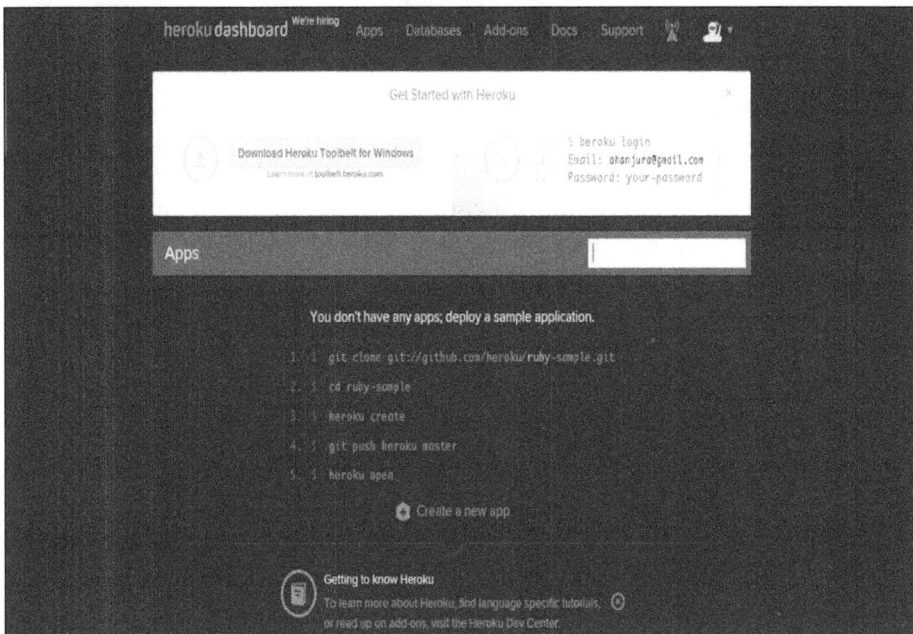

Installing the Heroku toolbelt

The Heroku toolbelt is the client software required to work with the Heroku platform. It can be downloaded from `https://toolbelt.heroku.com/` for Windows, Debian/Ubuntu, Mac OS X, and standalone platforms. For our example, we will use the Windows version as shown in the following screenshot:

Install the Heroku toolbelt by double-clicking on the downloaded executable and following the instructions.

The Heroku toolbelt contains the following components:

- **Heroku client**: This is the command-line tool to help create and manage apps.
- **Foreman**: This is a utility to give you the flexibility of running applications locally, especially sometimes when you want to troubleshoot.
- **Git**: This is the revision control system and relevant utility program that helps you push your code to Heroku or download it from remote repositories. You can also download a client specific Git UI to your operating system if you want a user interface to issue Git commands.

Logging in and generating a new SSH key

After installing the toolbelt, you can issue Heroku commands from the Heroku client command prompt. These commands (or code) are sent to the Heroku server and executed on the Heroku platform. However, Heroku needs to verify that the commands and code being sent to it are from an authentic user. Hence, you need to create a public/private key pair to push the code to Heroku.

Follow these steps to create the key and upload it to your Heroku account:

1. Generate the key on the local machine using the ssh-keygen tool (available at `http://www.openssh.com/`).

2. Add this key to the related Heroku account using the `keys:add` Heroku command.

   - In order to add the key manually, consider the following figure:

   ```
   $ heroku keys: add
   Enter your Heroku credentials.
   Email: test@example.com
   Password:
   Could not ?nd an existing public key.
   Would you ike to generate one? [Yn]        <Enter Y
   Generating new SSH public key.
   Uploading ssh public key /users/test/.ssh/id_rsa.pub
   ```

○ You can log in to the Heroku dashboard (`https://dashboard.heroku.com/account`) and add the key manually too, as shown in the following screenshot:

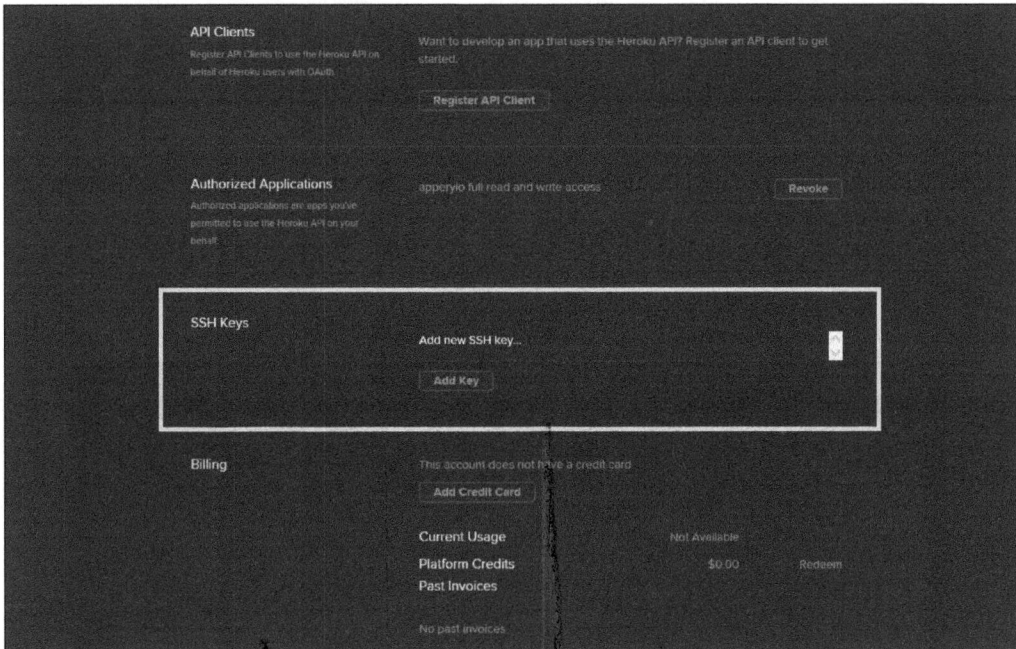

In our example, we use the Heroku command-line interface to create the key and add it to the Heroku account. If you have previously uploaded an SSH key to Heroku, Heroku will assume that you will keep using it and will not prompt you to create a new one.

Test driving Heroku

What fun is it to see a Ferrari and not drive it? So, let us put on our seatbelts and take Heroku for a spin. We assume that we are running the Heroku client on a Windows 7 machine. We assume that we have the Windows version of the Heroku toolbelt (download instructions in the prerequisites section). We have also created and added the SSH key to our Heroku account.

In this section, we will create a barebones Rails 3 app on the Heroku platform. You can use any other supported language, yet the steps won't change except for the language specific details (buildpack used). First and foremost, we need a few things up and running before we can create our first app on Heroku. These requirements are specific to the language we use here.

So, before we get started:

1. Ensure you have certain prerequisites for the Rails 3 example. You need:

    ○   Ruby 1.9.2 (the Ruby runtime toolbelt comes bundled with one)

    ○   Ruby gems (`http://rubygems.org`)

    ○   Bundler (`http://rubygems.org/gems/bundler`)

    ○   Rails 3 (`http://rubyonrails.org/`)

2. Check if the Heroku client is installed and in the path open the command prompt and type:

    ```
    $ heroku
    ```

    You will get the Heroku usage help as follows:

```
Usage: heroku COMMAND [--app APP] [command-specific-options]

Primary help topics, type "heroku help TOPIC" for more details:

    addons      #   manage addon resources
    apps        #   manage apps (create, destroy)
    auth        #   authentication (login, logout)
    config      #   manage app config vars
    domains     #   manage custom domains
    logs        #   display logs for an app
    ps          #   manage processes (dynos, workers)
    releases    #   manage app releases
    run         #   run one-off commands (console, rake)
    sharing     #   manage collaborators on an app

Additional topics:

    account     #   manage heroku account options
    certs       #   manage ssl endpoints for an app
    db          #   manage the database for an app
    drains      #   display syslog drains for an app
    git         #   manage git for apps
    help        #   list commands and display help
    keys        #   manage authentication keys
    labs        #   manage optional features
    maintenance #   manage maintenance mode for an app
    pg          #   manage heroku-postgresql databases
    pgbackups   #   manage backups of heroku postgresql databases
    plugins     #   manage plugins to the heroku gem
    ssl         #   manage ssl certificates for an app
    stack       #   manage the stack for an app
    status      #   check status of heroku platform
    update      #   update the heroku client
    version     #   display version
```

3. Log in using the e-mail address and password you used when creating your Heroku account:

    ```
    $ heroku login
    Enter your Heroku credentials.
    Email: xxxx@yyyy.com
    Password:
    Could not find an existing public key.
    Would you like to generate one? [Yn]
    Generating new SSH public key.
    Uploading ssh public key /users/xxxx/.ssh/id_rsa.pub
    ```

    Press enter at the prompt to upload your ssh key or create a new one.

4. Write a simple Rails 3 application:

    ```
    $ rails new sampleapp_rails3
    $ cd sampleapp_rails3
    ```

5. Edit your Gemfile (Gemfile is a file that contains the list of names of libraries/gem files your application needs to function correctly) and change gem 'sqlite3' to gem 'pg'.

    This change enables the application to use the newly introduced Heroku PostgreSQL database instead of SQLite.

6. Re-install your dependencies (to generate new Gemfile.lock):

    ```
    $ bundle install
    ```

7. Create your app in Git as shown in the following figure:

```
git init
git add
git commit -m "init"
•   Deploy the application on Heroku
•   Create the app on Heroku using:
heroku create
Creating pink-poppies-786... done, stack is cedar
http://pink-poppies-786.herokuapp.com/ | git@heroku.com:pink-poppies-786.git
Git remote heroku added
•   Deploy you code:
git push heroku master
counting objects: 67, done.
Delta compression using up to 4 threads.
Compressing objects: 100% (52/52), done.
Writing objects: 100% (67/67), 86.33 KiB, done.
Total 67 (delta 5), reused 0 (delta 0)

-----> Heroku receiving push
-----> Rails app detected
-----> Installing dependencies using Bundler version 1.1
        Checking for unresolved dependencies.
        Unresolved dependencies detected.
        Running: bundle install --without development: test --path vendor / bundle – deployment
        Fetching source index for http: //rubygems.org/
        Installing rake (0.8.7)
        ...
        Installing rails (3.0.5)
        You bundle is complete! It was installed into ./vendor/bundle
-----> Rails plugin injection
        Injecting rails_log_stdout
        Injecting rails3_serve_static_assets
-----> Discovering process types
        Proc?le declares types -> (none)
        Default types for Rails -> console, rake, web, worker
-----> Compiled slug size is 8.3MB
-----> Launching...done, v5
        http.//pink-poppies-786.herokuapp.com deployed to heroku

To git@heroku.com:pink-poppies-786.git
* [new branch]        master -> master
```

8. To open a Heroku app, type the `open` command on the Heroku CLI:

   ```
   $ heroku open

   Opening pink-poppies-786... done
   ```

9. Check the status of running Heroku processes, type the `ps` (process status) command as follows:

   ```
   $ heroku ps

   === web: `bundle exec rails server -p $PORT`web.1: up for 5s
   ```

10. To support more concurrent users, you need to scale up your application. Increase the web dyno count from the Heroku command line. Use the `ps:scale` command to scale up the web processes to 2 as follows:

    ```
    $ heroku ps:scale web=2
    ```

11. If you encounter any issues while running the Heroku app, you can use the `logs` command to get the details of most recent messages and use the information to troubleshoot pertinent issues as shown in the following figure:

```
$ heroku logs
2012-12-10T11:10:34.08:00 heroku[web.1]: State changed from created to starting
2012-12-10T11:10:37.08:00 heroku[web.1]: Running process with command: 'bundle exec rails server -
p 42383'
2012-12-10T11:10:40.08:00 app[web.1]: [2012-12-10 11:23:40] INFD WEBrick 1. 3. 1
2012-12-10T11:10:40.08:00 app[web.1]: [2012-12-10 11:23:40] INFD ruby 1. 9. 2. (2010-12-25) [x86_64-
linux]
```

That completes our test drive of Heroku. We created a Heroku account, added our SSH key to Heroku, and wrote a barebones Rails3 app and deployed it on Heroku. Finally, to troubleshoot, we used the `logs` command to see what was going on behind the scenes just in case something needed attention.

Summary

That brings us to the end of the introduction to Heroku. In this chapter, we built upon on our understanding of cloud computing, the different cloud service models and why cloud-based development makes so much sense in today's business environment. We were introduced to the magical Heroku platform as a service (PaaS), which provides an integrated build, deploy, and operate platform for web developers to deploy and easily manage their apps. We reviewed Heroku's platform architecture and understood the rich feature set of the platform. Finally, we test drove the Heroku platform, touching upon the toolset needed to connect to Heroku and build/deploy a barebones app on Heroku in the process.

In the next chapter, we will delve a little deeper into Heroku's platform architecture and understand how Heroku works under the covers. Specifically, we focus on the details of the Heroku stack, its process architecture, execution framework, and the logging architecture. And there is more—see you there!

2
Inside Heroku

Now that we have test driven Heroku and know a little bit about its feature set, it's time to understand some inner workings of the Heroku platform.

The Heroku cloud development platform provides you with the foundation for developing, deploying, and troubleshooting your cloud-based applications. It is comprised of the following components:

- **The platform stack**: This provides core components such as the operating system, language runtime, and supporting libraries.

- **Request routing mechanism**: This provides support to accept client requests and route them reliably to the running process.

- **The execution environment**: This provides the necessary runtime support to run your apps.

- **The Logplex logging framework**: This is an event logging system to collate application events that emanate from different processes for further processing.

- **The add-on ecosystem**: This provides the ability to easily plug in third-party libraries to provide value added services, such as performance monitoring, caching, or data storage for your application.

- **The Heroku Platform APIs**: This is a web service interface to programmatically perform Heroku operations from your code.

In this chapter, we review each of these foundational aspects of the Heroku platform in a little more detail. We will also get a deeper understanding of the Heroku process architecture—the core component of the Heroku runtime environment.

The Heroku platform stack

Heroku is a platform, that is, an environment that provides you with the foundation to run your applications without worrying about the nitty-gritty of how it all works under the hood. You build an application, push it to Heroku, and voila, the slug compiler builds your source into an executable and ready-to-run application. What's more, it also creates a URL for the application to use. While all this magic works for you in no time, there is a robust, highly available, scalable, and failure-proof foundation underneath that makes all this possible. The core element of the Heroku platform is the Heroku stack—a combination of the operating system, language runtime, and associated libraries that provide a complete execution environment for users to run applications of varying workloads and scale seamlessly.

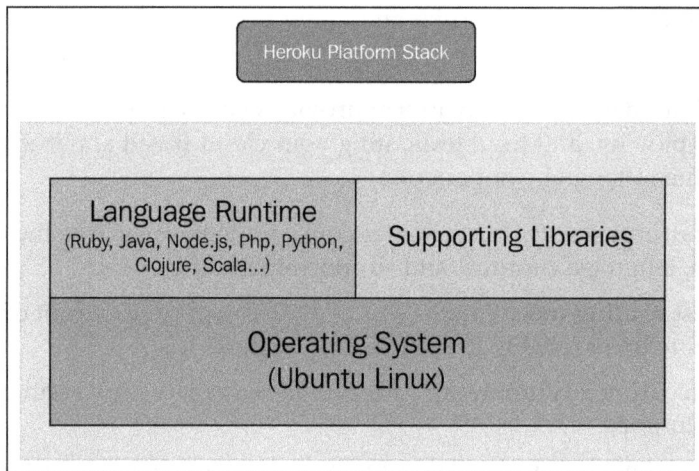

In the deployment stack, the operating system defines the base technology used by the Heroku platform, and it has varied across various releases of the Heroku stack. Each of these releases has supported a different set of programming language runtimes. The currently available Ubuntu 10.04 Linux operating system-based flavor of the Heroku stack is called the Celadon Cedar stack. With the adoption of the Celadon Cedar stack, Heroku has matured into a solid polyglot platform that natively supports the most popular language runtimes for application development. From supporting Ruby in its initial release, Heroku now natively supports six programming languages, and the list is growing.

Over the years, Heroku has supported the following three distinct deployment stacks:

Stack	Underlying platform	Supported runtimes
Argent Aspen	Debian Etch 4.0	MRI* 1.8.6
Badious Bamboo	Debian Lenny 5.0	REE** 1.8.7, MRI 1.9.2
Celadon Cedar	Ubuntu 10.04	REE 1.8.7, MRI 1.9.2, Node.js, Clojure, Java, Python, Scala

* MRI: Matz Ruby Interpreter

** REE: Ruby Enterprise Edition

Further details of Heroku's language support can be found at `https://devcenter.heroku.com/categories/language-support`.

The Celadon Cedar stack

Celadon Cedar is the default deployment stack for the Heroku platform going forward. Loads of applications deployed on Heroku may still be running the Badious Bamboo stack as Heroku supports it for backward compatibility. However, it is recommended that users migrate to the Cedar stack to leverage the latest features. It is also suggested that users should first test the application with the supported language runtime on a test (staging) environment before moving the entire application to production on Cedar.

The Cedar stack brings in many interesting enhancements to the Heroku deployment stack including the following stacks:

- **Multi-language support**: Cedar is a general purpose deployment stack, meaning it does not provide native support for any of the programming languages. It provides the ability to add support for a language virtually on demand through a build-time adapter mechanism called the **buildpack**. The buildpack can compile the application written in a particular programming language into a binary executable that is executable on the runtime provided by the Cedar deployment stack.

  Officially, Cedar provides support for REE 1.8.7, MRI 1.9.2, Node.js, Clojure, Java, Python, and Scala; though you could add a new buildpack for a language of choice and virtually run an application written in most of the programming languages on the Heroku platform.

The ease of using these custom buildpacks has led to developers providing support for many popular languages such as PERL, Go, and Common LISP. Running applications with a custom buildpack is as easy as specifying an environment variable BUILDPACK_URL and passing the buildpack URL at the application creation time like the following:

```
$heroku create --buildpack <BUILDPACK_URL>
```

- **The new process model**: The Cedar stack leverages the underlying UNIX process model to provide a seamless process execution environment that can scale on demand and provide fault tolerant application services. The process model framework provides detailed granularity to manage applications in a process execution environment that can span multiple machines. The process model introduces the concept of Procfile (short form for process file), which is a configuration file for your process formation. The various types of processes and how to run them can be specified in Procfile. The existence of Procfile gives great flexibility in choosing the right size of your application processes.

  The process model also enables you to run one-off processes on the command line, hence provides greater flexibility when running utilities or application just this one time. You can scale particular process types to run more processes on the fly, and the underlying execution environment takes care of starting the new instances automatically.

  The flexibility provided by Procfile also helps in replacing any executable with another, if an upgrade is required, for example, if you want to replace one web server with another due to application requirements.

- **Finer troubleshooting**: One extremely intelligent feature of the Heroku platform is its intuitive command reference to run, monitor, and manage application tasks. Unlike many other PaaS offerings, Heroku provides a UNIX-like command reference that is easier to learn and start using. Most common Heroku CLI commands on the Celadon Cedar stack are named after UNIX shell commands prefixed with Heroku to provide the distinction.

  For example, a simple command to check your Heroku process status is shown in the following screenshot:

```
$ heroku ps
=== web:  bundle exec thin start -p $PORT -e production
web.1: up for 3h
web.2: up for 2m
```

The output shows that currently two web processes are running for 3h and 2m respectively. The line with === shows the command being executed in the Heroku execution environment. Besides being close to the UNIX syntax whenever it can, Heroku also provides a straightforward syntax to manage processes. For example, to decrease the number of web process types and increase the worker process types, all that is needed is the following one liner:

Use the + (increment) and – (decrement) indicators to increase and decrease the number of respective Heroku processes, as shown in the following screenshot:

```
$ heroku ps:scale web-1 worker+2
Scaling web processes... done, now running 1
Scaling worker processes... done, now running 3
```

Checking the logs for troubleshooting applications or verifying the process flow is as simple as the following screenshot shows:

```
$ heroku logs
-[36m2013-01-27T10:48:08+00:00 heroku[api]:-[0m Starting process with command `date` by ahanjura@gmail.com
-[33m2013-01-27T10:48:12+00:00 heroku[run.2988]:-[0m Awaiting client
-[33m2013-01-27T10:48:12+00:00 heroku[run.2988]:-[0m Starting process with command `date`
-[33m2013-01-27T10:48:14+00:00 heroku[run.2988]:-[0m Process exited with status 0
-[33m2013-01-27T10:48:14+00:00 heroku[run.2988]:-[0m State changed from starting to complete
```

The last few (log tail) log statements can be viewed by the heroku logs -t command.

What's more, you can filter log messages for a particular process type. To filter log messages from the process worker.1 and list the corresponding log messages, use the heroku logs --ps worker.1 -t command.

Here, the user is trying to filter log messages for the worker.1 process only. This flexibility is extremely powerful in troubleshooting a large process formation by specific process instances.

- **Release management**: On new code deployment, whether it is configuration changes or modification (adding/removing) of resources, Heroku creates a new release and restarts the application automatically. Heroku provides the flexibility to list the history of releases and uses rollbacks to revert to prior releases, in case deployment or configuration went wrong. To list your releases, type what is shown in the following screenshot:

```
$ heroku releases
=== gentle-mesa-5445 Releases
v2  Enable Logplex   ahanjura@gmail.com  2012/12/03 03:39:37
v1  Initial release  ahanjura@gmail.com  2012/12/03 03:39:36
```

To demonstrate, how to modify your application, I have added a new configuration variable, as shown in the following screenshot:

```
$ heroku config:add TEST_ENV_VAR_EDHA=45
Setting config vars and restarting gentle-mesa-5445... done, v3
TEST_ENV_VAR_EDHA: 45
```

Verify that a new release is added by Heroku, as shown in the following screenshot:

```
$ heroku releases
=== gentle-mesa-5445 Releases
v3  Add TEST_ENV_VAR_EDHA config  ahanjura@gmail.com  2013/01/27 20:16:21 (~ 17s ago)
v2  Enable Logplex                ahanjura@gmail.com  2012/12/03 03:39:37
v1  Initial release               ahanjura@gmail.com  2012/12/03 03:39:36
$ heroku releases:info v3
=== Release v3
By:     ahanjura@gmail.com
Change: Add TEST_ENV_VAR_EDHA config
When:   2013/01/27 20:16:21 (~ 57s ago)

=== v3 Config Vars
TEST_ENV_VAR_EDHA: 45
```

Finally, I rollback the changes to Version 2 as shown in the following screenshot:

```
$ heroku rollback
Rolling back gentle-mesa-5445... done, v2
!    Warning: rollback affects code and config vars; it
     doesn't add or remove addons. To undo, run: heroku
     rollback v3
```

Request routing in Heroku

In the current deployment stack, an app named `myapp` will have the default hostname of `myapp.herokuapp.com`. The `herokuapp.com` domain routes any request to Heroku via the routing mesh and provides a direct routing path to the corresponding web processes. This allows for advanced HTTP uses such as chunked responses, long polling, and using an asynchronous web server to handle multiple responses from a single web process.

The routing mesh is responsible for directing a request to the respective dyno in the dyno manifold. The routing mesh uses a round robin algorithm to perform the distribution of requests to the dynos as shown in the following diagram:

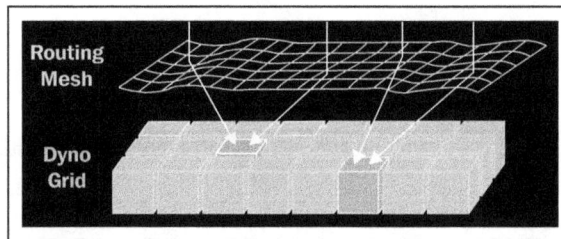

The HTTP request follows a timeout (30 sec) for the web process to return its response data to the client. If the web process fails to return the response within this time, the corresponding process log registers an error. After the initial communication, a larger (55 sec) time window is set for client or the server to send data. If neither of them sends it, the connection is terminated and an error is logged again. This scheme of rolling timeouts facilitates freeing up network connections when it is more likely that the communication will not occur in a reasonably practical time period. Less open connections mean better resource management and performance.

The Heroku stack also supports running multithreaded and/or asynchronous applications, which can accept many network connections to process client events. For example, all Node.js apps typically handle multiple network connections as per the process while handling client requests.

Cedar no longer has a reverse proxy cache such as Varnish, as it prefers to offer flexibility to developers to choose the CDN solution of their choice. Heroku's add-on architecture supports the enabling of such an option.

The execution environment - dynos and the dyno manifold

A dyno is like a virtual UNIX container that can run any type of process on the dyno manifold. The dyno manifold is a process execution environment that facilitates the execution of various dynos, which might cater to different client requests. The following diagram shows the various components of the Heroku execution environment:

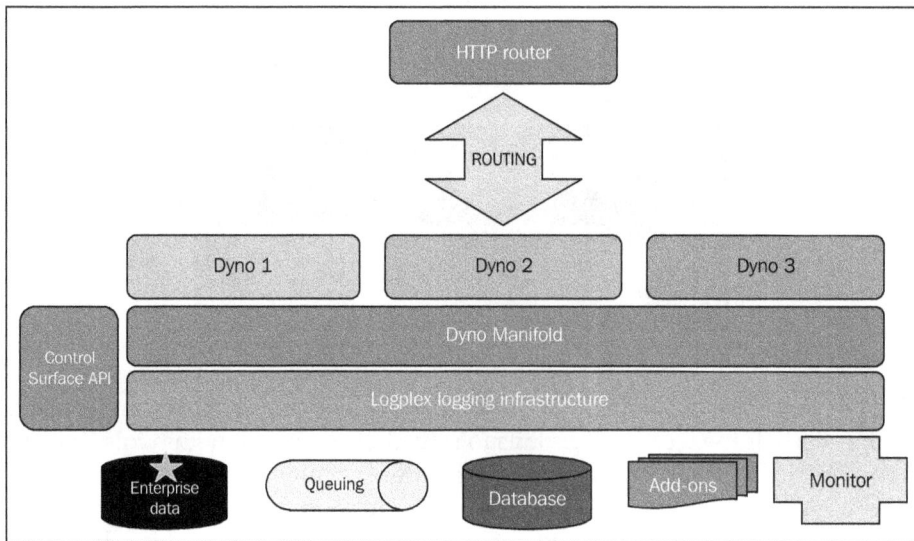

The dyno manifold infrastructure provides the necessary process management, isolation, scaling, routing, distribution, and redundancy required to run the production grade web and the worker processes in a resilient fashion.

The manifold is a fault-tolerant, distributed environment for your processes to run in full stream. If you release a new application version, the manifold manages the restart automatically, hence removing a lot of maintenance hassle. Dynos are recycled everyday or when resource constraints force dyno migration or resizing. The manifold is responsible for automatically restarting any failed dynos. If the dynos fail again and again, the manifold doesn't immediately restart them but waits for a delta and then tries to restart them. You can try starting the processes manually using the `heroku restart` command.

You can set global parameters and certain configuration variables in the environment `.profile` file as it gets called before the manifold starts the dyno. Each dyno is self-contained in the sense that it runs a particular instance of a web or worker process and has access to sufficient resources to handle client requests.

The dyno does have some restrictions in terms of the memory it can expend. There is a ceiling of 512 MB per dyno, exceeding which causes the process to log memory overuse warnings in the log file. If the memory exceeds a threshold of 1.5 GB per dyno, the dyno is rebooted with a Heroku error. Usually, it is recommended to design and size your application to use a maximum of 512 MB memory. If the application exceeds this limit, there is potentially a memory leak.

Dynos can serve many requests per second, but this depends greatly on the language and framework used. A multithreaded or event-driven environment such as Java or Node.js is designed to handle many requests concurrently.

Dynos execute in complete isolation and protection from one another, even when they are on the same physical hardware. Each dyno has (albeit virtually) its own filesystem, memory, and CPU that it can use to handle its own client requests.

Dynos could be running in a distributed infrastructure. The access and routing is managed by the routing mesh internally and usually none of the dynos are statically addressable.

Dynos use LXC (`lxc.sourceforget.net`) as the foundation to provide a lightweight UNIX container-like behavior to execute different processes in complete isolation.

Heroku's logging infrastructure – the Logplex system

The Logplex system forms the foundation of the Heroku logging infrastructure. It collates and distributes log messages from the application and other parts of the Heroku infrastructure. These entries are made available through a public API and the Heroku command-line tool. Due to the distributed nature of the Heroku platform, trying to manually access log messages across different application components and making sense out of those is practically infeasible. You cannot get a unified view of the entire system behavior if you collate these messages manually and try to troubleshoot problems. The Logplex integrated logging system provides an alternative in this case.

The Logplex system acts like a conduit that routes messages from log entry **sources**, that is, the producer of the log messages (for example, an application running on the dyno, the Heroku platform itself) to log entry **drains**, that is, consumers of log messages (for example, archival systems or post processors doing mining of information).

The Logplex system does not provide storage for the entirely generated log data but only keeps the most recent data that is good enough to extract relevant information from the application run. Typically, this data is of the size of about 1,500 consolidated log messages. If you have a business need to store more than the predefined limit, you would need to choose alternative storage services, for example, **Syslog drains** to archive all messages.

Logplex is designed with the ability to work with external tools and services such as Loggly. If any of these external tools or services is unable to consume messages generated by Logplex, they can lose some of these messages. However, Logplex does insert a warning entry anytime it has to drop messages due to the consuming service downtime.

The Heroku add-on architecture

Add-ons are one way to extend the capabilities of a Heroku application. The user can add a new service such as caching or data storage to the app by provisioning an add-on and consuming the service offered. Heroku users have two ways to provision the add-ons:

- The add-on marketplace
- The Heroku toolbelt client

The entire process of add-on provisioning and consumption is shown in the following diagram:

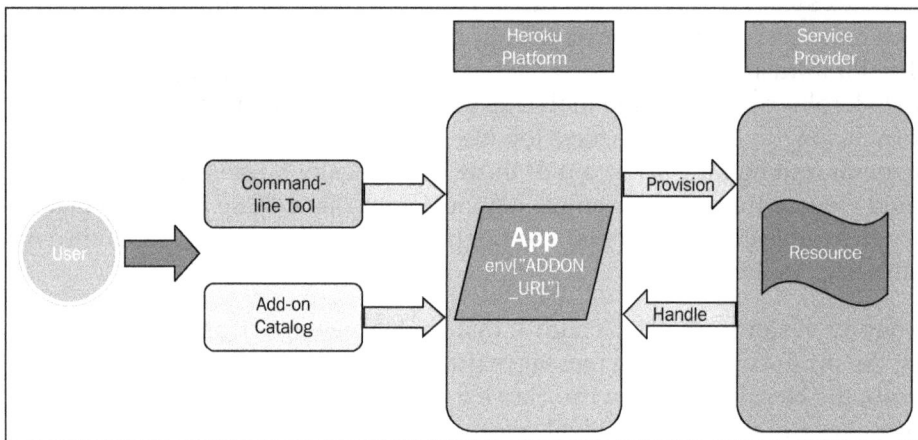

The following steps describe how a new add-on is provisioned and consumed by the Heroku app:

1. The Heroku user requests an add-on using either of the two ways indicated in the previous paragraph.

2. Heroku sends a provisioning request for the current account to the service provider for the given service.

3. The service provider validates the request and creates a private resource for the caller and returns a URL that specifies the exact location and the credential required to access the service.

    For example, the Amazon RDS service provider might return:

    ```
    MYSQL_URL=mysql://user:pass@mydbhost.com/database
    ```

4. At this point, Heroku adds the returned URL to the environment of the requesting app, rebuilds the app again, and restarts the related dynos for the app.

5. The app is ready to consume the services of the new add-on.

6. The app extracts the resource URL from the environment and issues a read/write request to the service, passing the necessary parameters.

7. The invoked resource within the service provider validates the authenticity of the requests and grants a privilege to execute the operation if the request is valid and the user is authentic.

8. The resource creates a response and sends it back to the app, which in turn uses the result to create a page or store the response in the app's memory for later use and continue.

Note that the request for service from the app could either be from the user making a request in the web browser or a worker dyno asking for some resource while performing a long running background job.

Programmatically consuming Heroku services

With Heroku Platform API, Heroku provides you with the ability to call the Heroku platform services to do virtually anything you need to do on Heroku—creating an application, checking the release history of your app, or plugging new add-ons in to your application. All this and more just by using simple HTTP. The following diagram depicts the interaction between a simple Heroku API client and the Heroku platform services. An API client can use the Heroku API to interact the core platform services of Heroku using a well-defined interface.

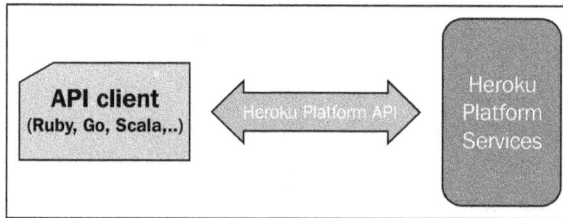

The Heroku Platform API allows you to do almost everything you can do with the Heroku command line or dashboard. This API is a powerful tool for application developers to leverage the capabilities of Heroku's features and gain complete control of their apps, from creating to monitoring them.

The Heroku Platform API

There are at least three important components of the Heroku Platform API as shown in the following diagram. These components define the behavior of the API to the external world.

The components are:

- Security
- Schema
- Data

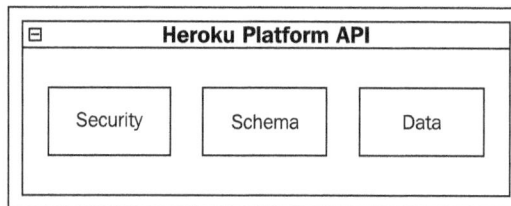

Security

Any application that wants to consume services provided by the Heroku platform via the Platform API should authenticate the users trying to access the service. Though basic HTTP authentication would work, if you are using your own scripts and don't expect to expose those to a wider audience, OAuth is the recommended way to provide authentication support for third-parties to access Heroku services. You can use the OAuth token to provide access to your account to every user including third parties. By gaining access through OAuth, third parties can then use your applications to provide many value added services such as monitoring, scalability, or application management.

Schema

To use the Platform API, the client needs to know a few things. For example, what resource is available, what is the corresponding resource location, how this resource is represented, and what operations are allowed on the resource? Only then a client can create a request to access the details of the resource as available on the Heroku platform via the API. Much of this information is provided by the API schema. This schema stored in the JSON format is machine readable and describes various aspects of the resource. The API schema, like other API resources, can also be accessed using the curl utility. Heroku also supports the validation and hypertext extensions for the base JSON schema to enable more powerful manipulation of the JSON data.

Data

Whenever the client receives a response from the Heroku Platform API, the response header contains the Entity tag (ETag). This tag is used to identify the precise version of the resource accessed, just in case the resource is needed again later. This ETag can be embedded inside the If-Not-Match header field in future requests to verify that the resource has indeed changed. If the resource hasn't changed, a return status of not modified is sent back to the client. If the resource has changed since the earlier request, the call performs normally and returns the new characteristics of the resource.

You can optimize the resource access by caching the resource response at the client side and issuing an API request for the resource only when the resource is indeed changed on the platform side.

Accessing the API

The client using the platform API calls standard methods defined for HTTP and passes parameters in the request body to the serving API. The API acts on the request, performs the specific operation, and returns results of the operation to the client via a response that is a JSON representation of the details of the resource requested.

API clients

Since the Heroku Platform API was recently released in Beta, API clients written in various languages that Heroku supports are slowly emerging on the development scene. Heroku supports an API client called Heroics for Ruby and there are more that have come up. There are known API clients for Node.js, Scala, and Go that could be used based on your app requirements.

Calling the API

API clients address the requests to `api.heroku.com` using HTTPS and specify the `Accept: application/vnd.heroku+json; version=3` Accept HTTPS header in the request. The client can also specify a User-Agent header to help with troubleshooting and tracking the request if required.

For the most part, you can use curl (`http://curl.haxx.se/`) as an API client in scripts or utilities to call the Heroku Platform API. The calling convention to access the Platform API is simple and the returned results are in the JSON format, so parsing and using them is very straightforward.

For other programming languages, all you need is a HTTP library and methods to call the API from your code and you are all set. Call the API, receive the returned data, parse it, and use it in your application. In this section, we use curl to show some samples to give you a basic understanding of how to invoke the API.

Response

The success or failure of the Platform API call is indicated by the status code returned by the API on completion. The API call can result in various actions, for example, the creation of a resource as in the case of a new application getting created or reviewing the history of a resource, for example, looking at the revision history of an application.

The API response is comprised of the shorter, relevant part of the HTTP header and the response details in the JSON body if required. The response header includes the current count of the remaining allowed API requests for the account.

Limits on API calls

The Heroku platform API allows the developer to control various aspects of the Heroku application development from within the application. The developer can manage application configuration, runtime (dynos), deployment, and user account management, besides a wide array of other functions. However, the platform puts a restriction on the number of API calls a user or developer can make per hour. This is essentially to protect against unnecessary overuse, ensure fair response handling of innumerable clients, and enforce security measures. With each API call, this token count is decremented.

The Heroku process architecture

A Heroku application is a collection of processes that run on the Heroku dyno manifold. Whether you are running a local process or a remote one on a distributed cluster of machines, a Heroku application is essentially a set of processes, each consuming resources like a normal UNIX process.

To add flexibility and have better control over how you define your process configuration, Heroku defines the concept of process type. Each process that you run as a dyno can be classified as a web process or a worker process type depending on whether it handles HTTP requests or does some background processing. You could also define a custom process type to add flexibility to your application definition.

Procfile

Heroku has a language agnostic, application centric method of defining your process types through a configuration file called Procfile — a format for declaring the process types that describe how your app will run.

Procfile is a text file named `Procfile` placed in the root of your application that lists the process types in an application. Each process type is a declaration of a command that is executed when a process of that process type is executed. All the language and frameworks on the Cedar stack declare a web process type, which starts the application server.

Here is the content of a sample Procfile for a Sinatra application:

```
web: bundle exec rackup config.ru -p $PORT
```

The part before : defines the process type, and the part after : defines the command to launch the process type when the dyno running the process boots up.

One can use environment variables populated by Heroku in the command as shown in the preceding command.

Another example of a Procfile command could be:

```
web: sh path/bin/webapp
```

In this example, when the web process is started, it will launch the web application server located in `path/bin/webapp` in a new shell. Note how similar it looks to running a UNIX process on the command line.

Declaring process types

A process type declares its name and a command-line command — this is a prototype that can be instantiated in one or more running processes. Usually, the Procfile will be in the application root. In case it isn't supplied or created, Heroku by default creates a web process to run the default application.

The main purpose of a Procfile is to declare different process types and associate an action with each type of process. Essentially, it is a declarative specification of what the individual process types available for this application are and how instances of those process types should be started or operated when needed. The process types could represent different types of worker processes, a clock job, or a Node.js server that runs and processes incoming events. While declaring new process types, it is recommended that we distinguish between the process type for a transient (running for a small period of time) job and the process type for a long running job. It helps when you create instances of each of these process types to run. You can easily scale the transitory jobs independently of the long running ones

The Procfile format

The Procfile format is one process type per line, with each line containing `<process type>: <command>`.

The syntax is defined as follows:

- `<process type>`: This is an alphanumeric string; it is a name for your process, such as web, worker, clock, or myproc
- `<command>`: A command line to launch the process, such as `sh path/bin/webapp`

The web process type is special and is the only process type that will receive HTTP traffic from the routing mesh. Other process types can be named arbitrarily.

A sample Procfile

Here is a sample Procfile for a Node.js app with two process types:

- `web`: This handles HTTP requests
- `worker`: This runs background jobs;

```
# Procfile

web: node server.js
worker: node bkgrnd.js
```

When you run the application that corresponds to this Procfile on Heroku, the platform detects the requested process types and boots them, as shown in the following screenshot:

```
$ heroku create --stack cedar
$ git push heroku master
...
-----> Heroku receiving push
-----> Node.js app detected
...
-----> Discovering process types
       Procfile declares types -> web, worker
```

Adding Procfile to Heroku

Procfile is not necessarily used to deploy applications. The platform can detect the type of application and the corresponding runtime to use. Though Heroku automatically creates a default web process type to boot the application server, it is recommended to create an explicit Procfile as that gives you a greater control on how your processes can execute in Heroku's execution environment. For Heroku to use your Procfile, add Procfile to the root of your application and then push it to Heroku, as shown in the following screenshot:

```
$ git add .
$ git commit -m "Procfile"
$ git push heroku
...
-----> Procfile declares process types: web, worker
       Compiled slug size is 10.8MB
-----> Launching... done
       http://gentle-mesa-5445.herokuapp.com deployed to Heroku

To git@heroku.com:gentle-mesa-5445.git
 * [new branch]      master -> master
```

Running applications locally

How often have we faced issues in the production environment that fail to reproduce in the development environment? Hence, it is critical that when developing and debugging an application, the code in a local development environment is executed in the same manner as the remote environment. This ensures that any differences between the two environments and bugs that hard to find are intercepted before deploying the code to production.

In a local development environment, you can run a small-scale version of your application by launching one process for each of the two process types: web and worker.

Foreman is a command-line tool used to run Procfile-based applications locally. It is installed automatically by the Heroku toolbelt (Heroku client package), and is also available as a gem.

If you don't have foreman installed, use the `gem install foreman` command to install it from the prompt.

Starting foreman is easy as shown in the following screenshot:

```
$ foreman start
09:27:10 web.1      | started with pid 22298
09:27:10 worker.1   | started with pid 22299
09:27:11 web.1      | Listening on port 5000
09:27:11 worker.1   | worker ready to do work
```

Since the Procfile has both web and worker processes, foreman will start one of each process type with the output interleaved on your terminal. Your web process uses port 5000, because this is what foreman provides as a default in the $PORT environment variable. The web process must use this value, since it is used by the Heroku platform on deployment as well. You can test the application now. Press *Ctrl + C* to send a signal to close down the application when it is done.

Setting local environment variables

Variables saved in the .env file of a project directory will be added to the environment when run by foreman.

For example, we can set SRCPATH_ENV to development in your environment, as shown in the following screenshot:

```
$ echo " SRCPATH_ENV=SMS" >>.env #Put the SRCPATH_ENV variable into the .env file

$ foreman run irb
> puts ENV["SRCPATH_ENV "]
> SMS
```

The command in the preceding screenshot runs the interactive shell and sets the value of the SRCPATH_ENV environment variable to SMS.

You can use the .env file for the local configuration as it has settings specific to your local environment. It does not need to be checked in or committed to Heroku.

Process formation

Each application's set of running processes on the dyno manifold are known as its process formation.

The default formation for a simple application will be a single web process, whereas more complex applications may consist of multiple copies of web and worker process types. You can scale the process types on demand as your application needs increase.

For example, if the application already has a process formation of three web processes, and you run the `heroku ps:scale worker=3` command, you will now have a total of six processes: three web processes and three worker processes.

Process scaling

In a production environment, your application may need to scale out to a much greater capacity. It is no longer a couple of web and worker processes that you typically need for your application deployed in the local environment.

Heroku follows a share-nothing process architecture. This enables the instantiation of each process type a number of times. Each process of the same process type shares the same command and purpose, but run as separate, isolated processes in different physical locations.

The `heroku ps:scale` command lets you scale your application to any size as your application demands increase as shown in the following screenshot:

```
$ heroku ps:scale web=20 worker=40
Scaling web processes... done, now running 20
Scaling worker processes... done, now running 40
```

The scale command instantiates 20 additional web and 40 worker processes to handle the increased application load.

Like `heroku run`, Heroku scale launches processes. But instead of asking for a single, one-shot process attached to the terminal, it launches a whole group of them, starting from the prototypes defined in the Procfile.

In the preceding example, the process formation is 20 web processes and 40 worker processes. After scaling out, you can see the status of your new formation with the `heroku ps` command, as shown in the following screenshot:

```
$ heroku ps
Process         State               Command
-----------     ------------------  ------------------------------
web.1           up for 3s           node server.js
web.2           up for 2s           node server.js
...

...
web.20......
worker.1        starting for 4s     node bkgrnd.js
worker.2        up for 2s           node bkgrnd.js
...

...
worker.40.....
```

The dyno manifold will keep these processes up and running in this exact formation, until you request a change with another Heroku scale command. Keeping your processes running indefinitely in the formation you've requested is part of Heroku's erosion resistance.

Scaling dynos quantities can also be specified as an increment from the existing number of dynos or processes as follows:

```
$ heroku ps:scale web+2
Scaling web processes... done, now running 22
```

Stopping a process type

To stop running a particular process type entirely, simply scale it to zero as shown in the following screenshot:

```
$ heroku ps:scale worker=0
Scaling worker processes... done, now running 0
```

Checking on your processes

Use `heroku ps` to determine the number of processes that are executed. The list indicates the process type in the left column, and the command corresponding to that process type in the right column, as shown in the following screenshot:

```
$ heroku ps
=== web: `bundle exec rails server -p $PORT`
web.1: up for 3m
```

Process logs

To get an aggregated list of log messages from all process types, type the code as shown in the following screenshot:

```
$ heroku logs
2013-01-26T01:24:20-07:00 heroku[slugc]: Slug compilation finished
2013-01-26T01:24:22+00:00 heroku[web.1]: Running process with command: `bundle exec
rails server mongrel -p 46999`
2013-01-25T18:24:22-07:00 heroku[web.1]: State changed from created to starting
2013-01-25T18:24:29-07:00 heroku[web.1]: State changed from starting to up
2013-01-26T01:24:29+00:00 app[web.1]: => Booting Mongrel
```

Use `heroku logs --ps worker` to view just the messages from the worker process type, as shown in the following screenshot:

```
$ heroku logs --ps worker
2013-01-25T18:33:25-07:00 heroku[worker.1]: State changed from created to starting
2013-01-26T01:33:26+00:00 heroku[worker.1]: Running process with command: `env
QUEUE=* bundle exec rake resque:work`
2013-01-25T18:33:29-07:00 heroku[worker.1]: State changed from starting to up
```

> Notice that the command has filtered the log messages and displays on `worker.1` messages in the log.

Running a one-off process

Heroku's process architecture enables you to run a group of processes (process formation) or a standalone one-off process. On your local machine, you can `cd` into a directory with your app, then type a command to run a process. On Heroku's Cedar stack, you can use `heroku run` to launch a process against your deployed app's code on Heroku's dyno manifold.

To run the `date` command on Heroku as a standalone dyno, type the code as shown in the following screenshot:

```
$ heroku run date
Running `date` attached to terminal... up, run.2963
Thu Jan 12 08:25:21 UTC 2013
```

The command displays the date on the terminal by running a standalone dyno with process ID `2963`. Each of these commands is run on a fresh, stand-alone dyno running in different physical locations. Each dyno is fully isolated, starts up with a clean copy of the application's ephemeral filesystem, and the entire dyno (including the process, memory, and filesystem) is discarded when the process launched by the command exits or is terminated.

Running anything

You can pretty much run anything on the Heroku platform. If you need additional features for your web app, you can use the supported add-ons and consume the add-on services from your app and provide newer capabilities such as monitoring (of the app) or data storage in your application. The possibilities are endless.

Let's say you want to swap the web server and worker system used for your Rails application and use Unicorn and Resque respectively instead.

You just need to change the Gemfile and Procfile, and that's it. You are ready to go!

The Gemfile changes are as follows:

```
gem 'unicorn'
gem 'resque'
gem 'resque-scheduler'
```

The Procfile changes are as follows:

```
web:      bundle exec unicorn -p $PORT -c ./config/unicorn.rb
worker:   bundle exec rake resque:work QUEUE=*
urgworker: bundle exec rake resque:work QUEUE=urgent
```

The `urgworker` is a new custom process type defined to signify tasks with an urgent `QUEUE` type. You get the flexibility of scaling these process types independent of each other when the need arises. So, if you want more `urgworker` process instances, all you need to do is call the `heroku ps:scale urgworker+1` command and voila, you are up and running with more number of urgent queue processing tasks.

Notice how the Procfile specifies two worker processes, one for the urgent queue and another one for the normal processing. Such flexibility is key to running large-scale application deployments.

Summary

In this chapter, we delved deeper into the various components that form the Heroku platform. We understood the foundation of the Heroku platform, its stack, and how the currently supported Celadon Cedar provides different capabilities that help build and scale web apps seamlessly. We also looked at how user requests gets routed and finally executed in the Heroku execution environment. We briefly covered Heroku's Logplex logging infrastructure that helps trace the internal proceedings of your web app. We also looked at Heroku's add-on architecture that helps developers extend the Heroku platform and build newer capabilities for their apps. We learned how to programmatically execute Heroku operations by leveraging the Heroku Platform API and finally we reviewed the process architecture of Heroku—the single most important subsystem of the Heroku platform.

Now that we have the required foundational understanding of the Heroku platform, we will start learning how to build real, robust, and scalable web apps on Heroku in our next chapter.

3
Building Heroku Applications

In the previous chapter, we took the first step in understanding Heroku. We learned the different components of the Heroku platform, starting with the platform stack and ending with the Platform API used to programmatically execute Heroku operations. We also delved deeper into the Heroku process architecture, which is in a way the heart of Heroku's platform architecture.

Now, we will take the next step. We will learn more about Heroku, including how to build scalable web apps on the Heroku platform including the mechanism used for configuration and providing language support for the app. But before we do that, we will also look at the key ingredients or principles that (should) govern the way SaaS web apps should be developed. This set of principles is called the Twelve-Factor App methodology.

At the end of this chapter, you will have a good understanding of the following factors:

- The application design principles for the Heroku platform
- The application creation and configuration process on the Heroku platform
- The role application buildpack system plays in enabling the language runtime support on Heroku
- How the code gets transformed into the slug and how the slug is optimized for faster, more efficient builds

Heroku's guiding influence – the Twelve-Factor App methodology

The understanding of Heroku won't be complete without understanding the methodology that is an outcome of the evolution of the Heroku platform. The **Twelve-Factor App (TFA)** methodology underlines certain key design principles that the developers should use to develop truly powerful SaaS web apps. The methodology is a result of solidifying the best practices for developing web apps on a PaaS such as Heroku, which architecturally focuses on the two most significant goals of simplicity and extensibility.

The TFA methodology (`http://12factor.net`) formulates key design principles to be used for building modern day SaaS apps. The web app could be written in any programming language and the same principles would be applied. Heroku enables the development of web apps based on this methodology by providing the necessary architectural foundation in the platform. In this section, we review these principles and relate their significance to the related parts of the Heroku architecture.

According to the TFA methodology, key characteristics of a good and modern web app are as follows:

- Make setting up an application easier and intuitive by employing declarative formats for setup automation

- Allow maximum portability of an app between execution environments by clearly defining the API between the platform and the underlying operating system

- Be suitable for deployment on any cloud platform, thereby eliminating the hassle of setting up or decommissioning servers

- Result in minimal differences between the development and production environments, helping perform continuous deployment

- Be elastically scalable, that is, should easily scale up or down when user load increases or decreases without any impact on the architecture, tooling support, or development practices

The TFA methodology is a philosophy and a set of practical guidelines that helps developers build well architected web apps. If one delves deeper into the philosophy of the methodology, one realizes that the principles are not new, per se. The idea of loosely coupled, configuration driven, plug and play, scalable, and concurrency driven architecture has been there for a while and has manifested itself in the most robust software designs over the years.

As we explore the different aspects of Heroku in this book, we will realize how important an influence this methodology has been on the Heroku architecture.

The TFA methodology consists of the following guidelines to help you develop robust, scalable SaaS web apps.

A codebase is always versioned and it can have multiple deploys

According to the TFA methodology, an app codebase is always tracked via a source code versioning system. The revision tracking database for the codebase is called the repository or repo in short. A codebase is a single repository (centralized source code control) or a set of repositories that share a base or a root version or commit (as is the case with the decentralized Git SCC system).

There is always a one-to-one correlation between a codebase and the web app. If there are multiple codebases, it is a distributed system with each component in the distributed system being an app. The TFA methodology then applies to each individual app that forms a part of the distributed app.

As a corollary to the preceding principle, multiple apps that have the same codebase violates the TFA methodology. If needs be, the common parts of the various apps should be abstracted into a library that can then be leveraged by the individual apps through a dependency manager.

This implies that your web application should have only one codebase but could have many deploys. The codebase is the same across multiple deploys. Even if different versions of the app are active in each deploy, the apps share the same codebase. It is possible that a developer has uncommitted changes or a staging environment has commits not yet pushed to production, but they all share the same code, thus making these (developer app or the staging app) appear as separate deploys of the same web application.

Declare and isolate dependencies explicitly (always)

The TFA methodology recommends declaring all dependencies of the application explicitly and completely, without relying on the implicit existence of system-wide libraries or packages. If you need a system library or tool, you should vendor that in your app, instead of relying on the surrounding system.

The TFA app should use a dependency declaration manifest that declares all the dependencies your app might have. Additionally, the TFA methodology requires you to use a dependency isolation tool during execution to make sure that no implicit dependencies seep in from outside.

The dependency specification so laid applies to all the different environments such as development and production uniformly. A common example for dependency declaration in a Ruby app is the Gemfile manifest. The dependency isolation part for the Ruby app is achieved through the bundle exec. Both dependency declaration and isolation are and should be used in tandem to conform to the TFA methodology. The obvious benefit of using both of these together is that when a developer starts a new project, all that is needed to get started is the language runtime and the dependency manager. The developer doesn't need to assume the existence of any libraries outside of these and doesn't have to install any package besides the runtime and the dependency manager. The developer's environment becomes self-contained in a sense. The environment has everything it needs to create an app, build, and deploy it.

Configuration should be stored in the environment

Come to think of it, the only difference between two deploys of an app is the configuration whether it is the database URL or the database flavor or the host name where the app is deployed. The TFA methodology bases its third principle on this very observation – the configuration should be separated from the code.

An app should never store the configuration inside the code because of the different deployment environment warrant changing these and that directly implies changing the code every time. This isn't efficient at all. This, however, doesn't apply to a configuration that stays the same between deployment environments. Usually, the apps following this principle can be easily open sourced without having to make any changes in the code.

The TFA methodology recommends storing the app configuration in the environment variables. This choice doesn't require code changes when you move between deploys. Also, an environment variable can control the app at the most granular level and should be independent of other environment variables. This model of defining configuration scales linearly as the number of deploys grow without any cross dependency on the code or the particular deployment environment. Alternatively, many developers try to group configuration into a name such as development or staging, depending on the deployed environment. This approach doesn't scale as well because over a period of time, these types of configuration groupings tend to overcrowd the system and become very hard to manage.

Backend services should be treated as attached (loosely-coupled) resources

The TFA methodology suggests treating backing services as loosely-coupled services that can be plugged in or out of your app without changing the code. This not only makes managing the app easier, it also helps scaling your app better when you need to. The methodology doesn't consider a third-party service any different from the local service. All that an app needs is a service locator through the configuration and it is all set. If the service provider changes, moving the app to the new service provider is easy and transparent to the user. All you need to do is to switch the service locator in the configuration. The app doesn't need to change at all.

Thus, the services or resources are attached to the app through the configuration and can be removed or detached when needed. No strings attached.

Strict separation of the build, release, and run stages of an app

A codebase undergoes many stages of evolution from getting written to getting executed during the runtime. A codebase is first built, then released, and finally run in an execution environment.

The **build stage** refers to the process of compiling the source code, deriving the dependencies, and building them into an executable. The **release stage** combines the executable with the specific configuration of the app (for that particular deploy) and makes the app ready to run. The **run stage** is where the app finds life and gets executed in the runtime environment. The app manifests itself into a set of running system processes specific to that deploy.

The TFA methodology strictly isolates these three stages from each other. Any executable code with its specific configuration defines a release and if the developer makes changes to the code or configuration, a new release is created. Each release is uniquely defined through a timestamp or a constantly incrementing sequence number (release number). A release can't be modified once created. A change to a release can either be a new release or an older release through a well-defined and implemented rollback process.

The run stage can be automated through tools as it can be triggered anytime without any changes to the app per se. The other two stages manifest themselves more frequent as developers continue to change code and/or config to trigger new releases. The run stage should have minimum complexity as the problems that can stop the process from running can crop up any time and it might be a while before anyone looks at them.

An app in execution is a process or many processes

A web app in execution can manifest itself as one or many processes running in tandem in the execution environment. The TFA methodology recommends that processes share nothing between them and are stateless. If the process needs to persist data for later use, the data should be written to a persistent store such as the database. The memory or filesystem cache can be used only for short duration transactions and the data contained within isn't assumed to exist to service a future request that could be routed to a totally new process. Any process restart will generally wipe out any local cache and memory. Hence, no persistence guarantees are given for this temporary state of a process. On the same lines, the TFA methodology also treats the use of sticky sessions as a violation of its principles as the app seems to assume that a previous state is available for a future request. Any type of compilation (for example, compiling assets) is done during the build stage with no impact on runtime of a TFA recommended process execution system.

Services should be exported through port binding

A TFA compliant web app exports a service, for example, HTTP service by binding to a port and the app listens to any requests arriving at that port address. According to the TFA methodology, a compliant web app is self-contained and doesn't depend on any runtime injection of a web server into the execution environment to build a web service to be consumed by users.

Depending on the deployment environment, these services can have different locators but these locators are not dependent on the code. For example, a developer can consume the service in a development environment from a localhost via the URL `http://localhost:1234`, whereas the same service when exposed in the production environment might be accessed through a different URL (including the port). In production, a routing layer could potentially handle incoming requests from a public hostname and bind them to port bound web services.

The port bound web services are implemented by declaring a dependency on the web server in your web app, so that the web server is a part of your build and the whole process is part of the user code. During runtime, the service is bound to a port and the end user can then request for service. One important manifestation of exposing services like this is that one service can be consumed by another by just accessing the service URL.

An app should scale out through its process model

There are many ways to run web apps. One of the ways is when the web server forks a new child process for every new client request (for example, Apache forking a process for PHP server-side processing). Another way is when the language runtime/virtual machine allocates a large chunk of system resources on startup and then manages those resources internally as new client requests come in (for example, the JVM in a Java web app). In either of these cases, developers have a very limited visibility of the processes running in the background servicing client requests. The TFA methodology provides guidelines on how to scale out your application's processes when the concurrent user base of the web app increases and scaling your web app is the only way to support the increased load.

The TFA methodology recommends using a **process type** to signify the type of work/processing being done. By using process types, a *web* app can distribute its workload based on the inherent nature of the incoming request. For example, if it is a HTTP request, then a particular process type called web could service requests of this type. The processes of this type could be scaled out independent of the processes of other process types. There could be a process type called *worker* that can be used to classify processes that are long running and can run in the background while your system readily processes other requests. The supported process types and all instances of those types together form what is called the **process formation**. As you can see, instances of each process type are isolated from instances of the other type and can be scaled independently. These principles could very well be applied to the more granular execution entities called threads. Threads exist within a process and do specific tasks with minimum overlap of shared resources with other threads in the same process.

The horizontal partition-ability and share nothing characteristic of these processes help scaling and allow adding more concurrency to the app very easily. According to the TFA methodology, an app can be comprised of multiple processes running on multiple physical nodes keeping up with the philosophy of processes being horizontally scalable. Conforming apps should always depend on the operating system's process manager to handle process related logistics such as responding to crashed instances and handling user initiated process reboots and shutdowns. A TFA compliant app doesn't daemonize processes nor does it use **process identifier** (PID — a unique way to identify a process instance in the system) files as a mechanism to store the state of process execution. This model is significantly influenced by the UNIX operating system's execution model for service daemons.

Faster startup and graceful shutdown is the way to app agility and scalability

According to the TFA methodology, processes of an app are disposable, that is, they can be started or shutdown at no notice at all. As a result, it becomes quite obvious that the processes should be architected to have a minimal startup time and shutdown gracefully when required. The apparent benefit being that processes can be scaled on demand and the move from development to production for the app would be faster.

The startup time signifies that time a process takes to start serving requests. Shorter startup times mean faster releases and better scalability. Also, the responsible process managers can easily switch processes to other physical machines when needed without holding back any new requests.

Graceful shutdown means a process receiving a terminate request from the process manager and it cleanly shutting down, cleaning up any temporary state it might have created in the interim. For web process handling HTTP requests, a graceful shutdown could mean completing the in-flight requests and stopping listening to new requests on the designated port. In some cases, the client of the server process may attempt reconnection when the connection to the shutdown process is lost. For a long running job or a worker process, a graceful shutdown could mean restoring the in-flight request to a previous state such as a checkpoint state from where processing can begin once the process restarts. This technique is also useful in case of sudden, abrupt shutdowns, for example, in the case of hardware failures where a TFA can use a robust queuing mechanism to restore pending jobs to a queue. The TFA methodology also recommends making the app fault tolerant and capable of handling unknown and ungraceful shutdowns.

Development and production (and everything in between) should be as similar as possible

One of the key issues and source of an operations team's agony in modern day code development is the discrepancy between the development and the production environment. Developers keep on changing the app, sometimes taking months to check-in new versions of the code (time gap) followed by the operations team deploying something they are least familiar with, in a very short span of time (skill gap) and finally the app having to use a completely new stack of tools — very different from the developer's environment (technical gap). This is a classic example of why things work in one environment and not in another though everything looks equal, well almost.

The TFA methodology attempts to resolve this discrepancy by formulating the principle that the gap between development and production should be as small as possible. This principle enables continuous deployment by having the developer not only write the code but also deploy it faster and actively engage with the operations in monitoring the code behavior in production. Additionally, the TFA methodology recommends using methods to keep the technical gap between the two environments to a minimum.

In many cases, the discrepancy between the development and production arises from the use of backend services used by the two environments. It is quite usual for developers to use a lightweight backend service in development whether it is a database (SQLite) or a cache (custom filesystem based cache). However, when the same system is deployed in production, the app has to use a production scale database (**PostgreSQL**) or a distributed cache (**Memcached**) to serve the load expected of the production environment. Though this makes a lot of sense given the complexity and scale needed to be supported in the relevant environments, the TFA methodology suggests the contrary.

A TFA compliant app should use the same backing services in a development and production environment, so that no untoward surprises come up when moving to the production environment even though the code remains the same.

Over the years, developers have used adapters to provide the flexibility to easily port apps from one environment to another even though the corresponding backing service could be different. Adapters provide flexibility but they don't necessarily circumvent issues that crop up from the use of the different backing services. Also, the incentive to use different types of backend services in development and production has become minimal. Many backing services (that usually were used for production only) have now become easily usable on the development environment through better install management tools.

In summary, for the overall lifetime of an app, maintaining dev/prod parity could work out better and provide many benefits compared to using different flavors of the backing services in different environments—continuous deployment and a happy operations team are a few of them.

The app should just log the event not manage it

Logging data is a window into the various behavioral characteristics of your app. A log is a continuous stream of time-ordered application events that are produced by your app while running. In most cases, the generated log either gets routed to the standard output for developer's review or gets persisted to the filesystem as a logfile.

The TFA methodology recommends that a compliant app should never be responsible for managing the log, whether it is about routing the log event or storing it. In development, the log messages could be routed to the developer's standard output for troubleshooting. Whereas in staging or production, the app just generates the log and lets the execution environment pick up the log events from various running processes, collate them in a time-ordered fashion, and then route them to either a terminal to be viewed or a filesystem for long term storage.

The execution environment completely manages the internals of where the logs are stored and how they are routed and persisted. The app has no visibility or ability to configure the specifics of the logging system. This approach provides great flexibility in terms of further processing of the app log data. The data could be sent in real time to an analytics tool to derive critical information about the app or to locate occurrences of specific events, besides triggering alerts when a certain condition is met on the aggregated or continuous form of log data.

App's administrative or management task should be run as a one-off process

As a developer or an operations team member, you sometimes need to run specific administrative or app management tasks. Such tasks may include database migrations or scripts to execute a one-time installation fix. These tasks, though different from the app's regular tasks in terms of the frequency with which they are run, are no different when it comes to how they are run. These tasks are part of the same app, run against a specific release and use the same configuration and code that regular long running tasks use on the system. The same rules of dependency isolation should be applicable to such tasks according to the TFA methodology.

The TFA compliant app runs tasks in a standard way in the same environment as the regular tasks, not differentiating between those that run many times versus those that run once. For example, the web process's startup process (runs more often) and database migration (runs one-off) use the same bundle exec directive/command followed by a specific task to perform seemingly different tasks.

The TFA methodology also recommends that the code for administrative or management tasks be shipped with the app to keep the codebase consistent and avoid discrepancies between various versions of the app.

Developers could use the TFA principles to build powerful web apps on the Heroku platform. Throughout this book, you will appreciate many Heroku features that lent themselves to the formation of these principles.

Now that we understand the governing principles for developing web apps, let's create one and see how it works.

Creating a Heroku application

Heroku started by supporting **Ruby on Rails (RoR)** as the default framework for developing web apps. With RoR was born the core philosophy of Heroku platform — convention over configuration. This philosophy means that a developer should not have to make too many decisions while developing an app and at the same time should not lose the flexibility of developing it in a way he or she deems appropriate. Over a period of time, Heroku added support for other languages such as Java, Node.js, and others while enabling the same underlying philosophy for developing apps on the Heroku platform.

Let's see a real manifestation of this philosophy by creating a web app. The process of creating a Heroku app could be broken down (for simplicity) into the following steps:

1. Knowing and satisfying the prerequisites for the application.
2. Writing the application — this is what the developer should ideally bother about most.
3. Adding pre-existing, reusable assets to the app through add-ons.
4. Configuring the application to set up the environment for the app.
5. Deploying the application on Heroku.
6. Monitoring and scaling the application if need be.

In this section, let us build RoR application and while doing so, understand the steps involved in developing a real-world web app on Heroku.

To get started, you need the following prerequisites:

- A Heroku account
- A Heroku client (toolbelt — `https://toolbelt.heroku.com`) installed on your machine
- Ruby, Rails 3, Rubygems, and Bundler installed on your machine
- The ability to develop a basic Rails app
- A basic understanding of how to push your code to Git

The following are the next steps that you need to take to create a RoR application:

1. Assuming you have installed Heroku toolbelt, you will have access to the Heroku **command-line interface (CLI)** from your machine. You can use Heroku CLI to issue commands to be run on the Heroku platform.
2. Open a Windows (or a Unix) command shell window.

3. Connect to the Heroku platform by using the `heroku login` command as follows:

```
$ heroku login
Enter your Heroku credentials.
Email: abcdef@ghijklm.com
Password:
Could not find an existing public key.
Would you like to generate one? [Yn]
Generating new SSH public key.
Uploading ssh public key /Users/abcdef/.ssh/id_rsa.pub
```

Type Y at the prompt to generate and upload a new public SSH key to the Heroku account. For details of how this works, please refer to *Chapter 8, Heroku Security*.

4. Write a bare bone Rails app or utilize an existing Rails app for deployment.

5. We will create a basic Rails app to satisfy the minimum requirements of this step as follows:

```
$ rails new herokuclouddevapp --database=postgresql
$ cd herokuclouddevapp
```

- The `--database` argument is passed to use the Heroku PostgreSQL database as the data store for your app. It is recommended that you use it instead of SQLite, which was the default development data store earlier. Choosing this database will help keep the development configuration as close as possible to the production configuration of the app, thereby reducing the probability of having any production issues related to the database type discrepancy.

- Ensure that the `config/database.yml` file for your Rails app points to the PostgreSQL adapter and contains the right settings and user credentials for the supported app environments.

```
development:
  adapter: postgresql
  encoding: unicode
  database: herokuclouddevapp_development
  pool: 3
  username: herokucda
  password:
production:
  adapter: postgresql
  encoding: unicode
  database: herokuclouddevapp_production
  pool: 3
  username: herokucda
  password:
...
```

- ◦ Update your project dependencies by running the `bundle install` command.

6. If you are on Rails 4, you may not need to do this but if you are on Rails 3 (as we are), you would need to do the following configuration in the `config/application.rb` file of your rails project:

```
config.assets.initialize_on_precompile = false
```

Now why is this required? Well, Rails 3 has a concept of asset pipeline, which is a method to concatenate and compress JavaScript and CSS assets available in the project. During the build process, Heroku precompiles your assets into the slug to make them easily available for deployment. To make the step of asset precompilation faster, it is a best practice to inform Rails to load your app only partially. Heroku does not provide the whole application environment to the build process, hence making this setting compulsory.

7. Initialize your Git repository and store your code there as shown in the following screenshot:

```
$ git init
$ git add .
$ git commit -m "first version"
```

8. Create your Heroku application as shown in the following screenshot:

```
$ heroku create
Creating herokuclouddevapp... done, stack is cedar
http://herokuclouddevapp.herokuapp.com/ | git@heroku.com:herokuclouddevapp.git
Git remote heroku added
```

9. Deploy your code to Heroku. The step that triggers the entire build process for your application is as follows:

- ◦ The user should be within the application directory to start pushing the code. The user issues a `git push` to start building the application as follows:

```
$ git push heroku master
Counting objects: 63, done.
Delta compression using up to 8 threads.
Compressing objects: 100% (49/49), done.
Writing objects: 100% (63/63), 26.03 KiB, done.
Total 63 (delta 2), reused 0 (delta 0)
-----> Ruby/Rails app detected
```

- ° Bundler — the dependency management tool for Ruby, tries to resolve the dependencies on other gems/packages and installs them as shown in the following command line:

```
Bundler will do a full resolve so native gems are handled properly.
      This may result in unexpected gem versions being used in your app.
-----> Installing dependencies using Bundler version 1.3.0.pre.5
      Running: bundle install --without development:test --path vendor/bundle --binstubs vendor/bundle/bin
      Fetching gem metadata from https://rubygems.org/..........
      Fetching gem metadata from https://rubygems.org/..
      Installing rake (10.0.3)
      Installing i18n (0.6.1)
      Installing multi_json (1.5.0)
      Installing activesupport (3.2.9)
      Your bundle is complete! It was installed into ./vendor/bundle
```

- ° Loads database configuration from environment (DATABASE_URL), completes Rails asset precompilation and plugin insertion as follows:

```
-----> Writing config/database.yml to read from DATABASE_URL
-----> Preparing app for Rails asset pipeline
      Running: rake assets:precompile
      Asset precompilation completed (11.90s)
-----> Rails plugin injection
      Injecting rails_log_stdout
      Injecting rails3_serve_static_assets
```

- ° Finally, the build process detects the supported process types (either by reading the Procfile or uses the default). Also, it calculates the slug size and launches the application from http://<application name>.herokuapp.com as follows:

```
-----> Discovering process types
      Procfile declares types      -> (none)
      Default types for Ruby/Rails -> console, rake, web, worker
-----> Compiled slug size: 9.0MB
-----> Launching... done, v9
      http://herokuclouddevapp.herokuapp.com deployed to Heroku

To git@heroku.com:herokuclouddevapp.git
 * [new branch]      master -> master
```

The slug that results from this build process can now be booted on the dyno manifold alongside applications written in other languages.

So, we are done building a simple Rails 3 application. Now, let us look at the concept of configuration variables, also called the config vars. The config vars is a way to influence the execution of your app depending on the deployment phase, for example, development, test, staging, or production. Config vars is the focus of the next section.

Configuring your Heroku application

Most application deployments can be a mess; multiple deployments—a production site, multiple test beds, staging environment, and who knows how many development environments are maintained locally by the developers. Additionally, there can be thousands of deployments for the most popular standardized open source packages. This poses a huge challenge for using configuration information of your application that might change depending on the environment one is working with. Even though the source code being run is the same, almost every time the configuration comprises of a large chunk of information that is environment specific. Typical examples include user credentials, database configuration, and so on. The use of property files is quite common to support such a requirement. However, such an approach has its pitfalls as property files quickly replicate themselves quite unmanageably.

Heroku provides a rich CLI-based configuration related API to manage application configuration information.

The Heroku application configuration API

Heroku uses the concept of configuration variables for application configuration much on the lines of environment variables, as used in Unix flavors.

The Heroku application configuration API consists of the following commands:

- `config:add`: This command adds a configuration parameter
- `config:get`: This command gets the value of a configuration variable
- `config:remove`: This command removes the configuration variable

The configuration variables take the place of environment variables for the app. These environment variables remain in place across deploys and app restarts and need to be set only once. If you want to change a configuration variable, you can use the `config:add` API and set the configuration variable to the new value. Any time you add or update a configuration variable (including remove a configuration variable), the app will get restarted.

The code can extract the configuration variable value based on the configuration variable name (which acts as the key) and execute a particular code flow; for example, if the developer wants to use a configuration variable named TRY_COUNT, which signifies the number of attempts an app should make to connect to a database before timing out and throwing an error, the `config:add` API can be used to set the config variable TRY_COUNT to some value, say 10. The code will try to connect to the database TRY_COUNT a number of times before throwing an error on the standard output.

Examples of using application configuration

Let's look at a few examples of using the configuration API. We will show the most common operations used while developing web apps. They are, adding, verifying, retrieving, and removing a configuration variable as given in the following steps:

1. To add a configuration variable, type the following command:

   ```
   $ heroku config:add GITHUB_USERNAME=whizkid

   Adding config vars and restarting myapp... done, v3
   GITHUB_USERNAME: whizkid
   ```

2. To check all configuration variables available to the app, type the following command:

   ```
   $ heroku config
   GITHUB_USERNAME: whizkid
   OTHER_VAR:       production
   ```

3. To retrieve a configuration variable, type the following command:

   ```
   $ heroku config:get GITHUB_USERNAME
   whizkid
   ```

4. To remove a configuration variable, type the following command:

   ```
   $ heroku config:remove GITHUB_USERNAME
   Unsetting GITHUB_USERNAME and restarting myapp... done, v4
   ```

The persistence of configuration variables

The configuration variables discussed in the preceding section are persistent—they will remain in place across deploys and application restarts. Unless you need to change these, you can create them once and use them repeatedly. Configuration variable data (the collection of all keys and values) is limited to 16 KB for each application.

Accessing configuration variables at runtime

You can read the variables at runtime using the language specific method. For example, to access an environment variable called DATABASE_URL in Ruby, type the following command:

```
ENV['DATABASE_URL']
```

After deploying to Heroku, the application will use the keys set in the config directory.

Limits on configuration data

There is an upper limit on the size of configuration variable data (including key and values) for each application on the Heroku platform. The current limit on the configuration variable data is set to 16 KB per app.

The Heroku plugin provides a way to retrieve all the configuration variables from an app and put them in the local environment of the developer. The reverse is also possible if needed.

Using the Heroku config plugin

To interactively pull your configuration, prompting for each value to be overwritten in your local file, type the following command:

```
$ heroku config:pull --overwrite --interactive
```

To push your local configuration to Heroku, use the `config:push` command as follows:

```
$ heroku config:push
```

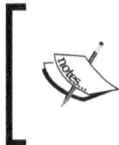

> One needs to be very discreet while pushing configuration to Heroku as it might accidentally overwrite your application's configuration in the Heroku environment—something you might not always want.

So, we wrote a simple Rails 3 app and learned how to set up configuration variables for the app on the Heroku platform. One question you might have is, how does Heroku map the code we send using a `git push` command to the language runtime to be used to build the code? Well, Heroku uses the concept of buildpacks to enable the needed language runtime for the app written in a supported language.

Introducing buildpacks

To support a language on Heroku, you need to build your application written in that language on top of a build-time adapter that can compile the application into an executable program suitable to run on the Cedar stack. This build-time adapter is known as a **buildpack** in Heroku parlance. The Cedar stack provides a universal runtime into which the language support is plugged in via the buildpack. A buildpack is responsible for building a complete working runtime environment around the application. This may include language VMs and other runtime dependencies that are needed by the application. Your buildpack will need to provide these binaries and combine them with the application code.

Heroku, by default, provides buildpack support for all natively supported languages. These default buildpacks are available to all Heroku applications during compilation and are downloadable from GitHub. When you push your application to Heroku, these buildpacks are searched in order to find the appropriate runtime to use for the application.

You can locate any buildpack at GitHub by following the following URL format:

```
https://github.com/heroku/heroku-buildpack-<Language>
```

For example, common buildpacks can be found at the following links:

Language	URL
Ruby	https://github.com/heroku/heroku-buildpack-ruby
Node.js	https://github.com/heroku/heroku-buildpack-nodejs
Clojure	https://github.com/heroku/heroku-buildpack-clojure
Python	https://github.com/heroku/heroku-buildpack-python
Java	https://github.com/heroku/heroku-buildpack-java

However, if you want to use a different buildpack for a supported language or want to add support for a new language, you can use/write a custom buildpack.

Using a custom buildpack

To use a custom buildpack, all you need to do is to override the Heroku default buildpack by specifying a custom buildpack in the BUILDPACK_URL configuration variable as follows on the Heroku CLI:

```
$ heroku config:add BUILDPACK_URL=https://github.com/heroku/heroku-buildpack-mylang
```

This command points BUILDPACK_URL to the custom buildpack using the Heroku command config:add. You can now use the buildpack for the language specified by mylang.

Specifying a custom buildpack at the app creation stage

We can specify a custom buildpack during the application creation step as follows:

```
$ heroku create myapp --buildpack https://github.com/heroku/heroku-buildpack-mylang
```

You can specify an exact version of a buildpack by using a Git revision in
BUILDPACK_URL as follows:

```
git://repo.git#master git://repo.git#v1.2.0
```

Buildpack URLs can point to either Git repositories or tarballs.

Third-party buildpacks

Third-party buildpacks contain software that is not under Heroku's control. If you
want to use these buildpacks, you need to carefully review the source code of the
buildpack and make sure it is safe to use and does not cause any kind of security
vulnerability. Also, these buildpacks may not be up to date with the latest version
or release of the language runtime.

The buildpack API

You can create custom buildpacks to deploy Heroku applications written in
languages not supported by default. Heroku offers a **buildpack API** to help
developers come up with buildpacks for newer languages and frameworks. Once
written, these buildpacks can be checked in to a common source code repository
such as GitHub and used by developers to build their Heroku applications.

Developers can even override the default buildpacks by providing an alternate
URL for the overriding buildpack during the build process. You can do this to use
an upgraded buildpack that might provide more recent support for the relevant
language while your existent buildpack might be dated.

Components of a buildpack API

A buildpack consists of three scripts; they are as follows:

Script name	Purpose
bin/detect	Detects whether this buildpack can be applied to an application
bin/compile	This script is responsible for converting the application to a runnable state on Heroku
bin/release	This script provides certain metadata information such as add-ons to install or default process types back to the runtime

The bin/detect script

The usage of this script is `bin/detect <build_dir>`. The following is its description:

- The `/bin/detect` script accepts a single argument

- This script accepts `<build_dir>` as an argument

- The script on execution should return an exit code of 0 if the application present in `<build_dir>` can be handled by this buildpack

- If the exit code is 0, the script should print a human-readable framework name to `stdout`

The following is the sample code:

```sh
#!/bin/sh

# this pack is valid for apps with a Makefile in the root
if [ -f $1/Makefile ]; then
  echo "GNU C application"
  exit 0
else
  exit 1
fi
```

The script checks whether `Makefile` exists in `<build_dir>` where the application code resides, and once the application `Makefile` is detected, it prints a message to the user on `stdout` and exits with an `exit` code of `0` (success). If `Makefile` is not detected, the shell script exits with a nonzero error code. A nonzero error code signifies an error condition that requires an action on the part of the developer. The developer should ensure in this case that the correct `Makefile` is present in the directory specified as the command-line argument.

The bin/compile script

The usage of this script is `bin/compile <build_dir> <cache_dir>`. The following is its description:

- `<build_dir>` is the location of the application

- `<cache_dir>` is the location that buildpack uses to cache build artifacts between multiple runs of the build process

The application in `<build_dir>` along with all changes made by the compile script will be converted into a slug that can be executed on a dyno in the Heroku environment.

The content of <cache_dir> is retained between builds to improve the build performance as this directory is used to cache the outcome of cumbersome and time taking tasks such as dependency resolution. The <cache_dir> directory is available only during slug compilation, and is specific to the application being built. The full content of the <cache_dir> directory is stored with the Git repository and must be shipped across the network each time the application is deployed; hence, this directory should be the right size to avoid causing significant delay to the build process. To use a cache, the application should create the <cache_dir> directory if it doesn't exist.

All output received on stdout from this script will be displayed to the user. The following is the sample code:

```bash
#!/usr/bin/env bash
# bin/compile <build-dir> <cache-dir>

set -e
set -o pipefail

BUILD_DIR=$1
CACHE_DIR=$2

function indent() {
  c='s/^/       /'
  case $(uname) in
    Linux) sed -u "$c";;
    *) sed -l "$c";;
  esac
}
cd $BUILD_DIR

# configure
if [ -f configure ]; then
  echo "-----> Configuring"
  ./configure 2>&1 | indent
fi

# make
echo "-----> Compiling with Make"
make 2>&1 | indent
```

This script changes the directory to the build directory where the application is stored and runs the configure script named `.configure` to set up the application. The `.configure` script checks if the necessary prerequisites for building the app are available. Once the configure part of compilation is over, the script runs the `make` utility to create an executable for your application.

The bin/release script

The usage of this script is `bin/release <build_dir>`, where `<build_dir>` is the location of the application.

The `bin/release` script provides certain metadata information back to the runtime.

The following is the sample code:

```
#!/bin/sh

cat << EOF
---
addons:
  - heroku-postgresql:dev
default_process_types:
  web: bin/node server.js
EOF
```

This script returns information about the add-ons to install and `default_process_types`, which is a hash of default Procfile entries. Now, let us see what it takes to write a new buildpack.

Writing a buildpack

Writing a buildpack consists of the following steps:

1. Writing three scripts: detect, compile, and release. Each of these scripts serves a different purpose for the build procedure.

2. Check-in the three scripts into GitHub in a standardized folder structure. For example, if the GitHub username is `johndoe`, then the buildpack can be stored in `johndoe/heroku-buildpack-mylang/bin`.

> A `README` file is recommended for the users to understand how to use your buildpack.

3. Use the following `config:add` command to add new `BUILDPACK_URL` for use with your app:

```
$ heroku config:add
BUILDPACK_URL=https://github.com/heroku/heroku-buildpack-
mybuildpack
```

4. You can also specify a buildpack during app creation as follows:

```
$ heroku create myapp --buildpack
https://github.com/heroku/heroku-buildpack- mybuildpack
```

After you have written, configured, and linked your app to the right buildpack, it is time to build the app and transform it into an executable that can be run on the Heroku platform. The slug compiler tool helps us with that.

The slug compiler

The slug compiler is responsible for creating an executable application from raw code by building the application, linking required binaries, and compressing the executable for faster deployment. The end product of the slug compilation process is what is termed as the **slug**.

Once the slugs are generated, they are compressed to decrease their size. Slugs are pre-packaged copies of the application optimized for quick distribution across the dyno manifold—Heroku's process execution environment. When we `git push` to Heroku, the code is sent to the slug compiler that transforms the user repository into a slug. Scaling an application then causes the slug to be downloaded and expanded for execution on a dyno.

The slug compiler is invoked by a Git pre-receive hook—a custom script that gets invoked when code is pushed to the Heroku platform by the developer. The slug compiler uses the following steps during its run:

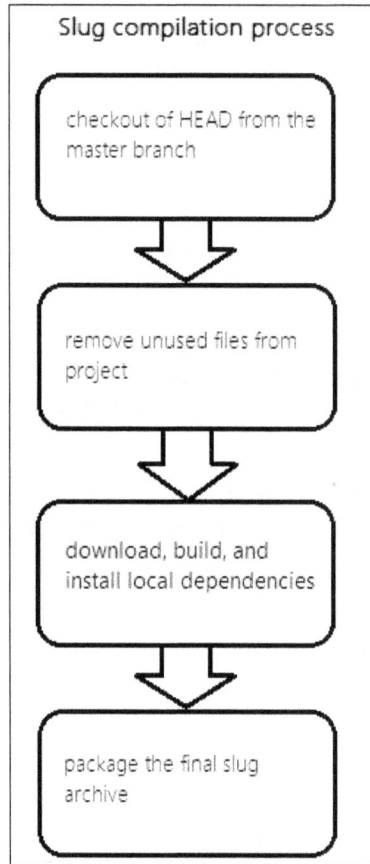

The following is the description of slug compilation steps:

1. Create a fresh **checkout of HEAD from the master branch**.

2. Remove unused files, including the .git directory, anything in the log and tmp directories, and anything specified in a top-level .slugignore file.

3. Download, build, and install local dependencies as specified in your build file with the dependency management tool supported by the language (for example, Bundler for Ruby).

4. Package the final slug archive.

Optimizing the slug

If your repository contains files not necessary to run your app, you should consider rightsizing or optimizing your slug by doing a few optimizations. You can prevent files in your repository from getting included in the slug by inserting the *to be excluded* filenames in the `.slugignore` file. These excluded files are typically files that contain unit tests, documents (PDF), or test data of the project that necessarily isn't required in the deployed app.

The following is an example of the contents of a `.slugignore` file:

```
*.pdf
/test
/spec
```

The `.slugignore` file causes files to be removed after you push the code to Heroku and before the buildpack runs. This lets you prevent large files from being included in the final slug. You can further reduce the number of unnecessary files (temporary or logfiles) by ensuring that they aren't tracked by Git, in which case they won't be deployed to Heroku either.

Size limits

The slug size is displayed after a successful compile. You could also type the `heroku info:apps` command to find the slug size once the slug is created. The maximum slug size is 200 MB; applications should ideally be much lesser than this to help faster deployment and execution. Smaller slugs can be transferred across the dyno manifold much faster allowing relatively instant scaling.

Slug size	Remarks
<15 MB	Small size, fastest to deploy and run
<50 MB	Average size, moderate deployment time
>90MB	Large size, best avoided, slower deploys and execution

If the application size gets beyond the largest size, it is recommended that the slug size be optimized by moving the larger files such as PDF or mp3 or video to asset storage, say a CDN, and remove unnecessary files and dependencies from the application.

To check the slug size, you can use the `apps:info` command as follows:

```
$ heroku apps:info
=== herokuclouddevapp
Addons:       heroku-postgresql:dev
Git URL:      git@heroku.com:herokuclouddevapp.git
Owner Email:XXXXXX@yyyy.com
Repo Size:    6M
Slug Size:    8M
Stack:        cedar
Web URL:      http://herokuclouddevapp.herokuapp.com/
```

The **repository (repo)** size has no predefined limits but very large repositories are discouraged as they cause transfer timeouts and slow code pushes. The build cache is also stored inside the repository, hence the repository might be larger remotely than locally.

Usually, checking in binary files into repository or large sized application development logs cause the repository to grow in size sometimes to nonrecommended levels. Files checked in by accident could optionally be removed by filtering them with Git filter-branch utility. Make sure that you force push the code next time after running this utility after coordinating with other developers.

Summary

This chapter was all about building web apps on Heroku. With the help of a simple example, we learned the steps involved in building a web app. We also reviewed the guiding principles for developing SaaS web apps on the Heroku platform. We looked at the configuration API provided by Heroku CLI to set and unset environment variables for your app in the Heroku platform. We also delved a little deeper into buildpacks—Heroku's way of identifying the language runtime to be used for building your app. Finally, we looked at the process of slug compilation that builds your code into something executable, linking with it the necessary libraries and other assets.

Now that we have a reasonable understanding of Heroku's features, the platform stack, and the build process, it is a good time to learn how to run applications on Heroku; appropriately the subject of the next chapter.

4
Deploying Heroku Applications

In the previous chapter, we learned about building Heroku applications. Specifically, we explored how the build process works, how the underlying Buildpack system enables the correct runtime to build your app, and finally, how configuration parameters, also called config vars, play an important role in your app's execution semantics.

Now, we will take the next logical step and understand the deployment phase of Heroku application's development life cycle.

In this chapter, among other things, we will look at the following:

- Understanding Heroku's deployment requirements
- Gaining familiarity with the Git-distributed version control used extensively with Heroku source code management
- Deploying your app to Heroku and learning how to optimize the slug
- Deciphering the concept of cloning and forking your Heroku app
- Optimizing the app deployment step
- Introducing and understanding the concept of regions for deployment
- Tracking application changes with deployment hooks
- Managing releases of your Heroku app

Deployment on Heroku

While many platforms today offer a rich set of tools and accessories to run web applications seamlessly, one area where Heroku stands out is its simple and efficient deployment model. The Heroku model of deployment is simple—focus on writing your app and leave the rest to Heroku.

Heroku deployment is comprised of the following:

- Getting a Heroku account
- Installing the toolbelt client kitLogging into the Heroku account using the Heroku client
- Writing your application
- Pushing your application to Heroku using Git version control

The pushed code gets built into a slug or self-contained executable by the slug compiler and executes as a dyno (the Heroku process) in the dyno manifold (the Heroku execution environment).

No matter what the programming language, the Heroku application deployment follows pretty much the same order of events from being just a piece of code to being a full-fledged production web app. The fact that a developer just needs to create the application and Heroku takes care of launching the app from there on is a very powerful aspect of the Heroku deployment model.

In this chapter, for the sake of completeness and consistency, we will cover each of the preceding elements and focus more deeply on the ones that have not been covered before.

Getting a Heroku account

The first step to start using Heroku is to sign up for a Heroku account. Go to `http://www.heroku.com` and sign up for a Heroku account.

You can choose one of the following:

- A free 750 hours of dyno per application, per monthly usage
- Buy the required hours of dyno as per your application's demand

On subscribing successfully, you can review your account details on the Heroku dashboard.

Installing the toolbelt client kit

Next, download the Heroku toolbelt kit from the Heroku website `https://toolbelt.heroku.com`.

The toolbelt kit contains the following components:

- **Heroku client**: This is a command-line tool that helps create and manage apps
- **Foreman**: This is a utility that gives you the flexibility of running applications locally, especially at times when you want to troubleshoot the Git revision control system and relevant utility programs that help you push/download your code to/from Heroku

Logging into the Heroku account

You can log in to your Heroku account by setting up a secure SSH session first.

Setting up SSH

If you don't use SSH already, you'll need to create a public-private key pair to push code to Heroku. This key pair is used to keep the channel of communication between the developer and Heroku secure.

Generating a public key is as simple as entering the following command:

```
$ ssh-keygen -t rsa
Generating public/private rsa key pair.
Enter file in which to save the key (/Users/ahanjura/.ssh/id_rsa):
Enter passphrase (empty for no passphrase):
Enter same passphrase again:
Your identification has been saved in /Users/ahanjura/.ssh/id_rsa.
Your public key has been saved in /Users/ahanjura/.ssh/id_rsa.pub.
The key fingerprint is:
a1:84:0a:08:72:90:c6:d9:d5:42:d6:e3:04:d5:6c:3e ahanjura@edha.pc
```

In this command, we are using the **RSA** encryption method to secure our credentials. With the RSA method, you can sign/verify and encrypt/decrypt your credentials for authentication purposes. Another reliable but slower security option you can use is the DSA algorithm that allows you to sign and verify the credentials. It is claimed that it is harder to crack a DSA key than an RSA key for a key of the same length.

Pressing *Enter* at both prompts makes a password-less key secure. As long as you keep the contents of ~/.ssh/id_rsa secret, your key will be secure even without a password.

You can read further details about the ssh-keygen tool at http://en.wikipedia.org/wiki/Ssh-keygen.

The first time you run the Heroku command, you'll be prompted for your credentials. Your public key will then be uploaded automatically to Heroku, allowing you to deploy code to all of your applications.

Your public key needs to be available on Heroku to let you connect.

You can remove old keys, which may not have been used for a while, using the following command:

```
$ heroku keys:remove ahanjura@edha.pc
Removing ahanjura@edha.pc SSH key... done
```

The key's name is the user@workstation bit that appears at the end of the key line in your public key file.

You can see a list of all of the keys, including the name, using the following command:

```
$ heroku keys
=== joe@example.com Keys
ssh-dss AAAAB8NzaC...DVj3R4Ww== joe@edha.pc
```

The long command-line option to Heroku keys command displays the longer form of the key details.

Once done, you can issue the command on the Heroku CLI:

```
$ heroku login
```

Connect to the Heroku server once you have entered your account credentials (e-mail and password). Now, you are ready to start pushing your application(s) to Heroku.

Writing your application

This step is really what a developer needs to be concerned with. You can create your application in a language of your choice—Ruby on Rails, Node.js, Clojure, Java, or any other supported language—and then push it to Heroku.

Pushing your application to Heroku

This step is the heart of deployment as far as Heroku apps are concerned. Deploying a Heroku app is as simple and uncomplicated as issuing the following command:

```
git push heroku master
```

And as they say, the rest is magic!

In this chapter, we will delve a little more into Git—the collaborative version control system used for Heroku application development. We will also touch on topics that are key to understanding deployment on Heroku and facilities in the platform, topics that help in making Heroku such an easy and efficient deployment platform.

The Git vocabulary

Heroku utilizes Git as the source code revision control system of choice for applications deployed on the Heroku platform. Git is a very powerful decentralized revision control system for managing code in a distributed development environment. Git has evolved to become the revision control system of choice for thousands of distributed software projects across the world.

To work with Heroku, one needs to be a little familiar with various Git commands. Hence, we will cover some Git concepts and commands to help you work with Heroku efficiently.

Getting started with Git

There are two scenarios that are relevant with respect to tracking projects with Git. They are as follows:

- Tracking a new project
- Using an existing Git project

Files that have not been added to Git have untracked status, as the repository isn't aware of their existence and has no reference to them.

Files that are already in the repository have a tracked status and are in the last snapshot of your repository. They can be reversed to an earlier state, changed to a new state, or staged and committed to the Git repository.

Tracking a new project

While tracking a new project with Git, you need to add the directory where your source lies to the Git repository. This is called initializing your Git project repository. You need to go to the respective directory on the filesystem where your code lies and type the following command:

```
$ git init
```

This creates a directory called `.git` on your local filesystem that contains a bare bone git repository structure inside with all of the necessary repository files. To start tracking your code with Git, you need to add the code to the Git repository using the `git add` command as shown in the following figure:

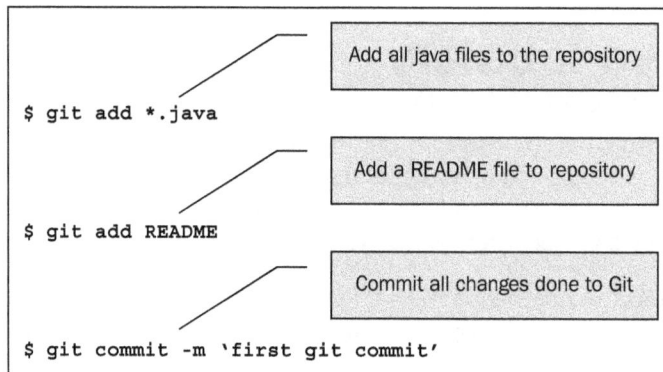

```
$ git add *.java           Add all java files to the repository

$ git add README           Add a README file to repository

                           Commit all changes done to Git

$ git commit -m 'first git commit'
```

Using an existing Git project

You can use an existing Git project and make changes to it, then later track these changes by using the Git commands. To use an existing Git project, you need to clone or copy the Git project to a directory on the local filesystem and then work on it locally. Once you are done, you can commit your changes to the Git repository, and Git ensures that your changes are stored in the repository consistently. To clone a Git repository, you need to use the `git clone` command in the following way:

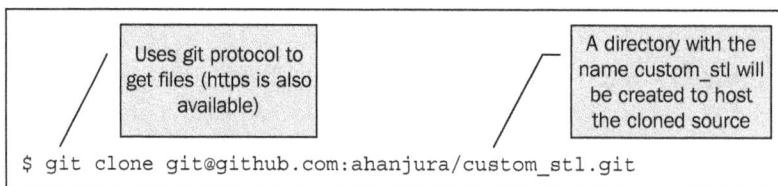

```
           Uses git protocol to              A directory with the
           get files (https is also          name custom_stl will
           available)                         be created to host
                                              the cloned source

$ git clone git@github.com:ahanjura/custom_stl.git
```

To use a custom directory name to check out the source, you can append the target directory name at the end of the command in the previous screenshot, which is separated by a space character, and run it. The source will be cloned in the directory specified by you in the command.

One thing worth noting is that the Git client supports different protocols to interact with the repository. The Git repository can use the `http(s)://` or `user@server:/path.git` format, which in turn uses the SSH transfer protocol.

The life cycle of an artifact in Git

A source file follows a typical workflow as it goes from being an untracked artifact (when nothing is added to Git) to a tracked and committed item (when the file is committed using `git commit`) in the Git version control system.

This workflow can be summarized as follows:

1. The developer first starts with a file that is unknown to Git and is hence untracked.
2. The developer adds the file to Git using the `git add` command. Now the file is tracked but unmodified.
3. The developer edits the file to make the necessary changes in the app. The file reaches the modified state.
4. You prepare the file to commit by optionally staging it. The file is ready to commit now.
5. The developer commits the file to Git using the `git commit` command.

You can further remove the commits (undo the changes) or remove the artifact itself depending on specific needs. You may need to edit the file many times before it takes its final shape, hence part of this workflow can be repeated many times.

Tracking files in a Git project

It is quite simple to track the status of your source files. Use the `git status` command to get the current state of your repository in the following way:

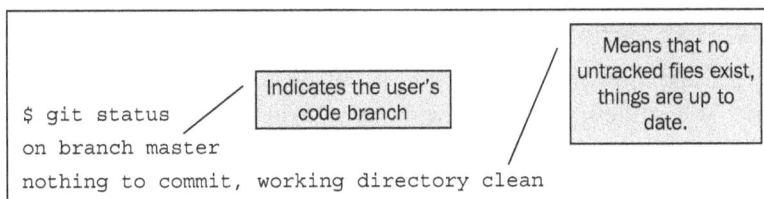

```
$ git status
on branch master
nothing to commit, working directory clean
```

Indicates the user's code branch

Means that no untracked files exist, things are up to date.

If you edit a new `test.rb` file and try the `git status` command, Git will report the untracked file as follows:

```
                    ┌─────────────────────────┐
              ╱     │     Edit a new file      │
             ╱      └─────────────────────────┘
$ vim test.rb ╱   ┌─────────────────────────┐
$ git status      │     Check git status     │
                  └─────────────────────────┘
on branch master
Untracked files:
    (use "git add <file>..." to include in what will be committed)
                        ┌──────────────────────┐
                   ╱    │  Git lists untracked │
                  ╱     │    file test.rb      │
        test.rb         └──────────────────────┘

nothing added to commit but untracked files present (use "git add" to track)
```

Let us add the `test.rb` file and verify that it is tracked now. Run the `git status` command as follows:

```
                  ┌──────────────┐
            ╱     │  Add test.rb │
           ╱      │ to repository│
          ╱       └──────────────┘
         ╱      ┌──────────────────┐
        ╱    ╱  │ Check git status │
       ╱    ╱   └──────────────────┘
$ git add test.rb
$ git status
On branch master
Changes to be committed:   ┌──────────────────┐
    (use "git reset HEAD<fi│ New file added to │ge)
                           │       repo        │
              ╱            └──────────────────┘
        new file:   test.rb
```

When you don't need Git to track your files

You can ignore the files that you don't want Git to add automatically to the repository or those that show up as being tracked, by using the `.gitignore` file. The `.gitignore` file lists all of the files (represented by filenames or regular expression-matching filename patterns) that you want to add to the excluded list. Files such as the log files or files generated during the build process fall under this category.

The `.gitignore` file follows certain conventions with respect to being interpreted by the Git system. If it contains a blank line or one started with a hash (#) character, the line is ignored.

You can use standard global patterns and end patterns with a forward slash (/) to indicate a directory or negate a pattern by using the negation operator (!) before the pattern.

A sample .gitignore file looks like the following:

```
# ignore all files in the temp/directory
temp/

# but do track setup.xml, even through you're ignoring .xml files
!setup.xml

# ignore the root SYSTEM file but not subdir/SYSTEM
/SYSTEM

# ignore man/ls.txt, but not man/server/ls.txt
man/*.txt

# ignore all .txt files in the win/directory
win/**/*.txt

# no .xml files
*.xml
```

The git diff command – knowing what changed

Type git diff in the following manner with no other arguments to check what you have changed but not yet staged:

```
$ git diff
diff --git a/test.rb b/test.rb
index abcdef0..ef65585 100644
--- a/test.rb
+++ b/test.rb
@@ -27,6 +26,10 @@ def main
            @commit.parents[0].parents[0].parents[0]
        end

+        foo_run(x, 'commits 1') do
+         git.commits.size
+        end
+
        foo_run(x, 'commits 2') do
          log = glt.commits('master', 7)
          log.size
```

The git diff command shows the lines where the changes are affected (+ sign at the start of the line).

Committing your changes

New or changed files that are not added again using `git add` since they were last modified won't go into a commit. They will continue to exist as modified files on your disk. Once everything is staged, we are ready to commit the changes.

To commit a change, use the `git commit` command from your source directory in the following way:

```
$ git commit -m "this is a sample commit"
```

This command will commit your source directory contents that you changed since the last checkout to git.

Deleting a file

To remove a file from Git, you need to remove it from the tracked files list and then commit the change using the `git commit` command. Use the `git rm` command to remove the file from the tracked list and also from the working directory, so that we don't see the file as an untracked file on running the `git status` command later.

If you delete the file physically from the filesystem, running the `git status` command will show that file as `changes not staged for commit`.

You need to run the `git rm` command to stage the file for deletion:

```
$ git rm test.rb
rm 'test.rb'
$ git status
On branch master
Changes to be committed:
  (use "git reset HEAD <file>..." to unstage)

        deleted:    test.rb
```

If you commit now, the file will be gone for good.

Moving a file

Git also provides a convenience `git mv` function to rename a file, which is as follows:

```
$ git mv src dest
```

This command is a shortcut for renaming a file outside Git, removing the old file from the repository, and adding the renamed one to Git. It is more of a utility function. One interesting thing about file movement is that Git doesn't store any metadata about the file movement to tell it that the file was renamed. However, if you check the status after renaming the file, Git has an *after the event* mechanism to identify that the file was renamed.

Viewing commit history

One of the most common encounters a developer has with Git is to check the history of code commits or modifications to the repository over a period of time. A developer may want to know how and when an artifact changed from its very first addition to the repository. The `git log` command comes in handy in such a situation. The `git log` provides great flexibility in showing only a partial list or a detailed explanation of changes for an artifact based on the command-line option passed to it.

You can use the `git log` command to review the commit history of the file in question as follows:

```
$ git log
commit aa82a6dff817ea66f44342007202620a23763242
Author: Anubhav Hanjura <ahanjura@abcdef.com>
Date:   Mon Mar 24 11:52:10 2008 -0700

    changed the version number

commit e77bef06e7f659402fe7567ebf99ed00de2209e6
Author: Anubhav Hanjura <ahanjura@abcdef.com>
Date:   Fri Mar 7 11:27:13 2008 -0700

    first commit
```

Undoing a change

To revert your file changes to the last committed version, you can use this variation of the `git checkout` command as follows:

```
$ git checkout -- <filename>
```

This command restores the filename to its last committed state and undoes all changes you had done in the interim.

You can use some Git help

To get help on a Git command, you can use one of the following commands:

- Option 1:

  ```
  $ git help <verb>
  ```

- Option 2:

  ```
  $ git <verb> --help
  ```

- Option 3:

  ```
  $ man git-<verb>
  ```

The `<verb>` parameter is a specific command that you need help for.

The local repository

Before you can push your code to Heroku, you will need to create a local Git repository and check in your files there. This repository serves as a local source code repository. The code will be pushed to Heroku for your application to build and run later.

Remote repositories

The commands we saw so far are generic commands to track your source code in your Git repository. However, in the context of Heroku cloud application development, we have to deal with code repositories that are hosted on the Heroku platform for build and deployment. Hence, it is important to understand concepts surrounding remote repositories.

Remote repositories (or remotes) are versions of your project hosted on a different machine than your local machine, typically, on a distributed system accessible via a set of functions to retrieve and update the source artifacts.

To see the remote repository of your project, you can use the `git remote` command as follows:

```
$ git remote -v
origin git://github.com/ahaniura/custom_stl.git (fetch)
origin git://github.com/ahanjura/custom_stl.git (push)
```

Creating a Heroku remote

Once the local Git repository is created, you need to create a Heroku remote to keep the source code pushed to the Heroku environment (using Git push). Heroku applications expect the application directory structure at the root of the repository. Failing to have the application files in the correct directory will cause failure on running the application.

The following figure shows the typical set of commands issued by the user of Git and the corresponding direction of flow of information:

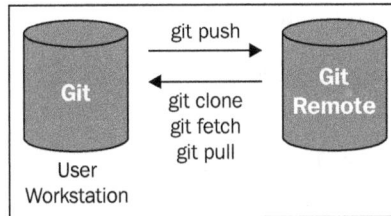

The heroku create command creates a new application on Heroku in addition to a git remote that is used to receive your application source files. The git remote command is just a reference to the remote source code repository. By default, the name of the remote created is heroku. It is possible to change the default name; however, this has to be done using a command-line parameter in the following way:

```
$ heroku create
Creating gentle-mesa-5445... done, stack is cedar
http://gentle-mesa-5445.herokuapp.com/ | git@heroku.com:gentle-mesa-5445.
git
Git remote heroku added
```

To verify the remote in your Git configuration, type the following command:

```
$ git remote -v
heroku      git@heroku.com:gentle-mesa-5445.git (fetch)
heroku      git@heroku.com:gentle-mesa-5445.git (push)
```

To associate a Git repo with an existing application, type the following command:

```
$ heroku git:remote -a gentle-mesa-5445
Git remote heroku added.
```

To name the remote as a custom name instead of Heroku, as done earlier, use the following option:

```
$ heroku git:remote -a gentle-mesa-5445 -r myremote
Git remote myremote added.
```

Renaming an application

It is possible to rename an application by using the `heroku:rename` command. The application becomes accessible by the new name immediately, and the old name should not be used anymore to address it.

For example, to rename the application as `foozball.herokuapp.com`, you can type the following command:

```
$ heroku apps:rename foozball
Renaming gentle-mesa-5445 to foozball... done
http://foozball.herokuapp.com/ | git@heroku.com:foozball.git
Git remote heroku updated
```

This command succeeded because we typed inside the application folder. If you want to change the application name from outside the Git checkout or application folder, you can type the following command:

```
$ heroku apps:rename newname --app oldname
http://newname.heroku.com/ | git@heroku.com:newname.git
```

Any Git remote that points to the old name needs to be changed or updated manually to reflect the application name change as follows:

```
$ git remote rm heroku
$ heroku git:remote -a foozball
```

Sending code to Heroku

Once you have created the remote, the Heroku remote in this case, you can push your code to Heroku by typing the following command:

```
$ git push heroku master
updating 'refs/heads/master'
```

The `git push` command effectively pushes the code to the Heroku remote environment. In this case, we pushed the code to the remote master as we pushed the code for the first time from our local environment.

If you want to push code from a local branch to a remote master, you can use the following command:

```
$ git push heroku somebranch:master
```

Alternatively, you can merge the code with the master and push your code to Heroku.

If you use the special remote name origin, then your push command doesn't have to explicitly specify the remote name, and you could just type the following:

```
$ git push
```

Here, `origin` is used as the default remote name.

Optimizing slug size

You may not want to push everything in your application to Heroku for a wide variety of reasons. For example, you don't really need to send logfiles or static assets to your remote Heroku environment because it is pretty much useless to store them on the remote as they would occupy disk space for no valid reason.

For this cause, Git provides you with a way to skip files or directories you don't want or those that you need to push to the remote environment. This ability is available through the `.gitignore` file, which contains the list of files that you don't want to push across. This list can be literal filenames or wildcard filenames. Git ignores these files when pushing the code to the remote Heroku environment. This has the added benefit of keeping the slug size smaller and speeding up the boot up time for the dynos.

While pushing your code to Heroku, ensure that unnecessary files aren't pushed across, for example, a log or a temporary working directory. As a user, you can configure Git to ignore those particular files, and if you like, remove them from your repository. This configuration can be done in a `.gitignore` file. Some of the currently available frameworks contain a `.gitignore` file by default, which list the pattern(s) of files or literal files they want to ignore while pushing the code to Heroku. You could additionally edit the `.gitignore` file in the application folder to further list additional patterns of files or filenames to avoid getting pushed.

For example, to ignore the temp directory completely, you can add the following in the `.gitignore` file:

```
$ echo temp >> .gitignore
$ git add .gitignore
$ git commit -m "ignored temp dir completely"
```

To ignore files with the extension log, that is, the `*.log` files, you can create a `.gitignore` file and add instructions to ignore it while pushing code to Heroku as follows:

```
$ mkdir log
$ echo '*.log' > log/.gitignore
```

The file `.gitignore` would contain the following details now:

```
*.log
```

To add the log directory to the repository, use the following command:

```
$ git add log
```

To delete files from your environment (for example, to remove everything from the log folder), you could type the following command:

```
$ git rm -r -f log
rm 'log/dev.log'
rm 'log/prod.log'
rm 'log/svr.log'
rm 'log/test.log'
```

Cloning existing Heroku applications

As a developer, you may want to create a copy of your Heroku application and try something radical with it while keeping the existing application intact to function as it is. This can be achieved by cloning your application using the Git facility.

Use `heroku git:clone` to create a clone of your application as follows:

```
$ heroku git:clone -a <NEW APPNAME>
```

This will create a new directory named after your application and automatically add a Heroku Git remote to enable future changes.

Forking an application

When maintaining most complex applications, it is a common practice to create multiple environments to support the development of various features independently, hence parallelizing the whole process and creating efficiency. It makes a lot of sense to use the stable production environment as a baseline for these multiple environments, what are being used to stage or test the application.

Using the `heroku fork` command allows you to do the following:

1. Copy an existing application.
2. Reprovision used add-ons (with the same pricing plan).
3. Copy configuration variables.
4. Copy any data from the Heroku Postgres database.

The following are the outcomes after successfully executing the command:

- The Heroku user executing the command is the owner of the new application.

- If the application uses any components that are not free, the owner of the application is responsible for the incurred charges. Hence, it makes a lot of sense to verify the source application for any chargable components before undertaking the task.

- Heroku Postgres data is automatically copied to the new application.

- Add-ons are simply reprovisioned, and any requisite data export or import for these services needs to be done manually. If the add-ons can't be provisioned because the original plan no longer exists, upgrade the plan on the source application and try the fork again. If you've already run `heroku fork`, you need to destroy the target app before retrying in the following manner:

  ```
  $ heroku destroy -a toapp
  ```

  For example, create the fork using the following command:

  ```
  $ heroku fork -a fromapp toapp
  Creating fork toapp... done
  Copying slug... done
  Adding pgbackups:plus... done
  Adding heroku-postgresql:dev... done
  Creating database backup from sourcapp... .. done
  Restoring database backup to toapp... .. done
  Copying config vars... done
  Fork complete, view it at http://toapp.herokuapp.com/
  ```

As with most commands, you need the Heroku toolbelt client utility installed to be able to run the `heroku fork` command.

Side effects of forking an application

The decision to fork an application versus cloning it is crucial in determining how your application performs over its lifetime. Hence, it is important to understand the side effects of forking a new application so that you use the forking capability judiciously when you have to. The following are the side effects of forking an application:

- Forked applications are just like new applications as they have the default dyno formation consisting of a single web dyno and no worker or other dynos. You can scale your forked application's dynos to meet your needs.

- The forking process reprovisions the SSL endpoint on the new application but it does not add any certificates automatically. If your application uses custom domains with SSL, you need to add new certificates to the SSL endpoint instance on the target application as follows:

```
$ heroku certs:add server.crt server.key -a toapp

Resolving trust chain... done

Adding SSL Endpoint to toapp... done

example now served by hawaii-9876.herokussl.com

Add a new DNS CNAME record utilizing this new endpoint URL to
serve requests via HTTPS.
```

- No custom domains are copied as part of the forking process as custom domains can belong only to one application. If you want to use custom domains in your new environment, you will need to add them manually and make the necessary DNS additions.

- You need to manually transfer the job schedule from one application to the other. Open the scheduler dashboard for both `fromapp` and `toapp`, compare them, and manually copy the jobs in the following manner:

```
$ heroku addons:open scheduler -a fromapp

$ heroku addons:open scheduler -a toapp
```

- When you fork an application, it doesn't automatically create a new Git remote in your current project namespace. First, create a remote manually and then deploy the newly forked application as shown in the following command:

```
$ heroku info -a toapp

=== toapp

...

Git URL:        git@heroku.com:toapp.git
```

Add a Git remote named `forked`, which represents the deploy URL for `toapp`:

```
$ git remote add forked git@heroku.com:toapp.git
```

Deploy to the new environment with:

```
$ git push forked master
```

- No users from the source application are transferred over to the forked app. You need to add collaborators manually as follows:

```
$ heroku sharing:add someoneelse@johndoe.com -a toapp
```

- The forking process copies all databases present on sourceapp but does not retain any fork/follow relationships between them. Remove extraneous databases yourself and manually re-establish any forks or followers.

- Any enabled Heroku lab's features on source application are not re-enabled on the target application.

Transferring Apps

You can transfer applications between Heroku accounts at any time via the Heroku dashboard.

The current application owner must initiate the transfer request. To initiate the transfer, the owner can navigate to the application's settings page on the dashboard. It looks like the following screenshot:

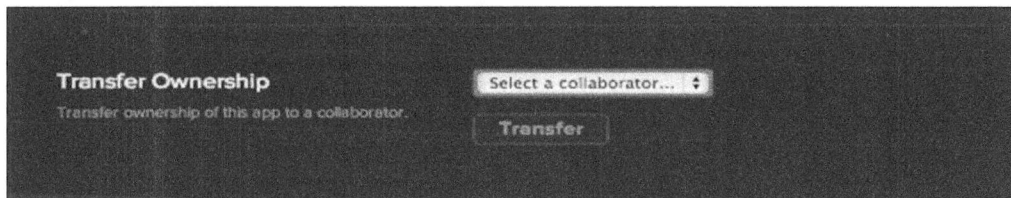

As the current owner, you can initiate the transfer request by selecting a collaborator to transfer the app to. The new owner can receive the transfer by accepting the pending transfer request at the top of the dashboard once it's initiated:

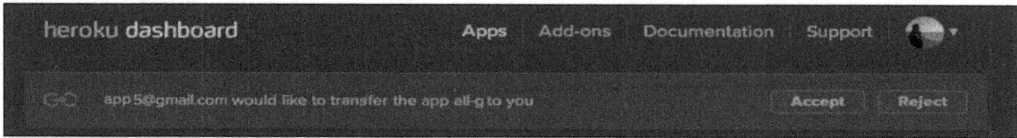

The new owner has the ability to accept or reject any transfer request. Additionally, the original owner of the request can cancel or change the transfer request before it has been accepted or rejected by the new owner.

Optimizing deployments

The simplest of the Heroku applications run in at least two different environments—your local development environment and the Heroku remote environment.

A given production application could have many developers working on it. You can have several developers interacting with the same production application when they want to push their local changes to it. Addtionally, developers may have additional code branches to test their applications or verify nonfunctional requirements such as performance.

All things work reasonably well as long as there is concurrency between the various environments you use, that is, similar configuration and common source code resulting in same functional behavior. However, in the real world, things get complicated as the size of a project increases and the number of developers working on it grows rapidly. Also, things can get complicated if applications are being developed locally on different operating systems or using peculiar environment settings. Such situations can cause strange results when you try to deploy the application on Heroku. To overcome such challenges, we need an effective way to manage deployment.

Development environments, which usually have newer features in them, may contain broken code or may point to different databases than production (for example, SQLite3 versus. postgres). Over a period of time, various environments begin to lead or lag production due to parallel streams of changes going on and there being no system in place to keep them in sync. Such a scenario, if not managed well, is a recipe for inconsistencies and failures for your application.

So, how do we make sure that we don't push buggy code to production or don't deploy something that breaks production and causes users a lot of heartburn?

One way to handle this issue is to use the concept of **staging** your application before moving it to production. The idea is to make the staging environment mimic production in all respects and route any changes to production via the staging. Unless things work as expected in staging, we don't move anything to an already well-functioning production environment.

Creating such an environment is quite easy in Heroku as follows:

```
$ heroku create --remote staging

Creating weak-mountain-783.... done

http://weak-mountain-783.heroku.com/ | git@heroku.com:weak-mountain-783.
git

Git remote staging added
```

Now, you can bring up the staging environment by using the following command:

```
$ git push staging master

...

$ heroku run rake db:migrate --remote staging

...

$ heroku ps --remote staging

=== web: `bundle exec thin start -p $PORT -e production`

web.1: up for 21s
```

To provide configuration variables specific to staging while using a **Ruby on Rails** framework (**RoR**), type the following command:

```
$ heroku config:add RACK_ENV=staging RAILS_ENV=staging --remote
staging
```

These configuration parameters are typically used by the application to figure out environment details. To enable the RoR application to use a staging environment, you need to create a `config/environments/staging.rb` file beforehand, coupled with the `RAILS_ENV` setting. You can boot your servers to use a staging environment for your application.

Since your application is up and running in staging, you can monitor it for any discrepancies, and if everything goes on well, you can now create the production version of the same by performing the following steps. You will also need to configure any add-ons, set up environment vars, or add contributors to both these applications as they evolve to keep them in sync:

```
$ heroku create --remote production
Creating fierce-ice-327.... done
http://fierce-ice-327.heroku.com/ | git@heroku.com:fierce-ice-327.git
Git remote production added
$ git push production master
...
$ heroku run rake db:migrate --remote production
...
$ heroku ps --remote production
=== web: `bundle exec thin start -p $PORT -e production`
web.1: up for 16s
```

Thus, we have the same source code running as two separate Heroku apps set up identically.

To make things easier, you can use the `git config` command to specify a default application instead of having to type application names every time you execute a Git command.

For example, to configure `staging` as your default remote, type the following command:

```
$ git config heroku.remote staging
```

This will configure `staging` as your default environment and add a section to the project's `.git/config` file that indicates the same.

To run a command on a different application, simply use the `--remote <env name>` option.

In many cases, it is possible that you started with a small application that wasn't very fussy and hence could be deployed directly to production. However, overtime, the application may have increased in complexity and scale and require closer monitoring. You may want to be more careful before deploying new enhancements to production now. You could follow the same approach of having a staging environment here as well.

To create a staging environment, you would need configuration parameters and add-on information for your production environment so that you can set up the staging environment using the same details.

You can type the following command in your production environment to capture configuration parameters:

```
$ heroku config
...list of configuration variables
```

You can type the following command in your production environment to capture add-on information:

```
$ heroku addons
...list of addons
```

Finally, create the staging environment by typing the following commands:

```
$ heroku create --remote staging --addons <add-on 1>,<add-on 2>,...


$ heroku config:add CFGVAR1=abc CFGVAR2=xyz
```

Additionally, you should copy your production database to the staging environment using available backup tools such as the PGBackups add-on.

The choice of a region

Heroku is currently being enhanced to support the concept of a deployment region, that is, you could choose the geographical region where your application will be deployed. This feature basically enables you to reduce the latency experienced by users of your application.

Currently, Heroku is available in two geographic regions: the US and EU. If most of your users are in Europe, it makes a lot of sense to deploy your application in Europe as access will be faster for them. All applications are created in the US region by default.

The easiest way to check your application's region is to use the following `heroku info` command:

```
$ heroku info
=== warm-current-5432
Git URL:        git@heroku.com:warm-current-5432.git
Owner Email:    user@test.com
Region:         eu
Repo Size:      164M
...
```

To verify the list of all of the available regions, type the following command:

```
$ heroku regions
=== regions
eu   Europe
us   United States
Specifying the region
```

You can use the `--region` flag to specify the region when creating the application:

```
$ heroku create --region eu
Creating warm-current-5432... done, region is eu
http://warm-current-5432.herokuapp.com/ | git@heroku.com:warm-current-5432.git
Git remote heroku added
```

There are a few aspects of your application that need to be considered while deploying the application in a specific region.

Add-ons with region support will be provisioned in the same region as the application. Provision them as you normally would by using the following command:

```
$ heroku addons:add <addon_name>
```

To verify supported add-ons for your region, type the following command:

```
$ heroku addons:list --region=<region_name>
```

Here, the region name could be `us` or `eu`.

You can also log in to `addons.heroku.com` and search for supported add-ons for your region.

Some add-ons may not require a low-latency connection to your application. Hence, it could be deployed in the default region if unavailable in your application region. If the add-on is latency sensitive and is not available in the same region as your application, provisioning will not complete and will fail in the following manner:

```
$ heroku addons:add cloudcounter
Adding cloudcounter on warm-current-5432... failed
!    This app is in region eu, cloudcounter:basic is only available
in region us.
```

Applications are deployed to the region specified on creation (which by default is us). It is easy to deploy your application. Any scheduler job, or one of the dynos, will be run in the same region where the application is deployed.

Use the git push in the following way to deploy, as in the case of a regular deploy:

```
$ git push heroku master
```

When you are developing an application that needs SSL support, you should provision an SSL endpoint for the application and upload the SSL certificates as follows:

```
$ heroku addons:add ssl
Adding ssl on yeppy... done, v1 ($20/mo)
add your certificate with `heroku certs:add PEM KEY`.
Use `heroku addons:docs ssl` to view documentation.


$ heroku certs:add server.crt server.key
Resolving trust chain... done
Adding SSL Endpoint to yeppy... done
yeppy now served by yeppy.herokuapp.com
```

If your custom domain is properly configured, no additional DNS configuration is required. All traffic to www.yeppy.com can now be served over SSL.

There is no difference between adding custom domains to your application running outside the US region or to applications in the US region. Using a different region is transparent to the application with custom domain and any user request is handled normally.

Tracking application changes

Sometimes, you want to track the changes being done to your Heroku application and are interested in knowing when a new version of the application is pushed to Heroku. Typically, in production grade applications, you may want to inform certain users about a new release or track a new deployment by logging its occurrence. For such cases, Heroku provides **Deploy Hooks**.

A Deploy Hook allows you to receive a notification whenever a new version of the application is pushed to Heroku. Setting up these hooks is simple enough, and the developer gets a wide variety of choices for the type of Deploy Hook that can be set up. Heroku provides Deploy Hooks in the form of e-mails to users and messages to a campfire chat room or a basecamp account to inform you about the new deploy. Deploy Hooks are inherently a notification mechanism that can be leveraged to integrate with other applications through the inbuilt messaging feature in the Deploy Hooks feature.

Setting up Deploy Hooks

Each Deploy Hook is its own add-on. Setting up a new Deploy Hook is just like adding a new add-on to Heroku. Let's discuss the different Deploy Hooks supported in Heroku.

Basecamp

The purpose of this Deploy Hook is to post a message to a Basecamp account you specify under a certain project and post category. Put your API Key under the username `param`.

The sample setup for Basecamp is as follows:

```
$ heroku addons:add deployhooks:basecamp \
    --url=http://testaccount.basecamphq.com \
    --username=00000000 \
    --project=weak-mountain-783 \
    --category=deploys \
    --title="{{user}} deployed weak-mountain-783" \
    --body="check it at {{url}}"
Adding deployhooks:basecamp to weak-mountain-783...Done.
```

Campfire

The purpose of this Deploy Hook is to post an automated message to a Campfire account when your app is pushed.

The sample setup for Campfire is as follows:

```
$ heroku addons:add deployhooks:campfire \
    --url=testsubdomain  \
    --ssl=1 \
    --api_key=0000000 \
    --room=devlounge \
    --message="{{user}} deployed weak-mountain-783"
Adding deployhooks:campfire to weak-mountain-783...Done.
```

E-mail

The purpose of this Deploy Hook is to send one or more e-mails with a subject and body. More recipients can be specified by adding e-mail addresses separated by a space.

The sample setup for e-mail is as follows:

```
$ heroku addons:add deployhooks:email \
    --recipient=john.doe@whereami.com \
    --subject="Weak-mountain-783 Deployed" \
    --body="{{user}} deployed app"
Adding deployhooks:email to weak-mountain-783...Done.
```

HTTP

The purpose of this Deploy Hook is to perform an HTTP post to the URL provided with parameters sent with a mime type of application/x-www-form-urlencoded.

The sample setup for HTTP is as follows:

```
$ heroku addons:add deployhooks:http \
    --url=http://whereami.org
Adding deployhooks:http to weak-mountain-783...Done.
```

IRC

The purpose of this Deploy Hook is to connect to the specified server and message the room; `nick` and `password` are optional. Set the server port by sending port = xxxx.

The sample setup for IRC is as follows:

```
$ heroku addons:add deployhooks:irc \
    --server=irc.freenode.net \
    --room=qahouse \
    --nick=testcomm \
    --password=secret \
    --message="{{user}} deployed app"
Adding deployhooks:irc to weak-mountain-783...Done.
```

Once the hooks are set up, `git push` will show that they are scheduled to run in the following manner:

```
$ git push heroku master
...


-----> Heroku receiving push
-----> Rails app detected
       Compiled slug size is 66K
-----> Launching...... done
-----> Deploy hooks scheduled, check output in your logs
       http://weak-mountain-783.heroku.com deployed to Heroku
```

The Hook output and errors appear in the application logfile as follows:

```
$ heroku logs
...
2013-03-15T15:04:23-05:00 heroku[deployhooks]: Sent email notification to
xyz@example.com
```

You can use variables to define a part of the Deploy Hook. For example, the variable {{app}}, when used in a message, will be replaced by the application name when the Deploy Hook is executed. Many other variables can also be used in the hook definition to add specific information about deployment when it happens.

Some of these variables are user (the user deploying the app), URL (the application URL), head_long or head (commit identifiers), or git_log (a log of commits between the last deploy and the current one).

Release management

When you push new code, make configuration changes, or modify resources, Heroku creates a new release and restarts the application automatically.

Through its robust release management mechanism, Heroku provides the flexibility to do the following:

- List the history of releases.
- Use rollbacks to revert to prior releases in case the deployment or configuration went wrong

Checking installed releases

To check the history of your application releases, you can type the following command:

```
$ heroku releases

=== gentle-mesa-5445 Releases

v2  Enable Logplex   ahanjura@gmail.com   2012/12/03 03:39:37
v1  Initial release  ahanjura@gmail.com   2012/12/03 03:39:36
```

The preceding output shows that the application has had two releases so far, the latest one being shown at the top.

Verifying the new release

A new release can be created by Heroku when you push new code or change some configuration parameters. For example, adding a new config param TEST_MAX_ARGS created a new release for the application. To check that the new release was indeed created, type the following command:

```
$ heroku releases

=== gentle-mesa-5445 Releases

v3  Add TEST_MAX_ARGS config  ahanjura@gmail.com   2013/01/27 20:16:21 (~
17s ago)

v2  Enable Logplex            ahanjura@gmail.com   2012/12/03 03:39:37
v1  Initial release           ahanjura@gmail.com   2012/12/03 03:39:36
$ heroku releases:info v3
```

```
=== Release v3
By:      ahanjura@gmail.com
Change: Add TEST_MAX_ARGS config
When:    2013/01/27 20:16:21 (~ 57s ago)


=== v3 Config Vars
TEST_MAX_ARGS: 45
```

The preceding output clearly shows that a new release v3 was created, and it also shows the log of the changes done. The configuration parameters changed are clearly demarcated under the v3 `config vars` header.

Rolling back the release

Sometimes, you need to rollback a particular release after you realize that it may break the application in some cases. You can issue the following command:

```
$ heroku rollback

Rolling back gentle-mesa-5445... done, v2
  !    Warning: rollback affects code and config vars; it doesn't add or
remove addons. To undo, run: heroku rollback v3
```

Alternatively, you can be specific and issue the following command:

```
$ heroku rollback <version name>
```

However, you should take precautions before you rollback an application release, as you may have to revert the state of your database as well to keep the two in sync. Reverse-migrate the database first and then apply the rollback to your application as done. To revert the database on an RoR app, you can use the `heroku rake db:rollback` command.

Summary

In this chapter, we reviewed various components of deployment under Heroku. We also reviewed the Git revision control system, which is central to application development under Heroku. Additionally, we understood how to optimize the application size by ignoring irrelevant application files before code push, and how to manage multiple environments to ensure that an application moves to production only after it has been certified that it works correctly in a similar environment. Finally, we reviewed how we can monitor new changes to the application through Deploy Hooks and how we can check release-specific information via Heroku's release management commands.

In the next chapter, we will focus on how to run Heroku applications and the considerations surrounding this.

5
Running Heroku Applications

In the previous chapter, we learned how to deploy Heroku applications. Specifically, we learned how to push code to and pull code from the Heroku environment, how developers of Heroku apps can use the Git distributed version control system to version their app, and how code deployments can be optimized. Finally, we learned how app releases can be managed in a Heroku environment.

Well, for the discerning minds, it makes a lot of sense to distinguish between deploying an app and running an app. Running an app is a subset of what goes on when you deploy a Heroku app. Running an app is more about operating an app using the available platform, troubleshooting the app in a test bed before deploying it in production, and finally monitoring it to verify if everything is working fine. In this chapter, we will focus on the running aspect of an app. We will discuss the typical lifecycle of a Heroku app and how we can run an app using the Heroku command-line facility (CLI). We will also explore the details of Foreman—the tool that we use for running an app locally before pushing the app to a Heroku platform. Then, we will review the Heroku dashboard—a tool that lets you look at your application at a holistic level.

To summarize, we will focus on the various ways in which Heroku applications can be executed or monitored.

We will perform the following tasks:

- Quickly review the Heroku app lifecycle.
- Learn how to use the Heroku CLI, which allows us to build and run Heroku applications from the command line, thus giving complete control over the behavior of your Heroku app.
- Review the Foreman tool that is used to execute your application locally before it is ready for the Heroku platform, thereby saving you the bandwidth and pain of rebuilding your slugs every time you change something on your local machine.

- Review the Heroku dashboard—a very useful tool to review and monitor your Heroku applications. The dashboard has a rich set of features that let you drill down into specific application details such as resource usage, and at the same time lets you change the configuration and behavior of your Heroku application as per your needs.

The Heroku app lifecycle

A Heroku application lifecycle can be represented by the steps shown in the following diagram:

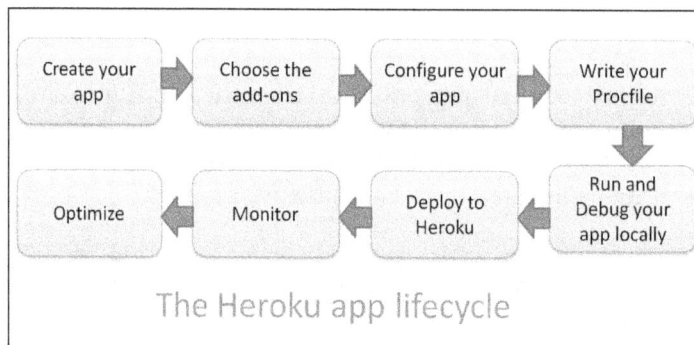

The Heroku app lifecycle

To create a Heroku app, a developer should perform the following tasks:

- Write an app in any of the supported languages as follows:
  - Create an app using the supported Ruby, Java, Python, Node.js, Scala, or Clojure programming language
  - Use a custom mechanism to build apps in other languages using custom buildpacks

- Select the add-ons to reuse components required to build necessary features as follows:
  - Choose the right add-on from a wide variety of supported add-ons (https://addons.heroku.com) depending on the functionality desired
  - For example, to add application monitoring using the popular New Relic tool (www.newrelic.com), a developer uses the Heroku CLI as follows:

    ```
    $ heroku addons:add newrelic:standard

    Adding newrelic:standard on myapp...done, v27 (free)

    Use `heroku addons:docs newrelic:standard` to view
    documentation
    ```

- Set up the configuration of the application using configuration variables as follows:
  - ○ Create the configuration or environment to be used for running the app by defining relevant configuration variables or parameters using the Heroku CLI as follows:

    ```
    $ heroku config:set GITHUB_USERNAME=<username>
    Adding config vars and restarting myapp... done, v12
    GITHUB_USERNAME: <username>
    ```

    In this example, the application will use the configuration variable GITHUB_ USERNAME; hence, the developer uses the config:set API to define it.

- Write Procfile (optional but recommended to gain a better control over the app execution) as follows:
  - ○ Provide a specification in a file named Procfile stored in the root of the application. This file contains a listing of the various process types of the app and information on how to run an instance of those process types. The contents of a sample Ruby app Procfile could be as follows:

    ```
    web:    bundle exec rails server -p $PORT
    worker: bundle exec rake jobs:work
    ```

    There are two process types defined here. The first one is web – the instance of this process type will handle all HTTP requests received by the app. The second type is worker – the instance of this process type will do all the heavy lifting for the app.

- Run the application locally using Foreman (recommended) or other tools as available:
  - ○ Boot the app locally using the Foreman tool to troubleshoot any impending issues before pushing the code to Heroku. To run the app locally, the developer uses the foreman start command as follows:

    ```
    xxxxxx@box:/local/bin$ foreman start
    14:03:02 web.1      | started with pid 1234
    14:03:02 worker.1   | started with pid 5678
    ```

- Deploy the app to Heroku as follows:

  ○ Push the app to the Heroku environment using the `git push` command as follows:

  ```
  git push heroku master
  ```

This Git command sends the code to the Heroku environment where Heroku builds it and deploys it to a running process called a dyno. The developer will access the application using a URL generated by the Heroku platform.

- Monitor the app as follows:

  ○ Check the log for any suspect events using the `heroku logs` command as follows:

  ```
  $ heroku logs

  2013-11-21T14:26:23.677020+00:00 app[web.1]: Processing
  PostController#list (for 208.36.131.14 at 2013-11-21
  14:26:23)
  [GET]

  2013-11-21T14:26:23.677023+00:00 app[web.1]: Rendering
  template within layouts/application

  2013-11-21T14:26:23.677902+00:00 app[web.1]: Rendering
  post/list

  2013-11-21T14:26:23.678990+00:00 app[web.1]: Rendered
  includes/_header (0.1ms)
  ```

The developer will optionally use the New Relic add-on to monitor the Heroku app and find interesting metrics such as response time for user requests, application bottlenecks, and overall performance of the app.

- Optimize the app to use more or less resources as needed as follows:

  ○ If the application expects increased user traffic, the developer will scale out the app using the intuitive `heroku ps:scale` command as follows:

  ```
  $ heroku ps:scale web=2 worker=2

  Scaling web processes... done, now running 2

  Scaling worker processes... done, now running 2
  ```

This command will set the number of web process type instances or dynos to 2 and set the worker process type instances or dynos to 2. Now, the app will automatically have double the capacity and be able to serve double the number of user requests compared to the earlier setting.

Now that we understand a Heroku app's lifecycle, let us look at the Heroku commands that help you build, deploy, and manage your app in the Heroku cloud platform. In the next section, we look at the Heroku CLI in detail and the specific commands (categorized by function) used to work with the Heroku platform.

The Heroku CLI

Heroku provides a rich CLI that developers can use to interact with the Heroku platform. The Heroku CLI provides full-featured support to build, deploy, and manage your apps. It also provides commands to manage your accounts and security information, as well as helping you operate your databases and monitor your app's health. The interface is very intuitive and reminiscent of the Unix style of running commands on the shell. The Heroku CLI provides you with direct control over your Heroku applications and lets you manage various aspects of the platform.

How to get the Heroku client tool

Heroku provides a package called toolbelt that contains the Heroku CLI. The toolbelt package can be downloaded from `https://toolbelt.herokuapp.com`.

The Heroku toolbelt package consists of the following:

- The Heroku client—a command-line tool for creating and managing apps, and more
- The Foreman tool—a utility for running your app locally
- The Git client—a source code control client tool for Git used to synchronize your code with a central Git repository

Verifying the tool

Once installed, you can verify the version of your client tool by typing the following command:

```
$ heroku --version
heroku/toolbelt/3.0.1 (i386-mingw32) ruby/1.9.3
```

Heroku shows you the current version of toolbelt installed on your system and the version of Ruby used.

How to get the latest Heroku client tool

Before you start using the Heroku CLI, it makes a lot of sense to make sure you are using the latest version of the client. To make sure that you have the latest version, you can run the `heroku update` command and get the most recent supported version of the Heroku CLI:

```
$ heroku update
Updating from 3.0.1... done, nothing to update
```

In this case, the version of the client is the latest one, so no updates are needed.

Where is the Heroku client stored?

Heroku stores the client in the `.heroku/client` path for your user (on Windows) or `~/.heroku/client` on Linux and Mac OS X. Whenever you run a Heroku command, a background process checks for a newer version of the client and downloads it if your current version is out of date. The background process that pools for the right client does the check at most once every five minutes to avoid performance degradation caused by frequent pooling.

When you run Heroku, it checks for the latest version of the client in the Heroku client directory before loading the system-installed version.

What if my client installation is corrupted or not working?

In case you find out that your client is not working and the installation is corrupted, you can uninstall the Heroku client package and reinstall it.

To uninstall, type the following command:

```
$ gem uninstall heroku --all
```

> This command will remove the Heroku client only if it was previously installed as a gem. You can run it to uninstall the old Heroku client before you use the newer toolbelt client. On Windows, you may have to remove some directories manually to do a clean uninstall of the client package.

Alternatively, you can remove the Heroku client using the following commands (on Linux):

```
rm -rf /usr/local/heroku
rm -rf /usr/bin/heroku
rm -rf /usr/local/foreman
rm -rf /usr/bin/foreman
```

The Heroku CLI commands

Heroku CLI commands are of two types:

- **General commands**: General commands apply to your account as a whole. For example, the `heroku apps` command is used to list all applications for the given account.

  ```
  $ heroku apps
  == My apps
  gentle-mesa-5445
  ```

- **Application commands**: Application (app) commands are run from within your local application directory. So, if you have an application called `sampleapp` under /home/you (on Linux or Mac OS X) or c:\users\you (on Windows), you would do something like this before executing app commands:

  ```
  $ cd /home/you/sampleapp OR c:\users\you\sampleapp
  $ heroku login
  ...system requests credentials...
  ...enter credentials...
  $ heroku apps:info
  ```

  The following screenshot shows the details of my application:

Heroku CLI commands by function

Heroku commands can be broadly categorized into the following groups based on the nature of the operation performed:

- **Application management commands**: These commands are responsible for doing the bulk of operations any Heroku user might need during the process of building, deploying, or managing apps. You can use the `heroku help` command to see the complete command list. The following table lists the various commands in this category and their purposes:

Command name	Purpose
apps	manage apps (create, destroy)
config	manage app config vars
domains	manage custom domains
addons	manage addon resources
maintenance	toggle maintenance mode
plugins	manage plugins to the heroku gem
ps	manage processes (dynos, workers)
releases	view release history of an app
run	run one-off commands (console, rake)
sharing	manage collaborators on an app
ssl	manage ssl certificates for an app
stack	manage the stack for an app

- **Account and user authentication commands**: This set of commands is responsible for managing the various account options, setting up login credentials, and managing authentication keys for the user. The following table lists the various commands in this category and their purposes:

Command name	Purpose
account	manage heroku account options
auth	authentication (login, logout)
keys	manage authentication keys

- **Database handling commands**: These commands are used to handle various database management operations for the data store attached to the application. The following table lists the various commands in this category and their purposes:

Command name	Purpose
db	manage the database for an app
pg	manage heroku postgresql databases
pgbackups	manage backups of heroku postgresql databases

- **Logging-related commands**: These commands are related to logging information provided by the Heroku platform. Developers use these commands to understand the application flow and troubleshoot errors when they occur. The following table lists the various commands in this category and their purposes:

Command name	Purpose
drains	display syslog drains for an app
logs	display logs for an app

- **Heroku platform commands**: These commands, when run, provide help information, information about the health of the Heroku platform, or information about the Heroku client currently being used. The following table lists the various commands in this category and their purposes:

Command name	Purpose
help	list commands and display help
status	check status of Heroku platform
update	update the heroku client
version	display version

Extending the Heroku CLI

Heroku provides the ability to extend the default capabilities of the Heroku CLI through **CLI plugins**. New commands can be added to the out-of-the-box commands using these plugins. The plugins are stored in the ~/.heroku/plugins folder on Linux distributions. This flexibility to customize the Heroku command list is an extremely powerful capability provided by the Heroku platform. Imagine writing your own commands against the available Heroku Platform API and adding them to the Heroku CLI on demand. How cool is that?

Let us explore the CLI plugins feature by running a few commands. The Heroku plugins library allows the following:

- **Listing the installed plugins**: To list installed plugins, type the following command:

  ```
  $ heroku plugins

  === Installed Plugins
  ```

  Presently, there are no plugins installed for the user.

- **Installing plugins**: To install a new plugin, use the heroku plugins:install <plugin URL/name> command. For example, the following command installs the heroku-accounts plugin to the user's account. The user can now use the operations available in the heroku-accounts plugin via the following command line:

  ```
  $ heroku plugins:install git://github.com/ddollar/heroku-accounts.git

  Installing heroku-accounts... done
  ```

- **Uninstalling plugins**: You can uninstall a plugin using the following plugins:uninstall command:

  ```
  $ heroku plugins:uninstall heroku-accounts

  Uninstalling heroku-accounts... done
  ```

- **Updating existing plugins**: To update all installed plugins, use the heroku plugins:update command. To update a particular plugin, pass the plugin name as an additional argument to the heroku:plugins update command as follows:

  ```
  $ heroku plugins:update heroku-accounts
  ```

The Heroku CLI and add-ons

Add-ons are third-party services that can be integrated with your Heroku app by using a few simple Heroku CLI commands. The Heroku CLI is one of the two ways in which add-ons can be used with your app, the other one being the Heroku dashboard (covered later in this chapter). The Heroku add-on mechanism is arguably one of the key features of the platform as a whole, and the Heroku CLI enables you to use it quite effortlessly; just enter a few CLI commands and you are ready to go. You can switch to (add-on) any required service from a rich set of add-ons currently supported by Heroku.

Let's review a few very useful Heroku CLI commands used to manage your app's add-ons:

- To list the add-ons currently in use by your app, use the `heroku addons` command as follows. In this example, I have the `heroku-postgresql` development version add-on installed in my account:

  ```
  $ heroku addons

  heroku-postgresql:dev
  ```

- To add a new add-on, simply use the `heroku addons:add` command as follows:

  ```
  $ heroku addons:add newrelic:standard

  Adding newrelic:standard on myapp...done, vX (free)

  Use `heroku addons:docs newrelic:standard` to view
  documentation
  ```

- Removing an add-on is as simple as typing the following command:

  ```
  $ heroku addons:remove newrelic:standard

  Removing newrelic:standard from myapp...done, vX (free)
  ```

- Upgrading to a higher version of an add-on is as simple as typing the following command:

  ```
  $ heroku addons:upgrade newrelic:professional

  Upgrading newrelic:professional to myapp... done, vY
  ($/dyno/hr)

  Use `heroku addons:docs newrelic:professional` to view
  documentation
  ```

- Downgrading to a lower version of an add-on can be achieved using the following `heroku addons:downgrade` command:

```
$ heroku addons:downgrade newrelic:standard

Downgrading to newrelic:standard on myapp... done, vX (free)

Use 'heroku addons:docs newrelic:standard' to view
documentation.
```

A note on Heroku CLI and security

Heroku helps secure developer interaction with the platform using three mechanisms. Each of these mechanisms can involve using the Heroku CLI to connect or authenticate a user to the Heroku platform. At any time, one of these mechanisms is operational based on the specific situation in which the developer is interacting with the platform.

These three mechanisms are as follows:

- **E-mail and password validation**: Heroku uses the user e-mail address and password to generate an API token. The `heroku login` CLI command is used to receive the e-mail and password of the user. The generated API token can then be used for authenticating future Heroku API requests to the platform on behalf of the user.

- **API token-based authentication**: The API token is used for authentication of the user requests to access the Heroku Platform API. The API token can be regenerated by the user on demand, thereby invalidating any existing tokens.

  You can display the token using the `heroku auth:token` command as follows:

```
$ heroku auth:token

f4ce94da15ea0544892c2cfd5ds4ead453567876
```

  The Heroku CLI stores the API token in the well-known `.netrc` file on most Linux distros. This file is usually found in the following location:

```
~/.netrc (Unix)

C:/users/username/__netrc (Windows)
```

  Any Heroku commands that need authentication services for executing the relevant platform API will either create or update the `.netrc` file. Tools such as `curl` use this file to access the Heroku platform API.

- **SSH key-based verification**: The SSH key is used for authenticating a user trying to push source code to the Git repository. When the user logs in to Heroku for the first time using the `heroku login` CLI command, an SSH key is created for the user and uploaded to the Heroku account for use. If the user doesn't configure an SSH key, a default key is created and uploaded for the user. The `heroku keys:add` CLI command can be used to add keys to the user account.

Running your cloud apps locally

It makes a lot of sense for cloud-based app developers to run their apps locally before pushing them to the cloud (production) environment. Doing so helps the developer understand the app characteristics and also predict other app needs (such as sizing) in the cloud environment. If the app developer follows the Twelve-Factor app (TFA) methodology recommended for Heroku web apps and keeps the development environment as close as possible to the production environment, potential issues (if any) show up during a local run of the app, and that gives an opportunity to fix issues before they hit production.

In this context, Foreman is the tool of choice for most Heroku app developers. Foreman is a utility that comes bundled with the Heroku client software (`https://toolbelt.heroku.com`). It helps run your Procfile-based Heroku apps in the local environment.

> A Procfile, as you know already, is a configuration file in which you name your process type and instruct Heroku to run an instance of the process type using the specified command line. You can have any number of process types in the Procfile. For more information on Procfiles, please refer to *Chapter 2, Inside Heroku*, where Procfiles are discussed in detail.

Foreman takes the complexity out of running multiple processes and lets you run your Procfile-based application locally before you deploy it on the Heroku platform.

Foreman lets you run the application locally in the following two ways:

- Direct execution using the `foreman start` command.
- Export the execution details to some other process management format. Foreman currently supports the `inittab`, `bluepill`, `runit`, and `upstart` output formats for export. This option is useful only when you deploy the application yourself. Since we use Heroku to deploy web apps, this option is not relevant for our case and is included for completeness.

Using Foreman to check Procfiles

Foreman can also be used to verify the correctness of a Procfile. To verify that the created Procfile format is correct, use the `foreman check` command as follows:

```
$ foreman check
```

Using Foreman to run apps directly

You can use `foreman start` to run your application directly from the command line. If you don't specify the concurrency in the command line, Foreman will run one instance of each process type defined in the Procfile.

To run Foreman, use the `foreman start` command as follows:

```
$ foreman start
```

To run an instance of a specific process type (`ptype`) for an application defined in the Procfile, type the following command:

```
$ foreman start ptype -p ~/app/Procfile
```

Running one-off commands

You can use `foreman run` to run one-off commands using the same environment as defined for processes listed in the Procfile. For example:

- You can run the Rails server using the following `foreman run` command:

  ```
  $ foreman run rails server
  ```

- You can run a rake task by using the `foreman run` command as follows:

  ```
  $ foreman run rake <task>
  ```

Foreman command-line options

You can use a wide variety of command-line options to control the behavior of the Foreman utility.

The following table shows the currently supported command-line options with a brief description of the purpose of each option:

Command-line option	Purpose
-c or –concurrency	Runs a specified number of instances for each process type. You should specify the concurrency in the *processname=number of instances* format.

-e or –env	Loads one or more .env files for use by the application. All processes will inherit the environment variables set in the .env file, but if you want to set a process-specific environment variable, use the env command in your Procfile as follows:
	
	```web: env CACHE=TRUE rake worker```
	```worker: env INSTANCES=1 rake worker```

-f or –procfile	Uses an alternative (and not default) Procfile as an input for process execution details.
	
	Example 1: To start processes using a specific Procfile, type the following command:
	
	```foreman start -f /home/apps/myotherapp/Procfile```
	
	Example 2: To start an instance of a particular process type using a different Procfile, you can type the following command:
	
	```$ foreman start gamma -f /home/apps/myotherapp/Procfile```
	
	Here, gamma is a specific process type.

-p or –port	Uses the specified port to use as the base for this application. The port number should be a multiple of 1000.

Heroku provides a unified web interface that gives the developer information about the deployed apps. This web interface is called the Heroku dashboard and can be accessed using the https://dashboard.heroku.com URL. Needless to say, you need a Heroku account to log in to the Heroku dashboard. There are some aspects of the Heroku dashboard that have a direct impact on the running aspect of a Heroku app. In this section, we explore those features of the dashboard that are related to running a Heroku application.

To log in to the Heroku dashboard, perform the following tasks:

- Open the `https://dashboard.heroku.com` URL in your browser
- Enter valid Heroku credentials to gain access

On successful login, you will be directed to the Heroku dashboard **Apps** page.

The Apps page

The following screenshot shows the **Apps** page for a registered Heroku user with deployed apps on the Heroku platform:

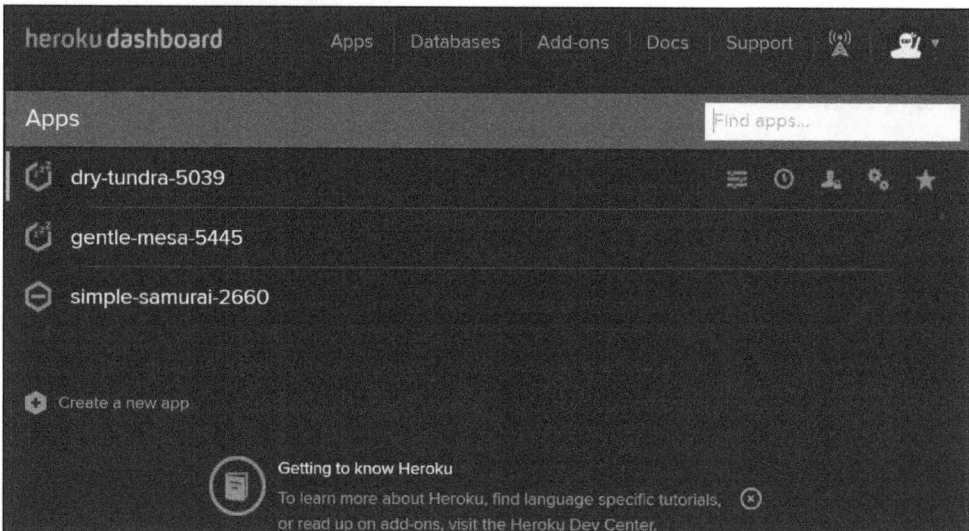

The **Apps** page lists two types of apps:

- Apps deployed by you
- Apps where you are a collaborator

The **Apps** page also contains a search text area where you can look up apps based on the following categories:

- App name
- App owner
- Buildpack
- Region
- Stack

The Resources tab

The following screenshot shows the **Resources** link available for each app shown on the **Apps** page:

On clicking on the **Resources** link for a particular application, you can see the resource usage for that application.

In the following case shown, the **dry-tundra-5039** application:

- Uses 1 web dyno and 0 worker dynos
- Uses the free Heroku Postgres :: Maroon version of the Postgres database
- Has an estimated monthly running cost of $0 since it is using just 1 web dyno, which is free for up to 750 hours of monthly usage, and other add-ons used are also free

This level of transparency is quite appealing for customers small and big who want to closely monitor the cost of running their applications on the Heroku platform.

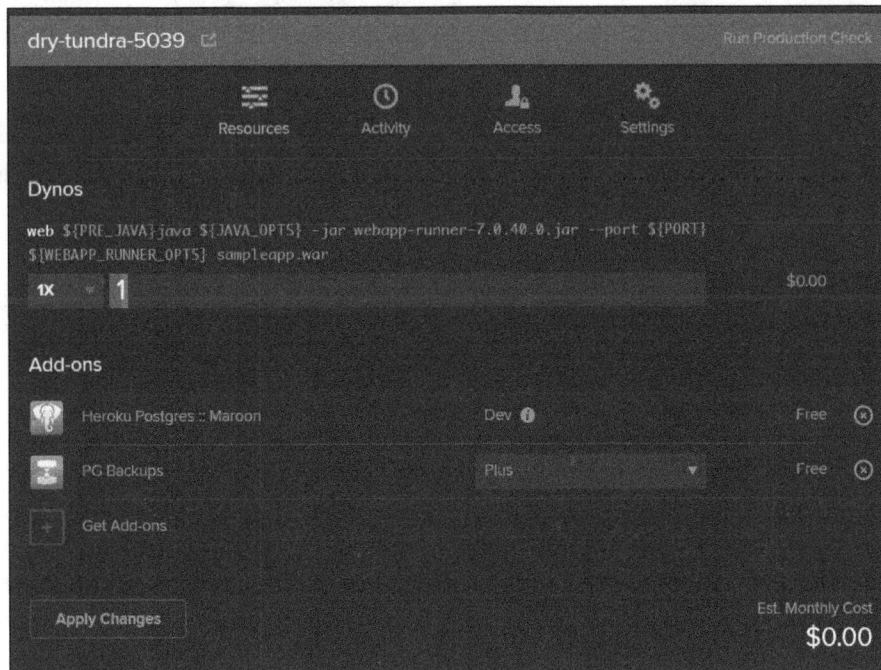

Managing resources

Ever imagined a situation where you anticipate unprecedented workload for your e-commerce shopping application during the holiday season? You don't need to worry. Just log in to the Heroku dashboard and scale your dynos at the click of a button. How effortless was that?

In the following screenshot for another Rails app, the user increases the number of web and worker dynos needed for the app to overcome an online shopping rush during the holidays. The user just moves the slider bar to the right and customizes the required number of dynos of each type. Scaling is so easy.

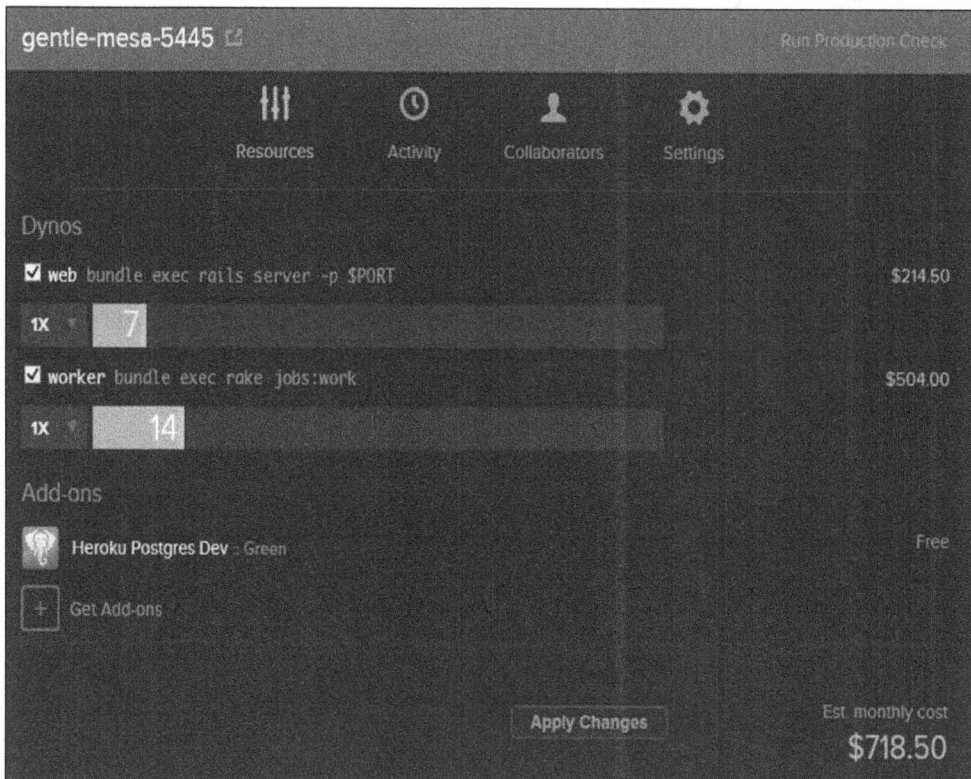

You can apply these changes by clicking on the **Apply Changes** button. If you have already registered a valid credit card with your Heroku account, you will be immediately billed for the new resources. Otherwise, you will be directed to the payment page to enter your payment information. On successful processing of the payment, Heroku will provision the required number of dynos for your application.

Many memory-intensive apps using standard dynos start slowing down once the app memory consumption crosses the 512 MB threshold. The logs are flooded with warnings and eventually errors pointing to constant page swapping and slowed performance. In cases such as these, it makes a lot of sense to audit the performance of your app using tools such as New Relic (http://www.newrelic.com) to identify the memory bottlenecks. If memory is indeed the problem, you can scale up your dyno memory by using 2X or PX (performance) dynos. These recently available memory configurations help your app perform way better and provide app users with much better response times.

The following screenshot shows how to configure your web or worker dynos to use 2X or PX memory by selecting the required configuration from the dropdown for dyno scaling:

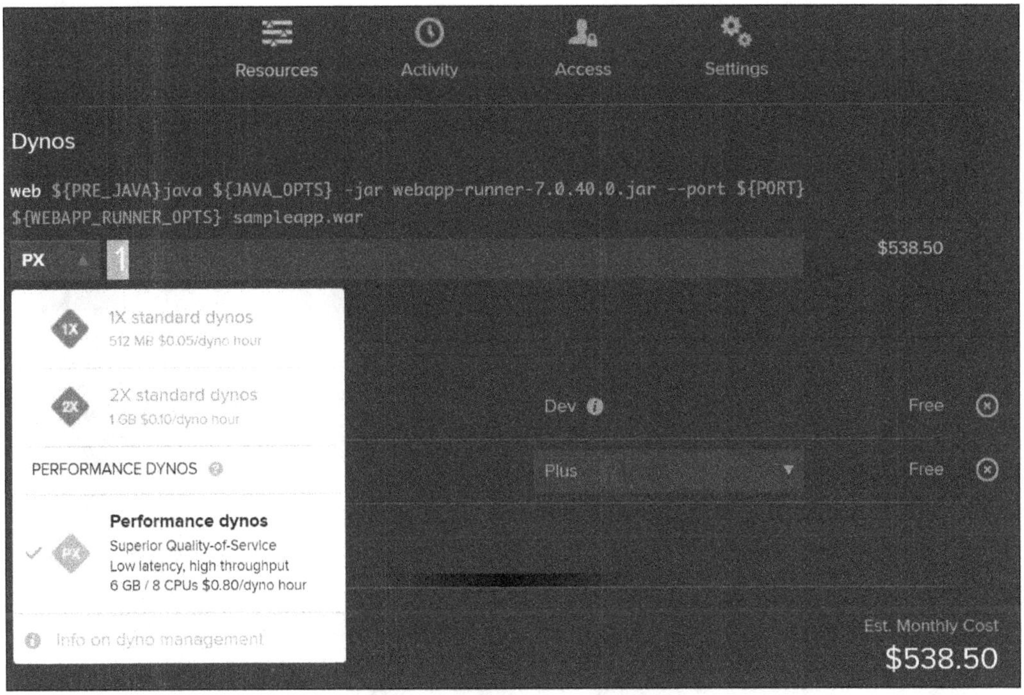

The Activity tab

The **Activity** tab of the app lists all events that took place since the app was deployed or shared with the account owner. When an app starts behaving unexpectedly, you can look at this activity log to check if a particular event resulted in the app's altered behavior. The following screenshot shows the location of the **Activity** tab on the **Apps** page:

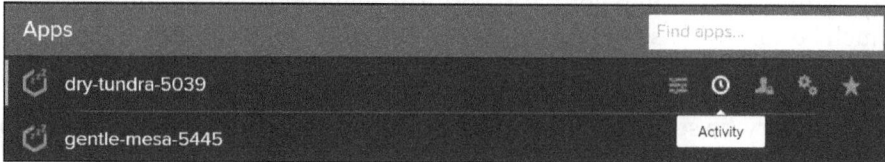

On clicking on the **Activity** tab for a particular app, the user is directed to the activity log as shown in the following screenshot:

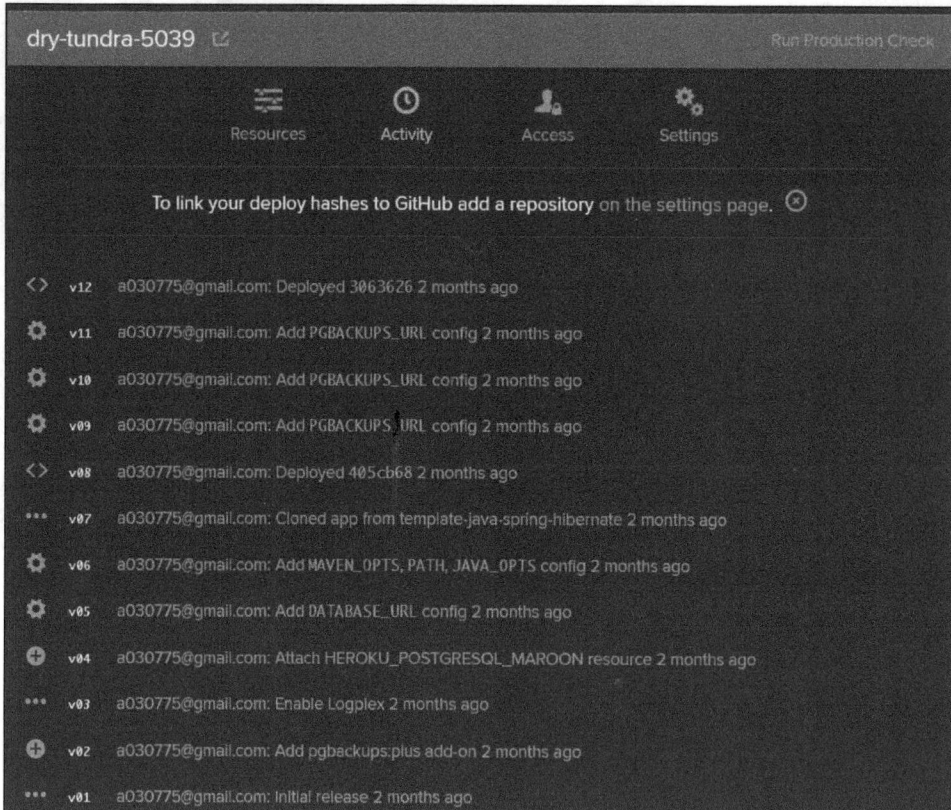

The Access tab

The **Access** tab lists the owner of the app as well as the collaborators working on the app. The following screenshot shows the location of the **Access** tab on the **Apps** page:

When the user clicks on the **Access** tab for the app, the user gets directed to the **Access** page as shown in the following screenshot:

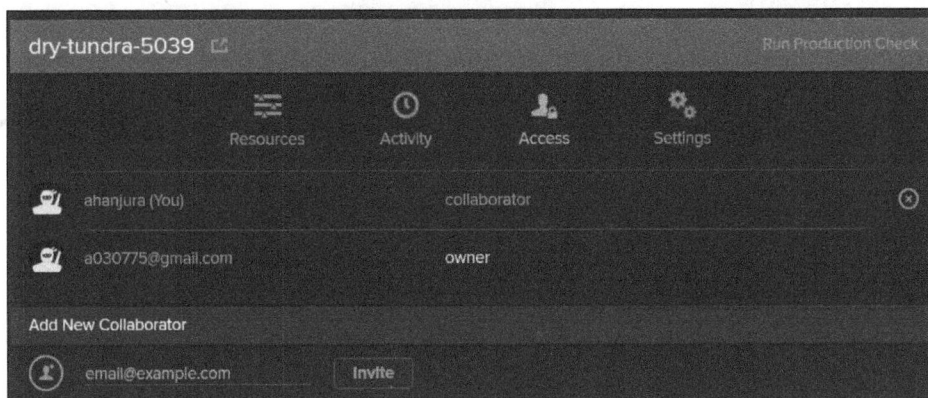

You can invite or remove collaborators on this page. The collaborators added using the **Access** tab can push the app's code to Heroku and create releases. They can't however attach paid add-ons to the app.

The Settings tab

The **Settings** tab provides detailed app configuration information including the app region, domain, stack, app error pages, and more. The following screenshot provides the location of the **Settings** tab on the **Apps** page:

The following screenshot shows the settings information for the **dry-tundra-5039** app:

The **Settings** tab provides specific information about the application as follows:

- Application name
- Application information (**Region, Stack, Framework, Git URL, Repo,** and **Slug size**)
- GitHub repository details (GitHub repository path — username/repo-name format)
- **Domains** (the current application domain URL is listed here with an option to enter a custom domain too)
- **Error Pages** (if the application is down or under maintenance, the redirect pages can be specified here)
- **Transfer Ownership** (you can choose one of your collaborators to be the new owner using the drop-down list)
- **Delete App** (you can delete the app, which internally deletes all related add-ons and database resources)

The Run Production Check tab

The **Run Production Check** tab lets you run a series of sanity tests on your application. The **Run Production Check** link is available on an app's detail page as shown in the following screenshot:

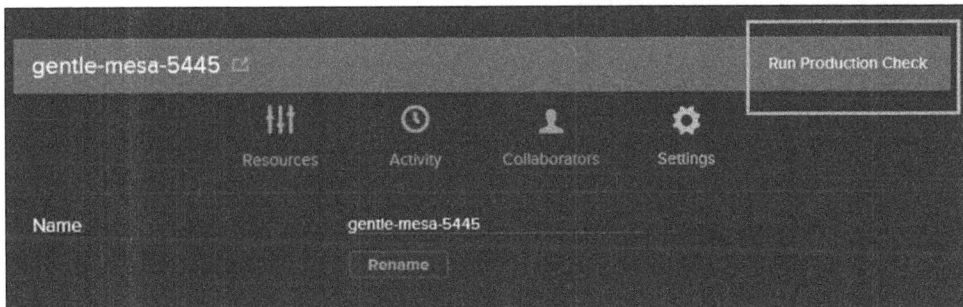

The check covers all components currently used by the production application and provides real-time diagnostic information about the possible failures. It also suggests appropriate solutions to those likely failures. This check serves as a handy tool for application administrators to identify the gaps in an application's configuration and validate the app's health.

The following screenshot shows the potential errors thrown by the **gentle-mesa-5445** app when **Run Production Check** was used with it. The Heroku platform readily provides some suggestions on how to resolve these errors. An online help link is also available for each of these topics as highlighted with a rectangular box in the following screenshot:

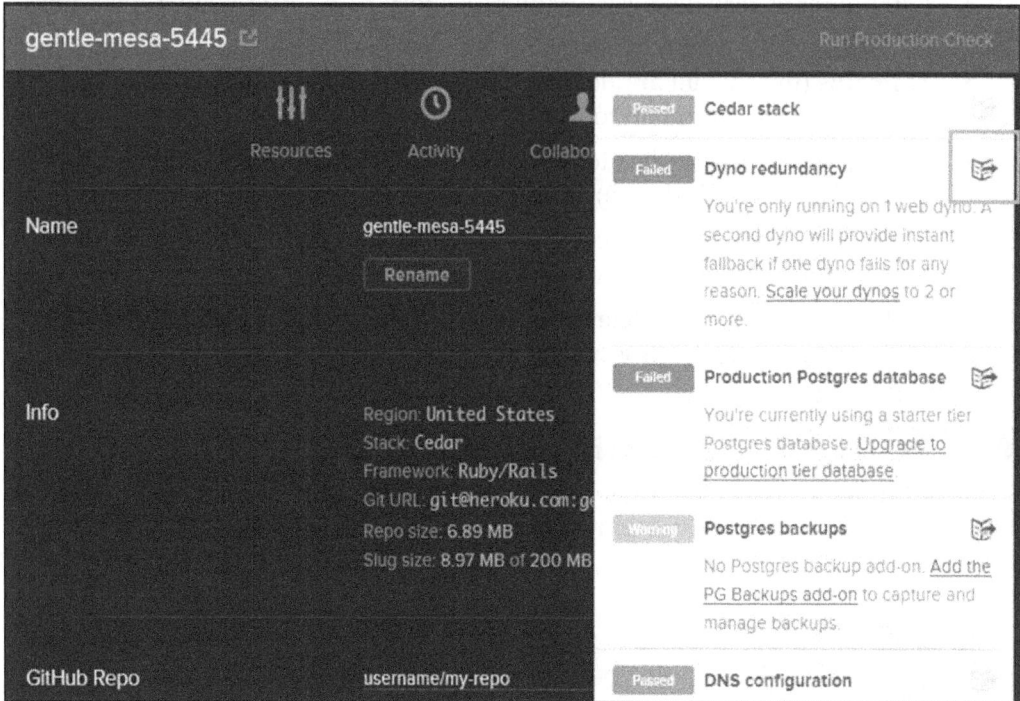

Heroku support

There may be instances when your app stops behaving all of a sudden. User requests don't seem to move faster, databases seem to be painfully slow, and you need immediate help. In cases such as these, you can get instant help by searching for specific topics of interest in the Heroku dashboard's **Support** section. The **Support** link is available in the top navigation bar of the Heroku dashboard page, as shown in the following screenshot:

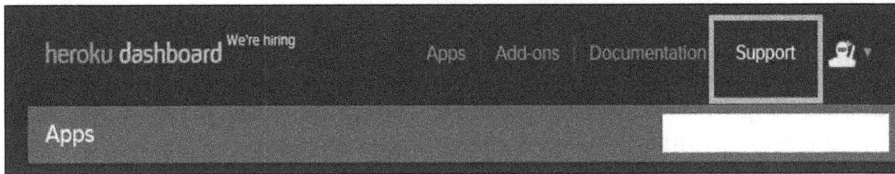

On clicking on the **Support** link, the user will be directed to the help page where you can enter specific search strings to look for more information on topics of interest. The help center page, as shown in the following screenshot, lists the most common issues and links to their resolution as well as showing the current production and development status of the Heroku platform. All this information on a single page is enormously beneficial for developers to troubleshoot ongoing issues with their app. The help center page is shown in the following screenshot:

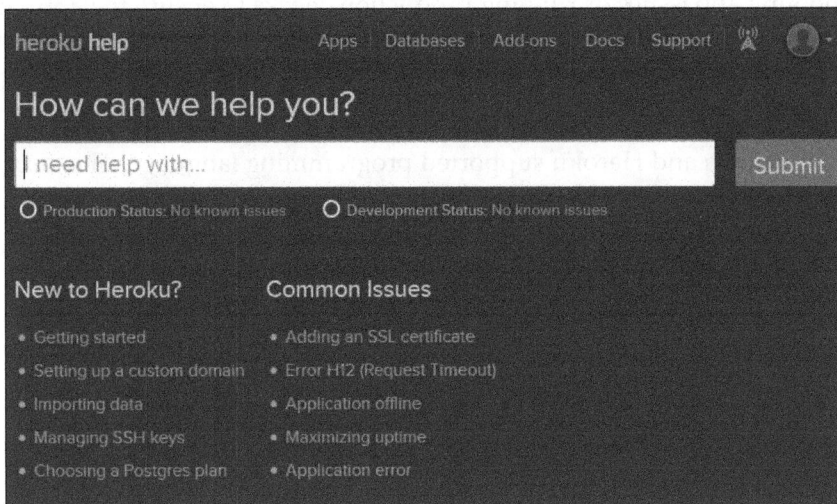

Summary

In this chapter, we reviewed the Heroku app lifecycle and learned how an app goes from the stage of creation to the stage of deployment and finally to the stage of monitoring and optimization. We looked at the Heroku CLI—the way most developers issue commands to create and run apps on the platform. Then, we familiarized ourselves with the Foreman tool, which is used to run your apps locally before pushing them to the Heroku platform. Using Foreman saves you a lot of trouble by helping you understand the app characteristics while in development and by helping you to make the right choices in terms of sizing and configuration before you take your app to production. Finally, we looked at Heroku's web UI for app execution and management; that is, the Heroku dashboard. We specifically looked at those aspects of the dashboard that deal with running an app on the Heroku platform—be it managing your app resources or looking at the activity log to troubleshooting app issues or running production checks to ensure the app's health. The Heroku dashboard hides the complexity of the platform by giving an intuitive web interface for developers and administrators alike to manage their apps.

In the next chapter, we combine our new skills and develop an app end to end using a well known and Heroku supported programming language. The next chapter nicely illustrates how you can develop and deploy cloud apps almost effortlessly using the available app development ecosystem which integrates very well with the Heroku platform. See you there.

6
Putting It All Together

One of the core strengths of the Heroku platform is its ability to function as a polyglot platform, where developers can virtually pick and choose any supported programming language and develop their feature-rich web apps. The Heroku platform also supports these languages by providing add-ons to include specific features (for example, caching pages) in these web apps. Web apps are deployed seamlessly, monitored, and shared with other developers at the click of a button.

Earlier in this book, we focused on specific aspects such as building and deploying apps on the Heroku platform, and learned how various techniques can be employed to perform useful tasks with the platform.

In this chapter, we provide a round-up of everything we have learned so far. We will learn the following:

- How to add Heroku support and deploy Java apps on Heroku using Eclipse
- How to manage Heroku apps and perform all the app management operations inside Eclipse

We could have done this with any other language and any other IDE. The choice of language is really immaterial. The key point is how rapidly cloud application development is enabled using Eclipse as a development and deployment tool for Heroku.

Heroku's support for Java

Heroku started focusing on supporting Ruby as the programming language of choice. Most features and samples deployed on Heroku were written in Ruby. Even the Heroku build system used Ruby build tools as the default toolkit for building and deploying web apps on Heroku. Soon, Heroku extended its language support to include more programming languages, thereby making it a true polyglot platform—one where you could write apps in any of the supported programming languages.

Besides Ruby, Heroku started supporting Java, Python, PHP, Clojure, and other languages. Heroku's support for these languages combined with Heroku's Plug and Play architecture has helped Heroku reach a much larger audience. Heroku has now evolved into one of the best choices for developing and deploying web apps very easily and quickly. Heroku has found followers of its polyglot approach across the developer community — from freelancers to larger web software companies trying to rapidly build useful web apps.

In this section, we will review Heroku's support for one of the most popular programming languages in the software world — Java.

General support for Java

The Heroku Cedar stack can run various types of Java web apps. The Cedar stack uses Maven as the build system for compiling Java source code into an executable application. By establishing the presence of a `pom.xml` file, the Heroku system detects that a particular code push is a Java app. Heroku uses the OpenJDK toolkit to run Java apps. Currently, the Heroku Cedar stack supports OpenJDK 6 and 7.

Database support for Java apps

When you build Java web apps on Heroku, a Postgres database is automatically provisioned for the app. If the default Postgres plan doesn't suit your app needs, you can upgrade the database's add-on plan depending on your business needs. You can find more details of the available plans at `https://devcenter.heroku.com/articles/heroku-postgres-plans`.

Environment configuration

When you deploy your Java web app for the first time, Heroku sets the following configuration or environment variables for your application:

PATH	This is the set of directories where executables will be looked up by the build process or other steps of application deployment and execution, for example, `/usr/bin:/bin` (UNIX variants) and `C:\<JAVA_HOME>\bin;C:\Windows`.

JAVA_OPTS	The following are the command-line options for the Java compiler: • `-Xss512k`: This option sets the Java stack size • `-Xmx384m`: This option sets the maximum heap memory to be allocated • `-XX:+UseCompressedOops`: This option allows references to be 32-bit in a 64-bit JVM and access close to 32 GB of a heap This can be manually adjusted to suit the specific needs of the application environment. For example, in Heroku, there is an upside limit to the dyno memory, so the maximum heap size needs to be adjusted for it to be below the dyno memory limit in order to allow for the optimal execution of your app.
MAVEN_OPTS	Command-line options for the Maven Build tool are as follows: • `-Xss512k`: This sets the Java stack size • `-Xmx384m`: This sets the maximum heap memory to be allocated • `-XX:+UseCompressedOops`: This option allows references to be 32-bit in a 64-bit JVM and access close to 32 GB of a heap This option can be manually adjusted to suit the specific needs of the application build environment.
PORT	This is the HTTP port to which the web process will bind.
DATABASE_URL	This is the database connection URL to be used by the application.

> If you needed more dyno memory for your app and started using 2X dynos to meet your application's memory requirement, this change would not be automatically reflected in your app's configuration. You would need to manually edit JAVA_OPTS and MAVEN_OPTS to reflect the change.

Integrating Eclipse with Heroku

In the steps that follow, we show how to configure the Heroku development environment in Eclipse. Eclipse is one of the most popular and powerful integrated software development platforms on the market today. Millions of developers use Eclipse to write and deploy enterprise and other Java apps using Eclipse for the JEE edition.

In this section, we first list the prerequisites for enabling the development of a Heroku cloud application using Eclipse, and then show a step-by-step approach to configuring the Eclipse plugin for Heroku. Finally, we create a sample web app in Java and deploy the app. We also show you how to manage and monitor the Java web app using features of the Eclipse plugin for Heroku.

Prerequisites

Before you begin your journey of deploying Heroku apps using Eclipse, perform the following steps:

1. Get a Heroku account at `www.heroku.com`.

2. Download Eclipse. Go to `http://www.eclipse.org/downloads/` and download the Eclipse IDE for Java EE developers. Unzip the downloaded ZIP and restore the contents of the package to `C:\Eclipse` or any other directory.

Configuring Heroku in Eclipse

It is quite straightforward to add Heroku support for writing, deploying, and managing Heroku web apps from Eclipse. If you have not used Heroku before and you are a Java developer, using Eclipse is your best bet to instantly get started with Heroku. There are instructions available to do the same via Heroku CLI at `https://devcenter.heroku.com/articles/getting-started-with-java`.

Let's get started then.

Installing the Eclipse plugin for Heroku

The first step to writing and deploying a Java web app on Heroku is to install the Eclipse plugin for Heroku. This fairly straightforward procedure helps you set up the Eclipse Heroku plugin which can then be used to help you interact with your Heroku environment from Eclipse. So, all set? Perform the following steps to install the Eclipse plugin for Heroku:

1. Open Eclipse and navigate to the **Help** menu, and within it, select the **Install New Software** menu option as shown in the following screenshot:

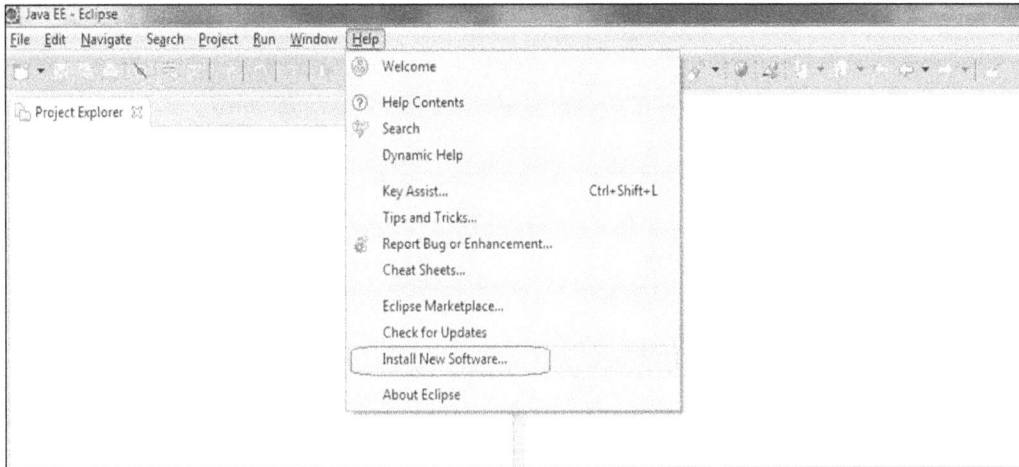

2. Enter the URL of the Eclipse Heroku plugin, `https://eclipse-plugin.herokuapp.com/install`, and click on **Add** as shown in the following screenshot:

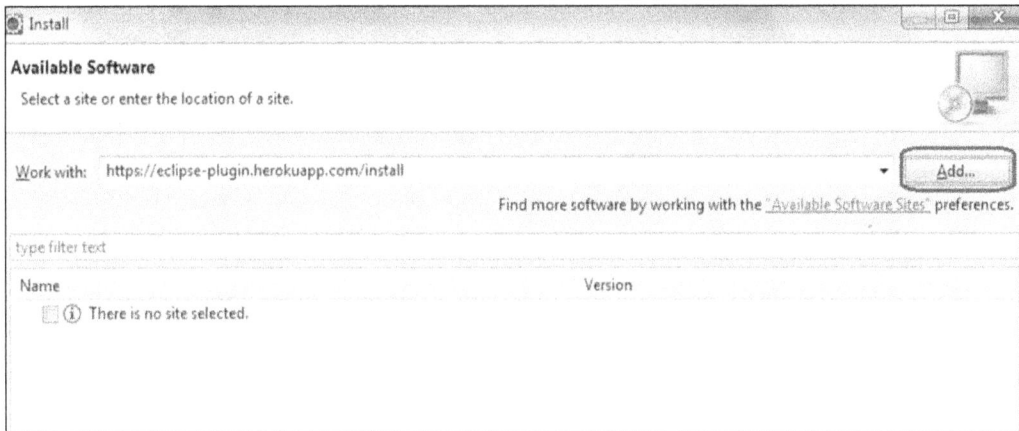

3. Enter the repository name as `Heroku` and click on **OK** as shown in the following screenshot:

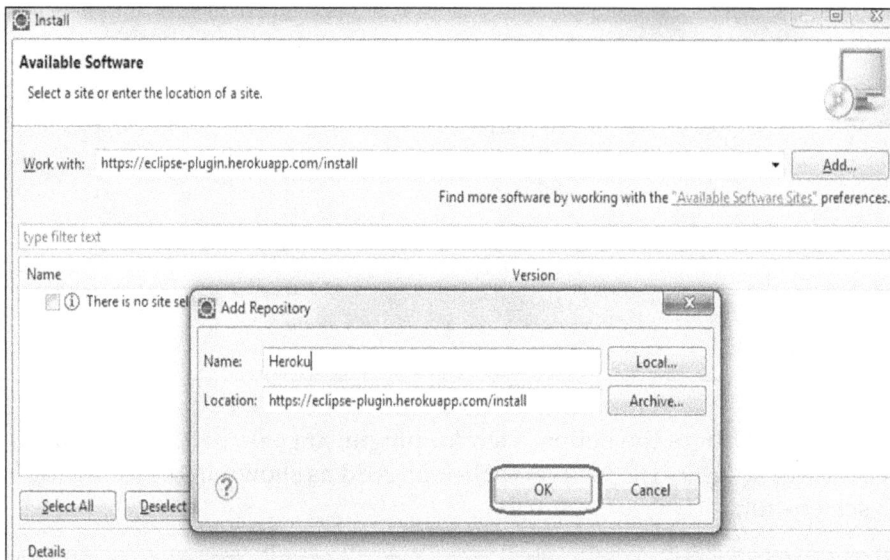

4. Check the plugin name **Heroku Eclipse Integration** and click on **Next** as shown in the following screenshot:

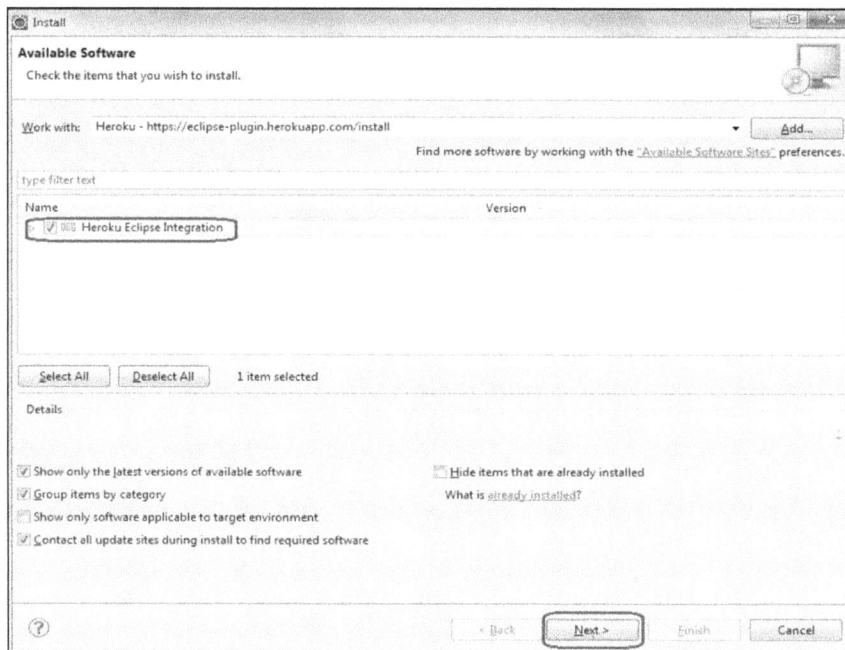

5. Review the details of the plugin and click on **Next** as shown in the following screenshot:

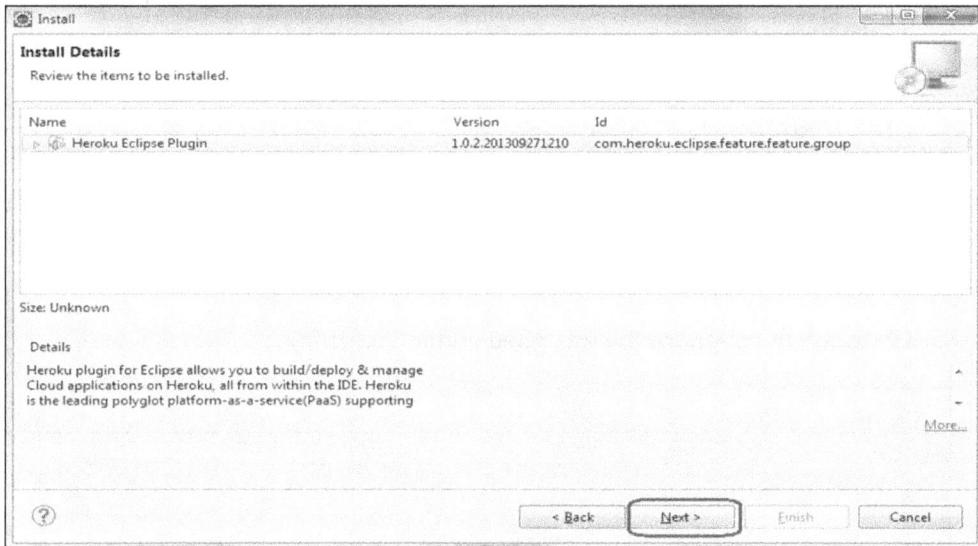

6. Accept the license agreement and click on **Finish** as shown in the following screenshot:

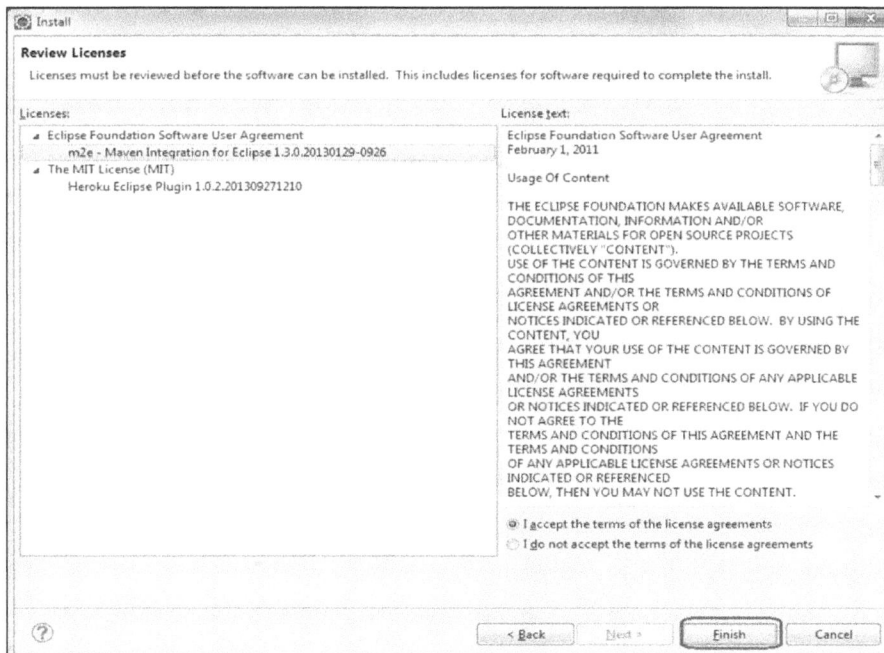

7. The Heroku software is now being installed.

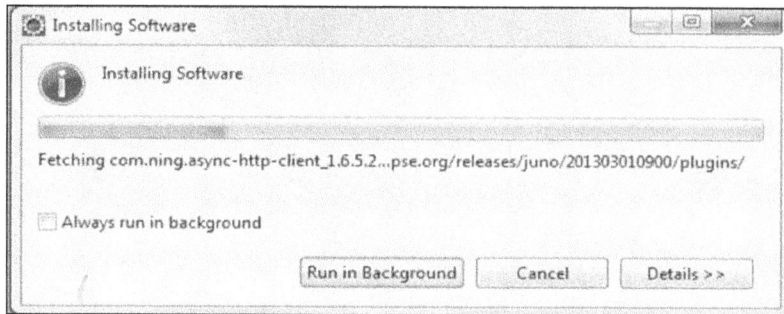

> **Installing Software**
>
> ⓘ Installing Software
>
> Fetching com.ning.async-http-client_1.6.5.2...pse.org/releases/juno/201303010900/plugins/
>
> ☐ Always run in background
>
> Run in Background | Cancel | Details >>

8. Click on **OK** to ignore the unsigned content warning.

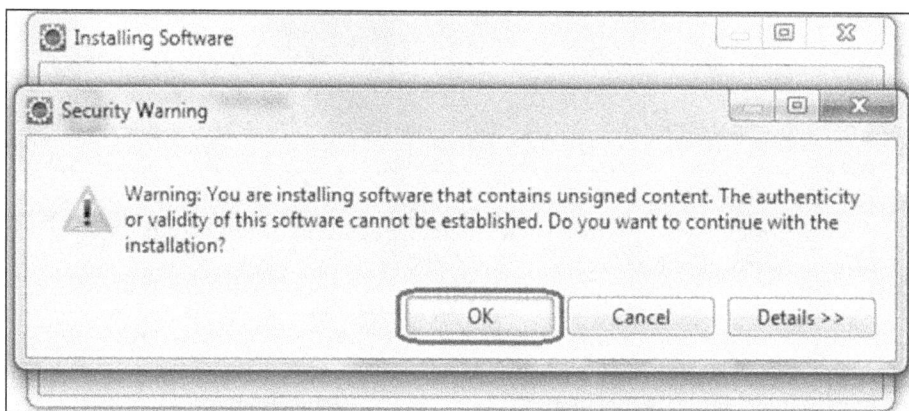

> **Installing Software**
>
> **Security Warning**
>
> ⚠ Warning: You are installing software that contains unsigned content. The authenticity or validity of this software cannot be established. Do you want to continue with the installation?
>
> OK | Cancel | Details >>

9. Click on **Yes** to make the changes effective.

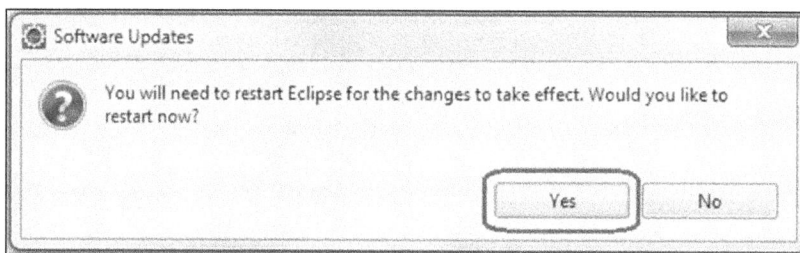

> **Software Updates**
>
> ❓ You will need to restart Eclipse for the changes to take effect. Would you like to restart now?
>
> Yes | No

10. The Eclipse IDE will restart. You can go to **New | Other** to verify whether Heroku support has been added.

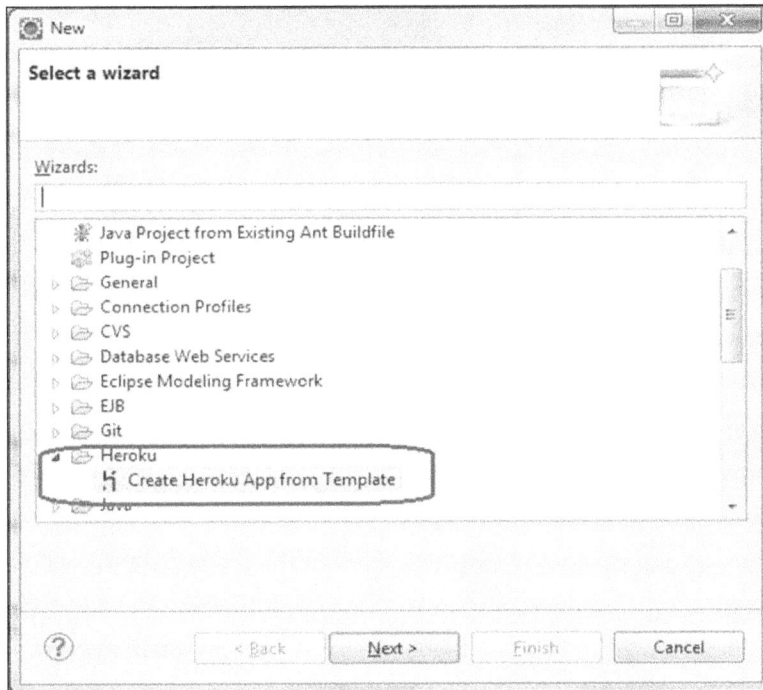

Setting up Heroku for development

Developing apps based on Java using Heroku is as easy as writing your Java apps on premise. Well, it is quite transparent as far as setting up Heroku support is concerned. You need a plugin and you install it. That's it. We tell Eclipse which Heroku account to use for newly created apps and what security credentials are needed to access API services and push/pull code from the Heroku platform.

Setting up SSH support

As discussed in the earlier chapters, SSH is used as a security mechanism to transport your changes to and from Heroku. You can configure SSH for the development of your Heroku application in the following two ways:

- Creating a new key by navigating to **Windows | Preferences | Heroku**
- Loading an existing SSH key that is already set up for the machine you are working on

As I am already working on Heroku using the **command-line interface (CLI)**, I already have an SSH key. Generating a new one is equally straightforward. We will look at how to load an existing SSH key in the following steps:

1. Open Eclipse.
2. Go to **Windows | Preferences | Heroku** and click on **Load SSH key**.

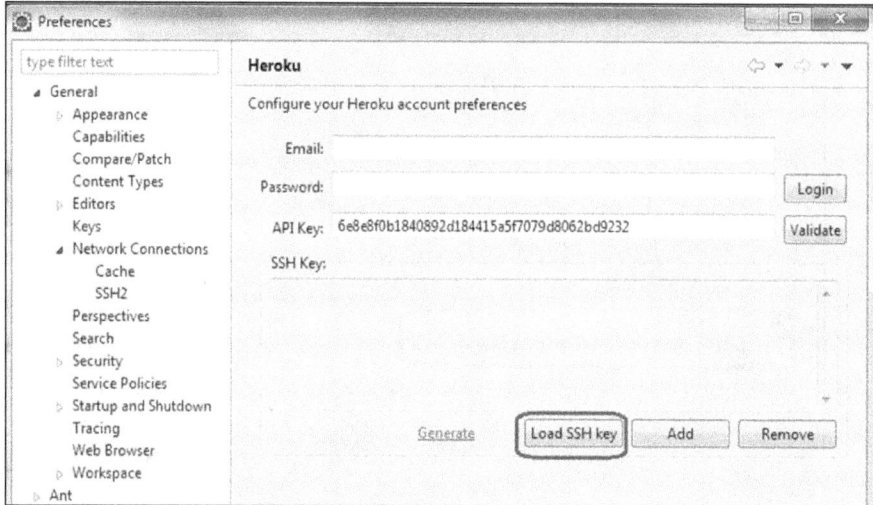

3. Select the file from the `.ssh` folder of your user directory.

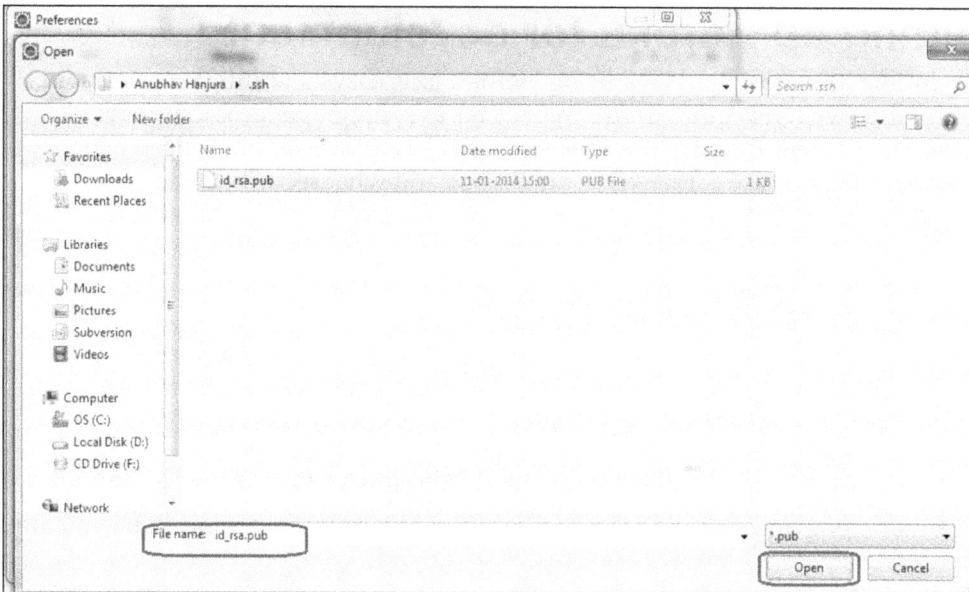

This will load the SSH key into Eclipse Heroku preferences. As I already have an API key, I will log in to my Heroku account to retrieve the key by navigating to **Account | Show API Key**.

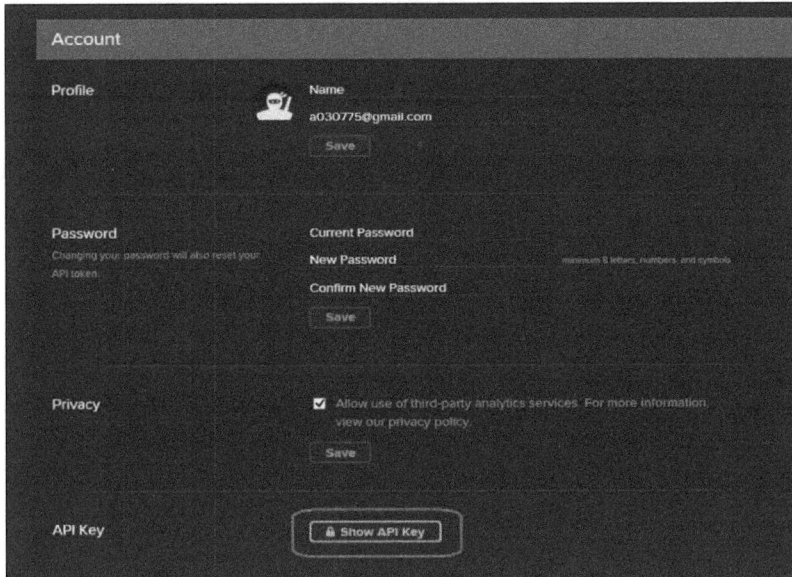

4. Enter the retrieved API key in the **API Key** section and click on **OK**.

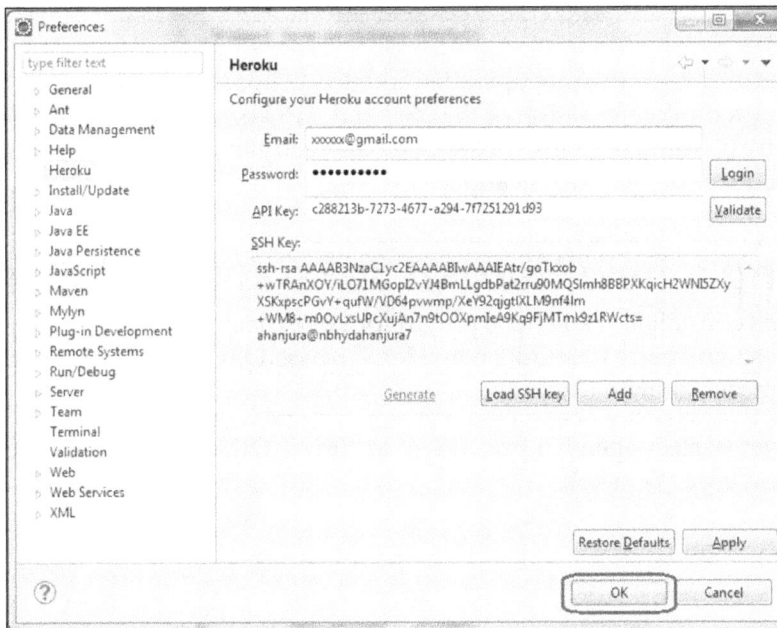

Heroku will validate the entered information including the API key and will return errors, if any.

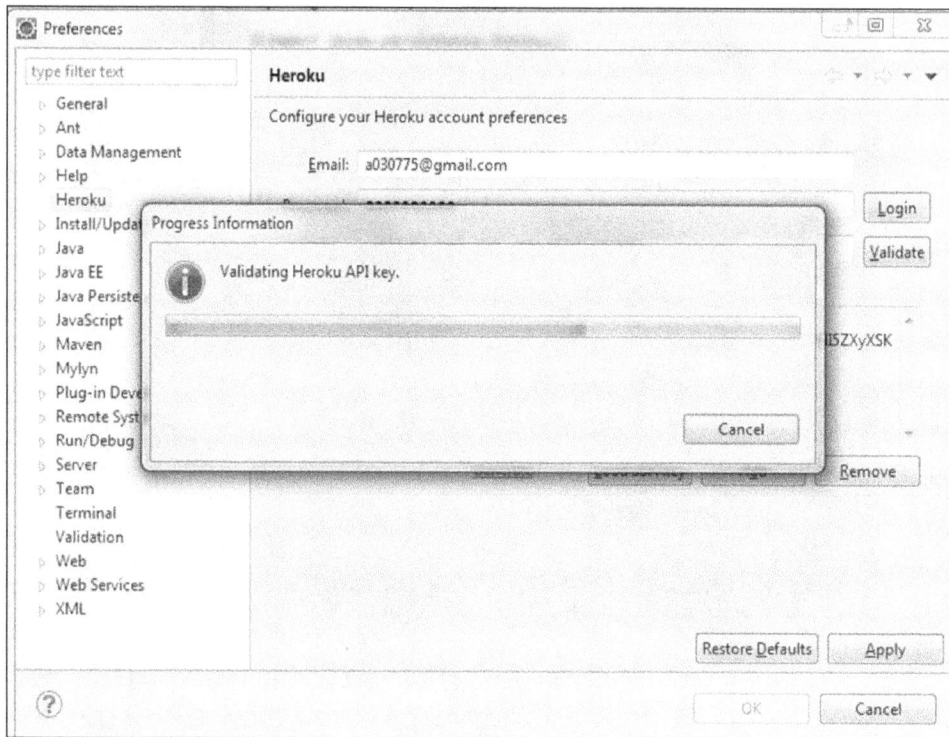

The SSH and API keys are now uploaded into the Eclipse configuration. This completes the configuration of the SSH and API keys for deploying your Heroku web app through Eclipse. Now, you are ready to go and write your first Eclipse-based Heroku web application.

Creating a new Heroku Java app in Eclipse

Once you have installed the Eclipse plugin for Heroku and set up SSH and API keys in Eclipse, you are ready to build a new Heroku-based Java web application. To do this, perform the following steps:

1. To get started, open Eclipse and go to **New | Other** as shown in the following screenshot:

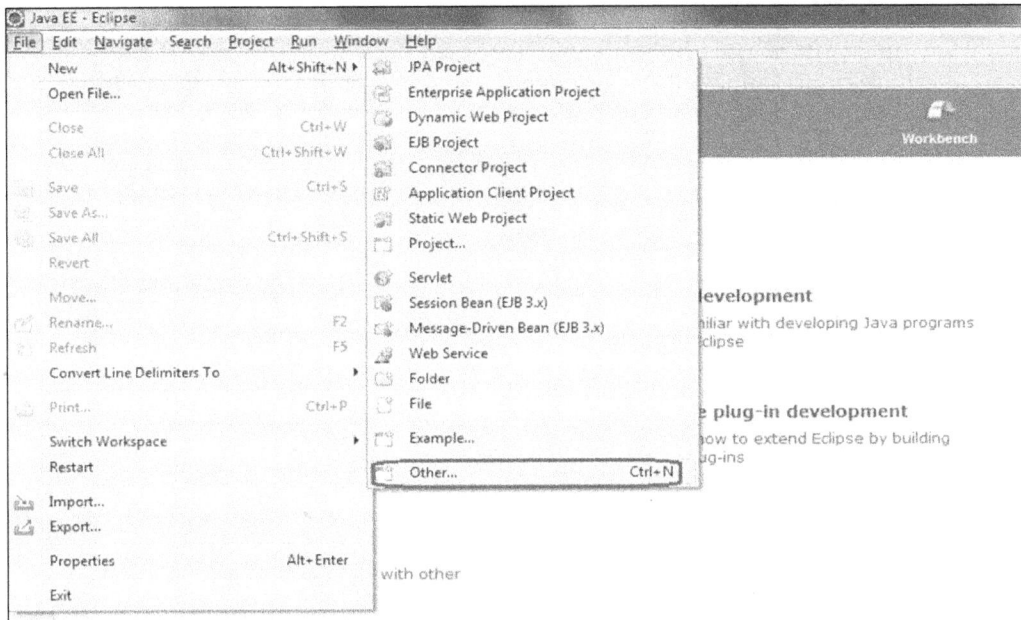

2. Click on the **Create Heroku App from Template** option.

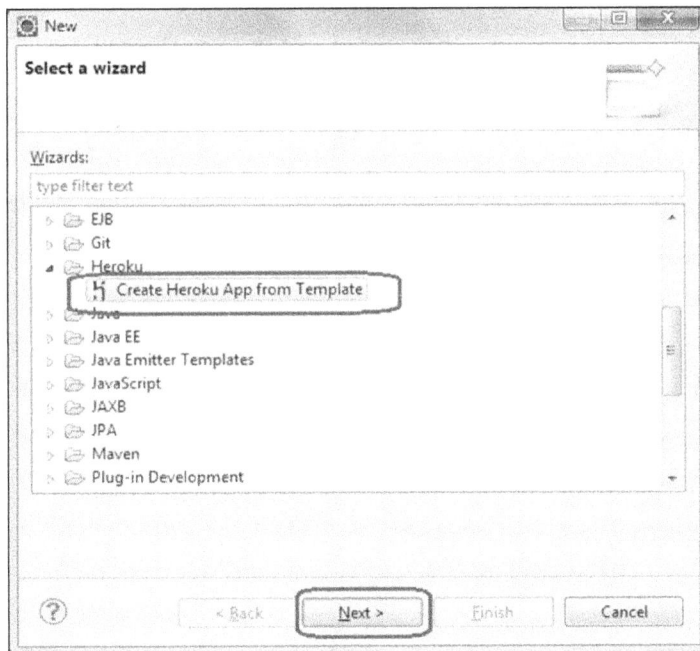

3. You can create an application from the list of template apps that are already available in Eclipse. Enter the name of the application (or leave it blank, in which case a name will be autogenerated for the app) and click on **Finish**.

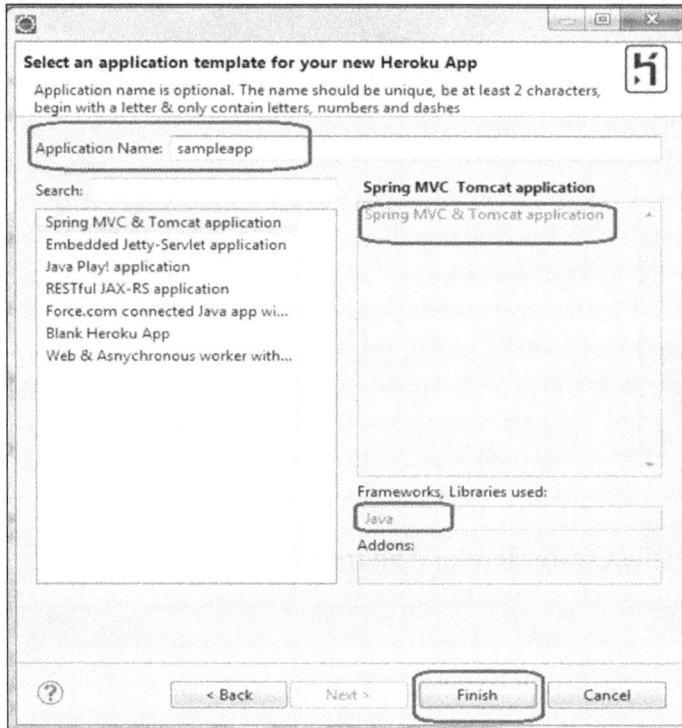

A new application, `sampleapp`, will be created for you. Once the application is created, the plugin will pull down the source code's repository as a local Git repository.

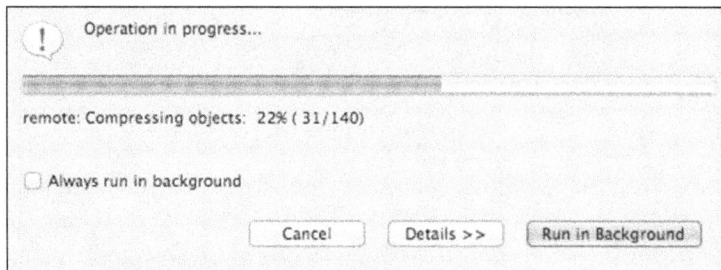

4. Once the application is created, you can open Eclipse's **Package Explorer** folder and notice the newly created directory structure for the app.

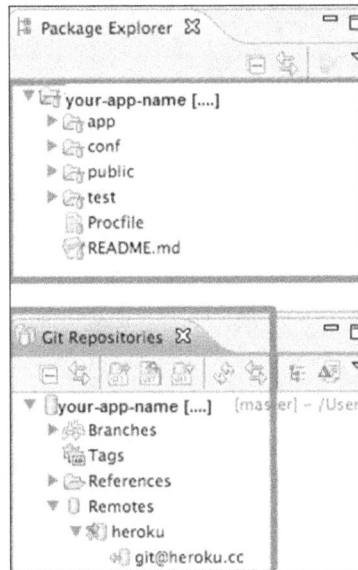

Now you are ready to make changes to your web app. Once done, you can push the updates to Heroku using operations provided by Eclipse. Using Eclipse, you can pretty much do anything you could do using the Heroku command-line interface. You can view the application's information, deploy the modified app, monitor logs, scale the app, refresh the application, and much more. We will soon experiment with each of these useful aspects of Eclipse-based cloud app development.

Using an existing Heroku application

Heroku imposes a limit on how many apps you can have in your Heroku account in order to avoid abuse by users who can choke the Heroku infrastructure by running a large number of apps, thereby making heavy use of Heroku's system resources such as memory, CPU, and network bandwidth. The limit is 100 apps for verified accounts and five apps for unverified ones. Therefore, it is beneficial to reuse existing apps that might no longer be actively used and are eating up resources. We could use these existing Heroku apps and transform them to create useful web apps.

To import an app from your Heroku account, you can perform the following steps:

1. Navigate to **File | Import**.

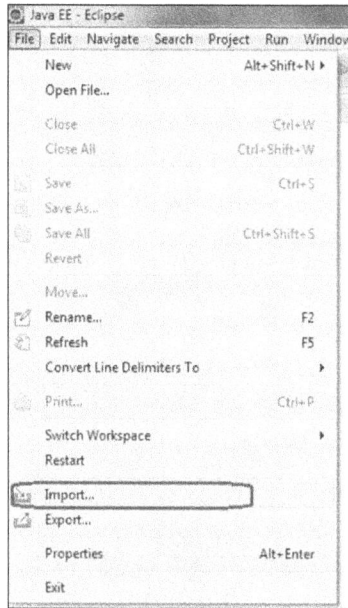

2. Select the **Import existing Heroku App** option in the **Import** menu.

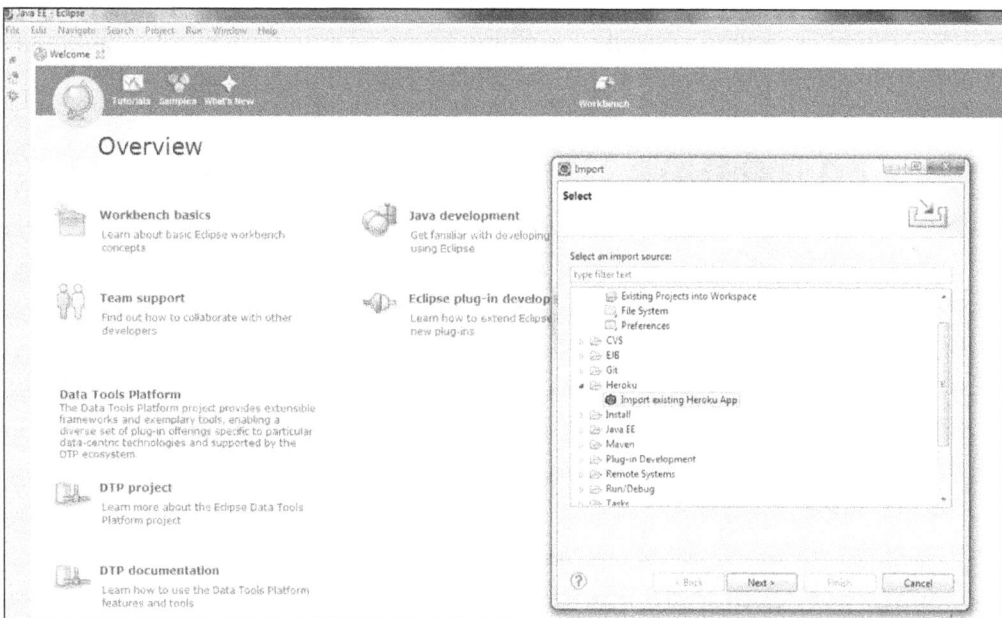

3. We will see a list of Heroku apps that can be imported into your workspace. Select **dry-tundra-5039** and click on **Next**.

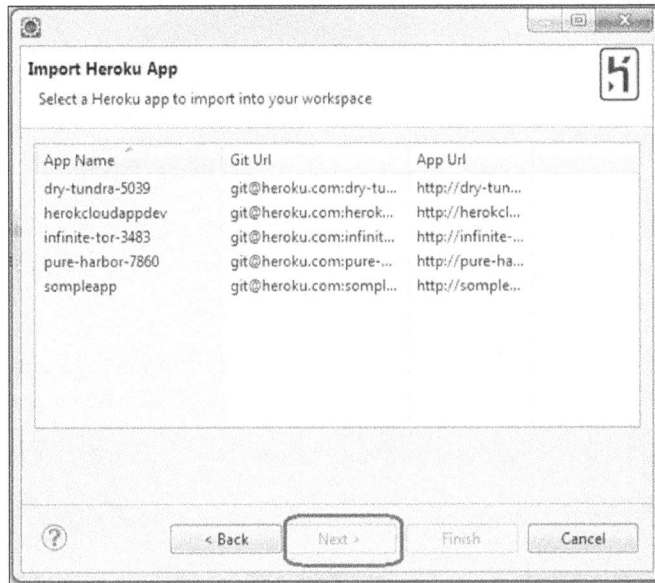

4. During the import, Eclipse can detect the type of project (optionally based on the developer's choice) and accordingly apply the characteristics of that type to the imported project. Our project was built using Maven. While importing the project, Eclipse will apply the properties of a Maven project to our project. Choose the **Auto detected project** option and click on **Finish**.

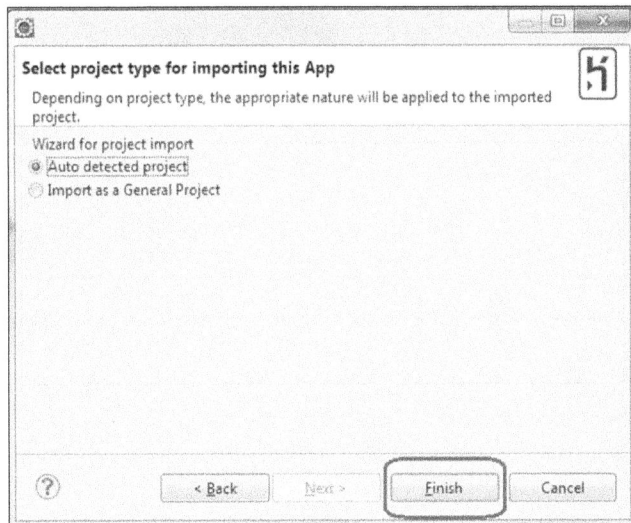

Eclipse will import the selected project and create the necessary project settings.

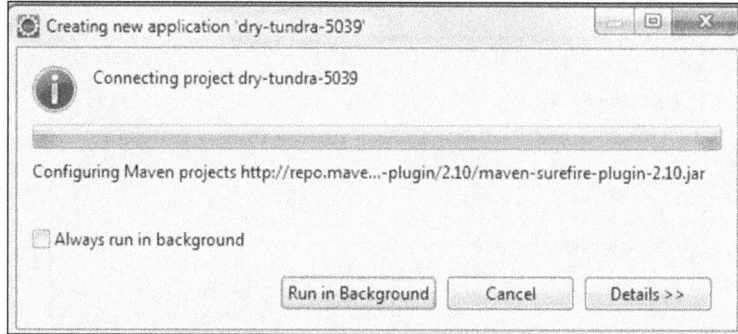

5. Go to the **Project Explorer** view by navigating to **Window | Show View** on the Eclipse menu and then clicking on **Project Explorer**. Verify that the imported project is available for use and editing, as shown in the following screenshot:

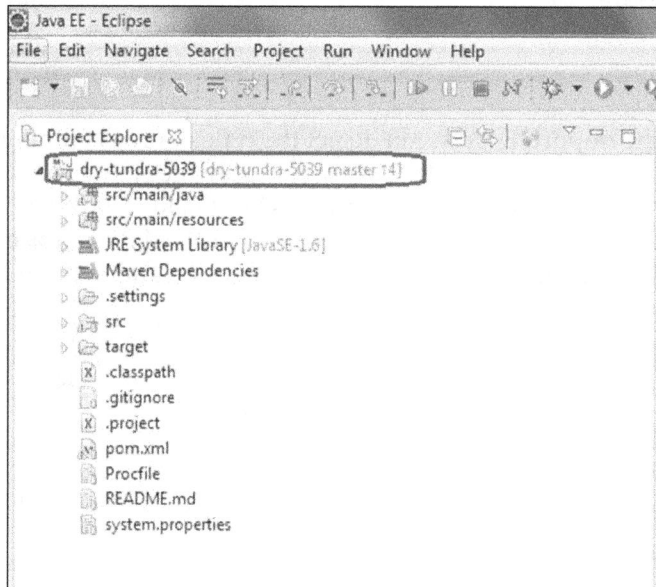

We have successfully imported a Heroku app into Eclipse. We can now edit the source code located in the `src` folder.

Pushing code to Heroku

Now that we have a working project in Eclipse, let's modify the source code and then push the changes to Heroku by performing the following steps:

1. Open Eclipse and go to the **Project Explorer** view by navigating to **Window | Show View** on the Eclipse menu and then clicking on **Project Explorer**.

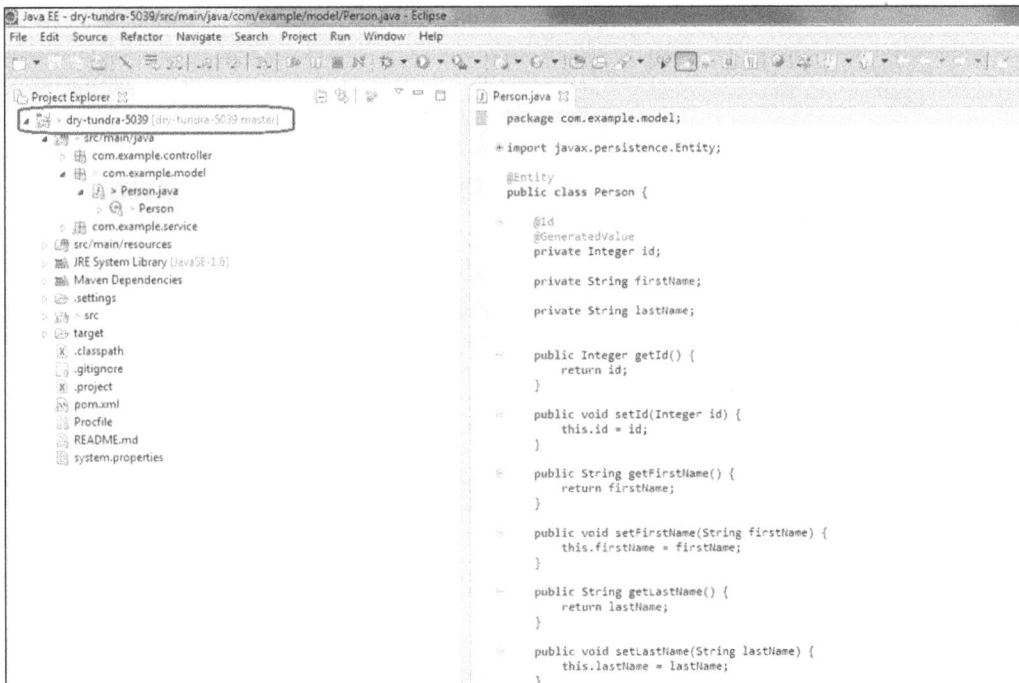

2. Change the `Person.java` source file by adding a new method at the end of the `Person` class as shown in the following screenshot:

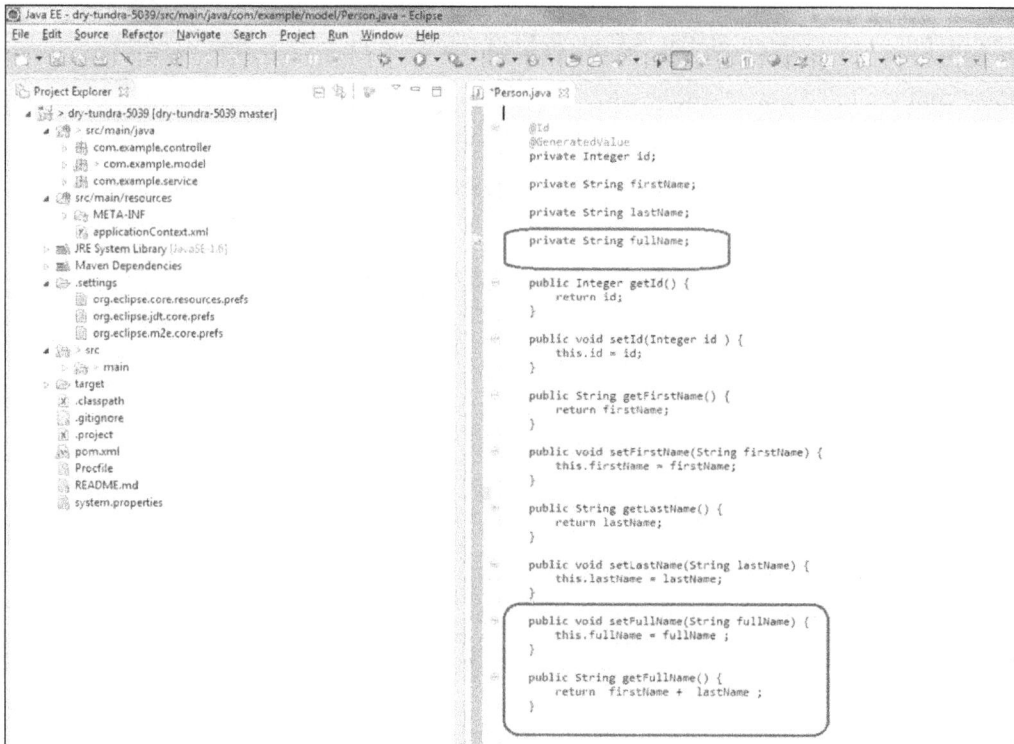

3. After making the necessary changes and saving them, select the project in the **Project Explorer** view and then navigate to **Team** | **Push to Upstream**, as shown in the following screenshot:

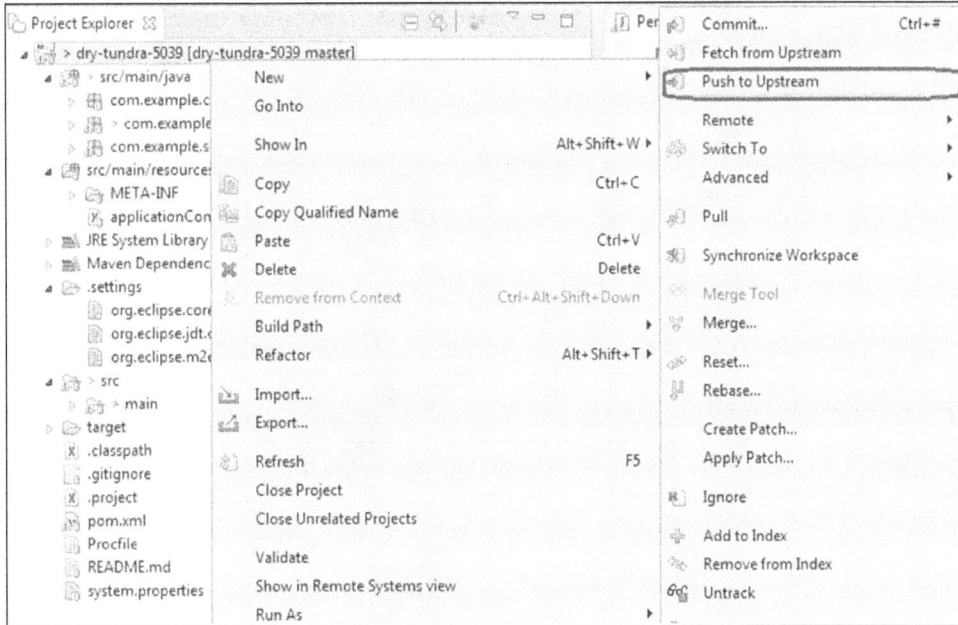

By clicking on the **Push to Upstream** menu option, the changes in your code will be pushed to your app's remote repository.

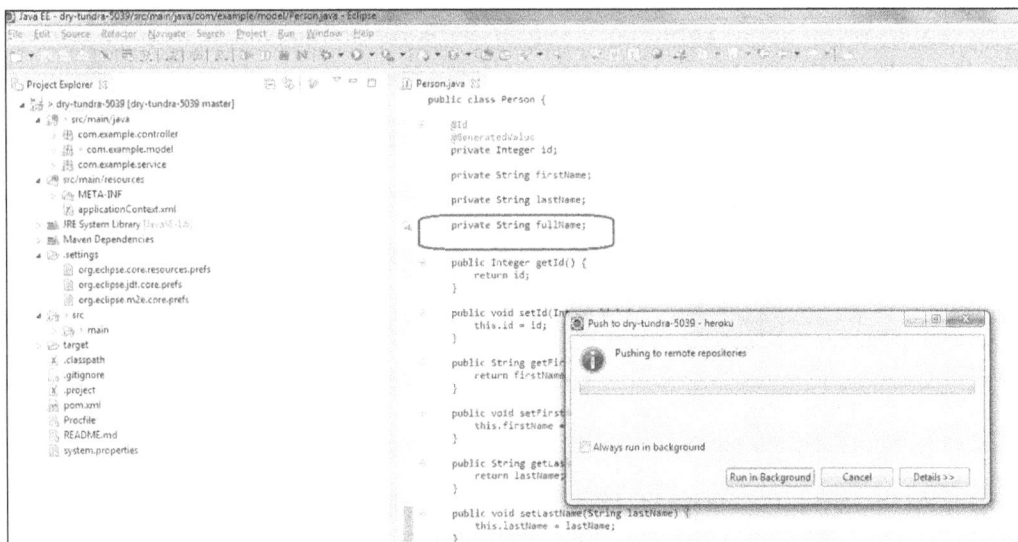

4. Finally, Eclipse displays a successful push message. Click on **OK** to complete the process of pushing your code to Heroku.

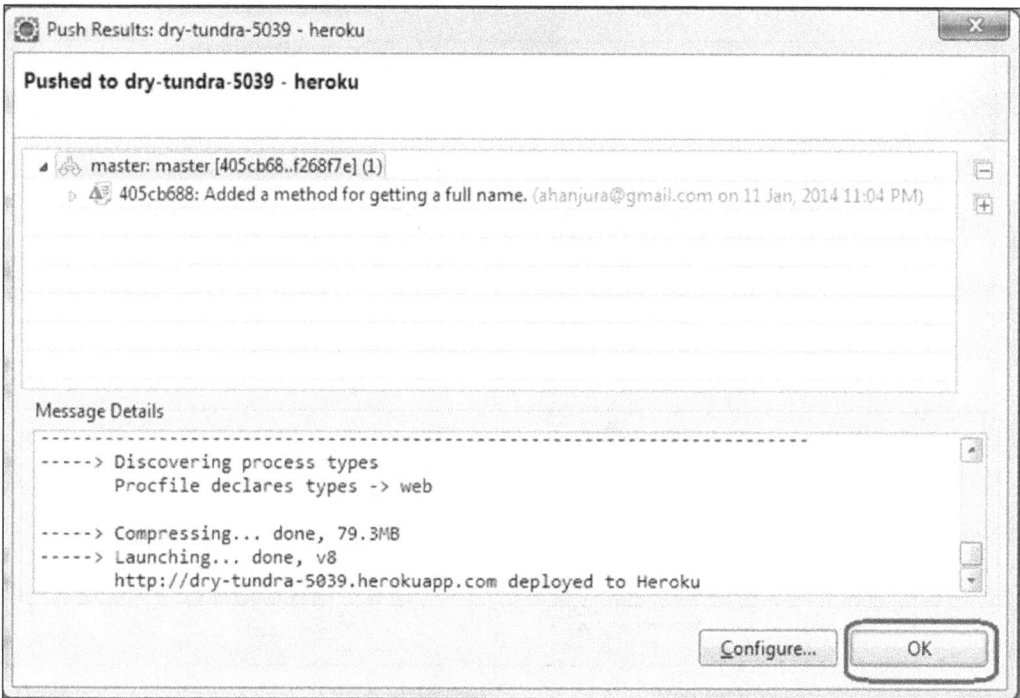

Pushing code to the Git repository

Eclipse allows you to push your code to the Git distributed version control system just like any other Git client.

You can select the code to check in, enter your Git repository's credentials, and then enter your commit message (optional). Click on **OK**, and voila, you are done. This is illustrated as follows:

1. Open Eclipse and navigate to **Window | Show View** on the Eclipse menu and click on **Project Explorer**.

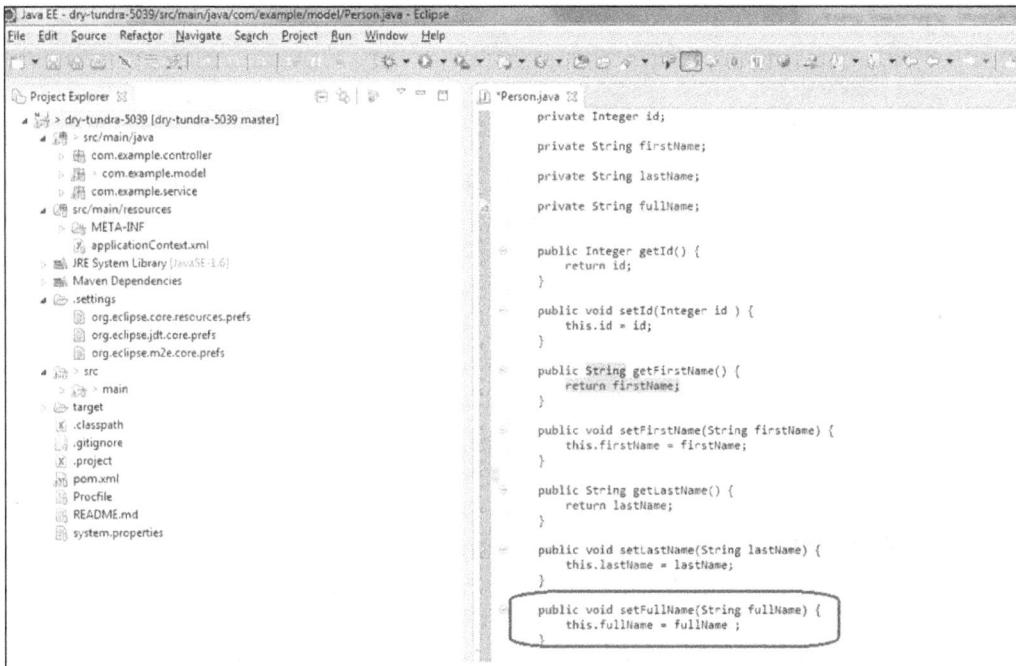

2. Make changes in the code and save it in Eclipse. Right-click on the project and navigate to **Team** | **Commit**.

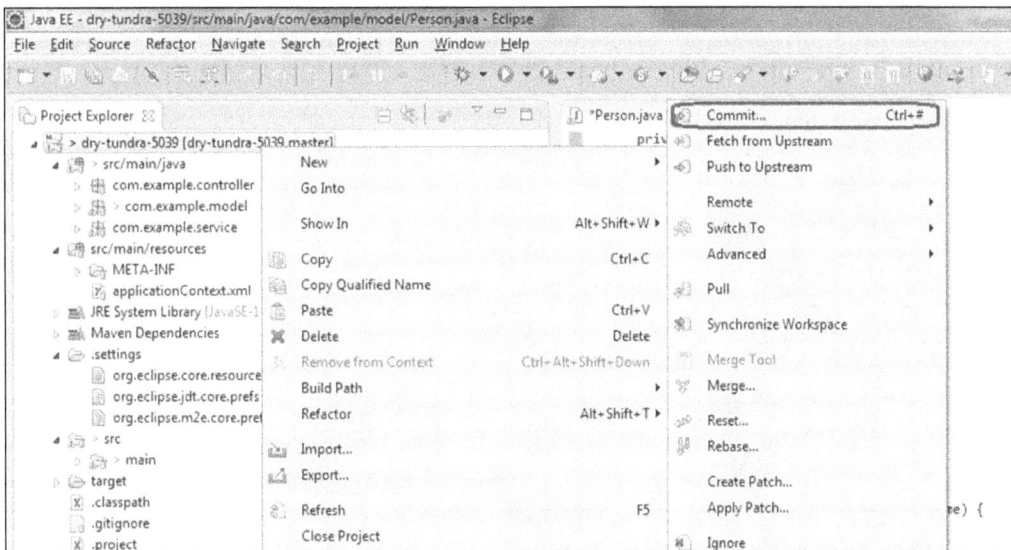

3. Enter your Git credentials to access your Git repository.

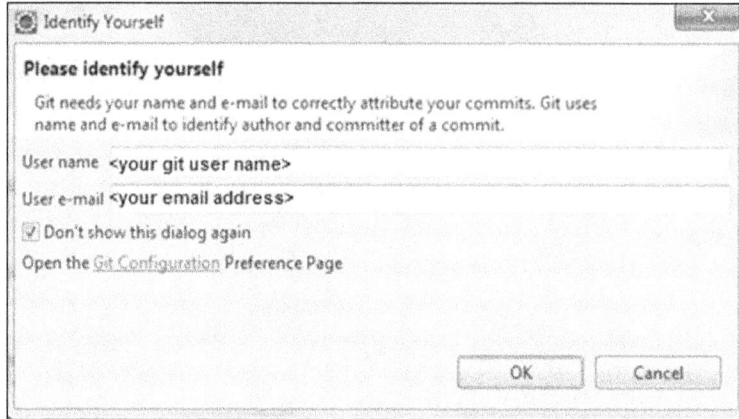

4. Enter a commit message for the changes you have made and click on **Commit**. Note that there is a **Commit and Push** option as well. This option will commit your changes to Git and push them to Heroku in one go.

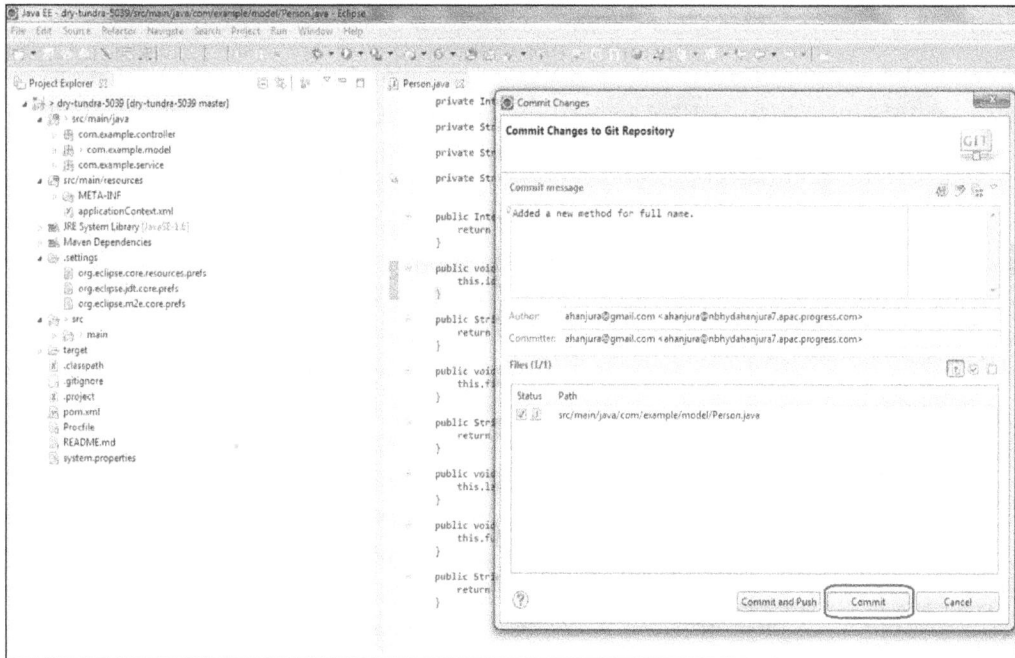

Now, your code changes will be synced with the Git repository and ready for use by other developers.

Managing Heroku apps in Eclipse

You can have many Java web apps deployed on Heroku at any single point of time. You can log in to your Heroku account and manage these web apps, or you could use the facilities provided within Eclipse to do everything you need to manage your web app. In the current section, we will see how to use Eclipse to do the most common tasks to manage your web apps.

Viewing your Heroku application

Eclipse makes the monitoring and management of your Heroku web app extremely simple by providing a Heroku view in the **Window** menu option. With the click of a few buttons, you can easily review the list of Heroku applications you have. This can be done by performing the following steps:

1. Open Eclipse, go to **Window** | **Show View** | **Other,** and then select **My Heroku Applications**.

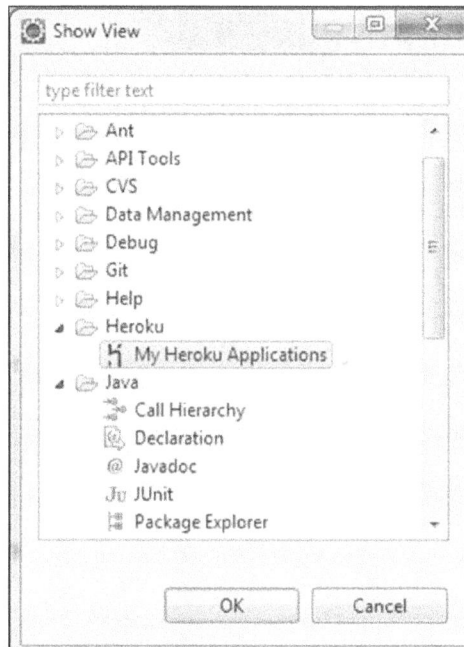

2. Eclipse will display a list of Heroku apps that belong to your account, or you are a collaborator on, along with other relevant information such as the app name, Git URL, and application URL for that app, as shown in the following screenshot:

Markers	Properties	Servers	Data Source Explorer	Snippets	Search	My Heroku Applications	

Name	Git URL	App URL
dry-tundra-5039	git@heroku.com:dry-tundra-5039....	http://dry-tundra-5039.herokuapp...
herokcloudappdev	git@heroku.com:herokcloudappd...	http://herokcloudappdev.herokua...
infinite-tor-3483	git@heroku.com:infinite-tor-3483....	http://infinite-tor-3483.herokuapp...
pure-harbor-7860	git@heroku.com:pure-harbor-786...	http://pure-harbor-7860.herokuap...
sompleapp	git@heroku.com:sompleapp.git	http://sompleapp.herokuapp.com/

Getting to the application's details

In Eclipse, it is quite straightforward to review the details of various Heroku apps and perform various operations on them, like we do using the Heroku command-line interface. Eclipse is a one-stop console and development platform for building and managing Java-based Heroku apps. You can manage all of the application's resources including add-ons, database connections, and additional libraries from Eclipse.

Reviewing the application's details

To review the list of operations that are available for a particular application, right-click on the application. The list of operations available for each app is very similar to the list that is available from the Heroku command line, but is more easily found within Eclipse. The next screenshot shows the list of available operations for the **dry-tundra-5039** application:

Markers	Properties	Servers	Data Source Explorer	Snippets	Console	Search	My Heroku Applications	

Name		Git URL	App URL
dry-tundra-5039		git@heroku.com:dry-tundra-5039....	http://dry-tundra-5039.herokuapp...
herokcloudappde	Refresh	u.com:herokcloudappd...	http://herokcloudappdev.herokua...
infinite-tor-3483		u.com:infinite-tor-3483....	http://infinite-tor-3483.herokuapp...
pure-harbor-7860	App Info	u.com:pure-harbor-786...	http://pure-harbor-7860.herokuap...
sompleapp	Import	u.com:sompleapp.git	http://sompleapp.herokuapp.com/
	Deploy...		
	Open		
	Restart		
	View logs		
	Scale		
	Destroy		

The set of operations available for each app includes:

- **Refresh**: This refreshes the Heroku application list with the latest updates.
- **App Info**: This provides a list of the following application-level options to the user:
    - ○ **Application Info**: This lists the name, URL, Git repository URL, and domain name of the application. You can rename the application as well.
    - ○ **Collaborators**: This reviews and manages the list of developers working on this application.
    - ○ **Environment Variables**: This reviews and manages the list of environment variables / configuration variables available in the application.
    - ○ **Processes**: This provides the details of dynos associated with this application based on the process type.
- **Import**: This imports the web app into Eclipse.
- **Deploy...**: This deploys the application to Heroku.
- **Open**: This opens the application in the browser.
- **Restart**: This reboots the dynos of the application.
- **View logs**: This views the application logs for the given app.
- **Scale**: This upscales or downscales the web app by increasing/decreasing the number of web dynos.
- **Destroy**: This destroys/cleans up the web app and releases all the associated resources.

Going deeper into the application information

To get more detailed information about a particular application, go to the **My Heroku Applications** tab and then follow these steps:

1. Right-click on the particular application that you are interested in and click on **App Info**.

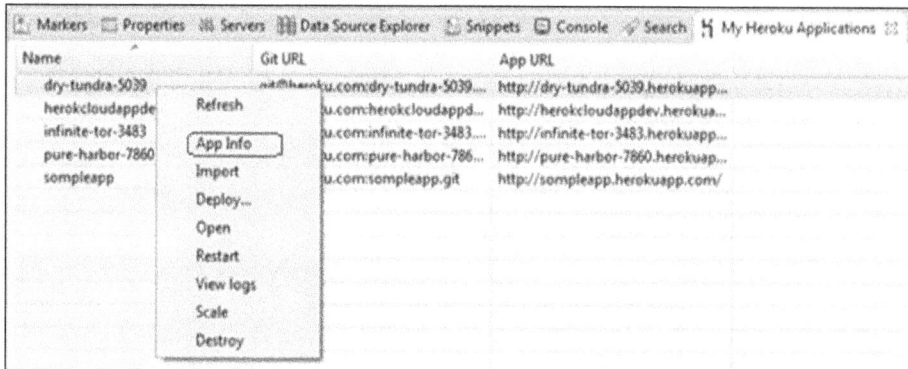

2. The **Application Info** tab provides details about the name, website URL, Git repository URL, and domain name of the application. You can also rename the application using the **Rename** button.

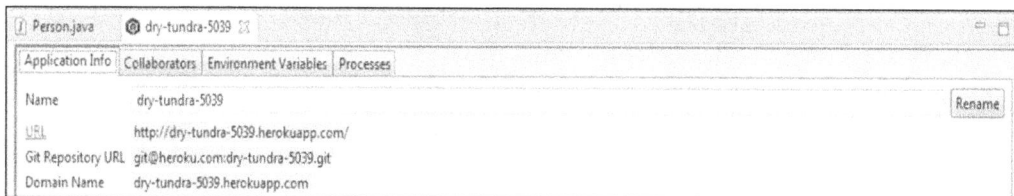

Adding collaborators to the application

Adding collaborators helps you share your project with other developers who may be interested in contributing to the development and management of your app. Adding or managing collaborators is fairly easy using Eclipse. To do this, perform the following steps:

1. Go to the **Collaborators** tab and click on the **+** button to add a collaborator to the current project.

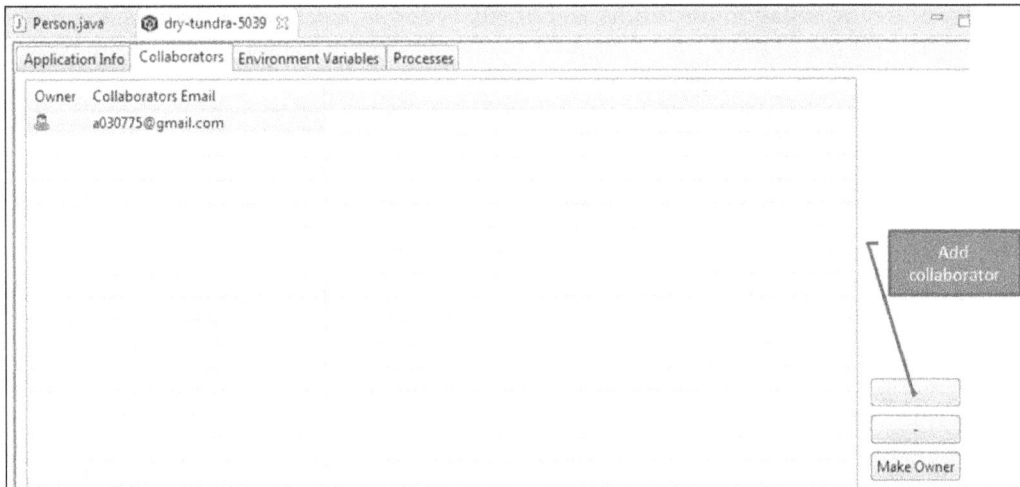

2. Add the e-mail address of the new collaborator and click on **OK**.

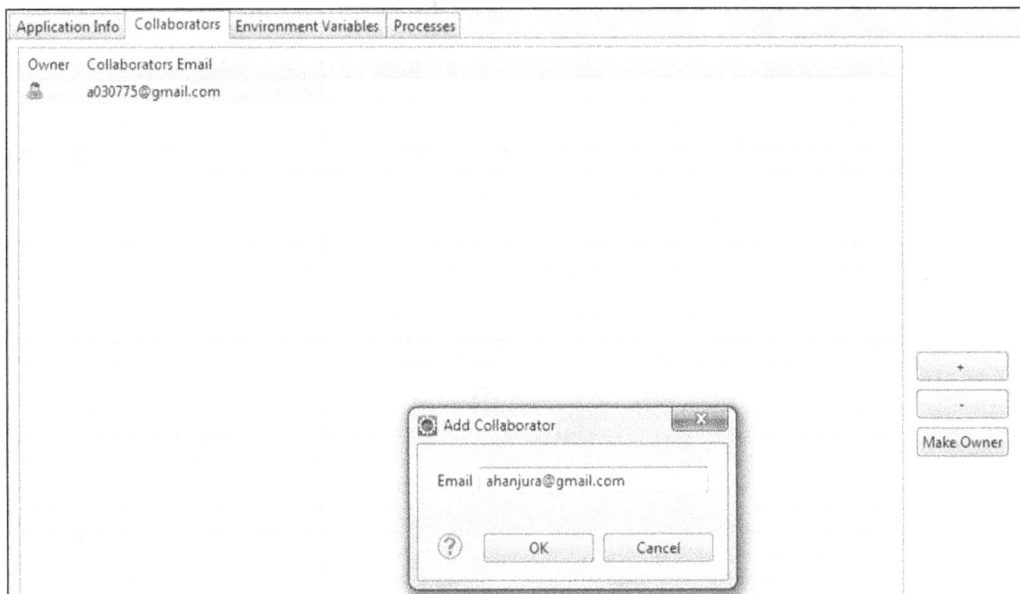

3. The new collaborator is added to the list of collaborators for the given project. The owner of the app is indicated by an icon in the owner field as shown in the following screenshot:

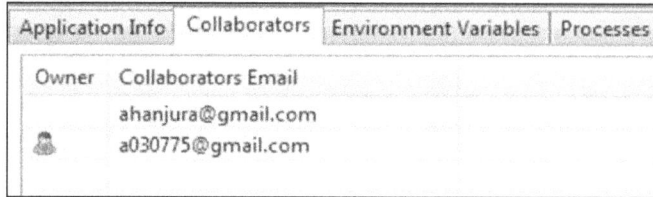

You can also delete a collaborator by selecting the name and clicking on the - button, which is located just below the add button. To reassign the owner of the app, select the collaborator and then click on the **Make owner** button.

Changing the environment variables

Clicking on the **Environment Variables** tab will list the set of existing environment variables or configuration variables that are available to the application. Select a particular environment variable and click on the **Edit** button to modify the environment variable. You can click on the **+** button to add a new environment variable. To remove a particular environment variable, select the environment variable and then click on the **-** button. Confirm your choice to remove the environment variable permanently.

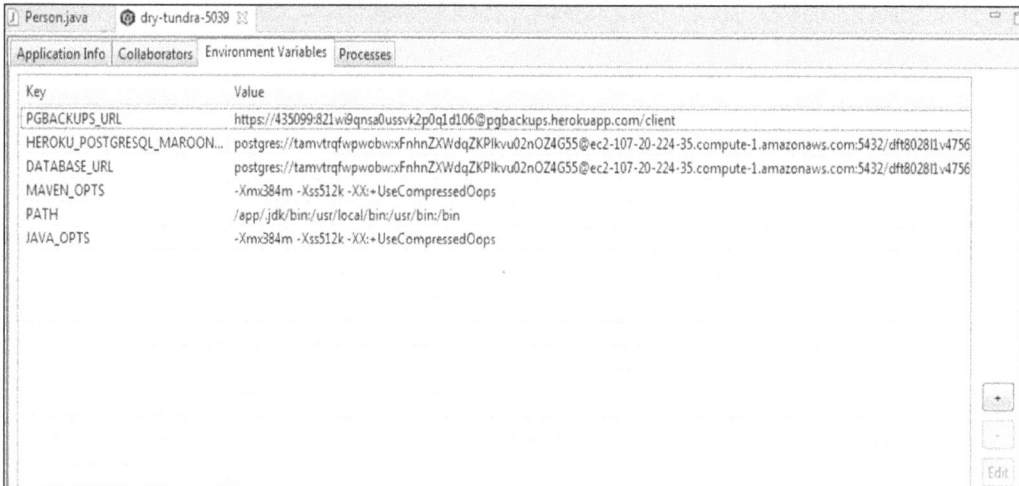

Heroku's process management in Eclipse

One key advantage that sets the Heroku platform apart is the ease of using it. The Eclipse IDE also provides a very intuitive interface for managing Heroku processes from the **Processes** tab of the web app.

Click on the **Processes** tab. You will see process-related information that is very similar to the Procfile format. The right palette also provides additional operations that can be executed for the selected app.

The Eclipse interface provides the following process-related operations on the **Processes** page:

- **Scale**: This allows you to scale up/down the number of dynos of a particular process type for the current app
- **Logs**: This shows the application logs for the particular web app
- **Restart**: This reboots the dynos related to the web app
- **Refresh**: This updates or refreshes the current Heroku application with the latest configuration information

Let's explore each of these process-related operations one after the other.

Scaling your app dynos

To scale up/down the dynos for a particular process type of your web app, select the process type and enter the scale value, that is, the number of dynos you need for optimum app performance. Click on **OK** to confirm the change.

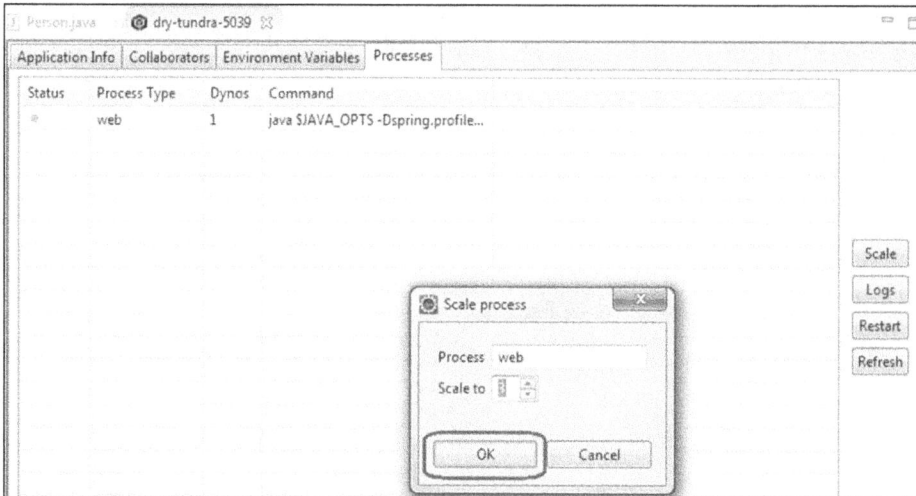

Switch to the **Logs** view to see the updates made by Heroku. Heroku scales up the dyno count for the web process type and creates two more web dynos for your web app.

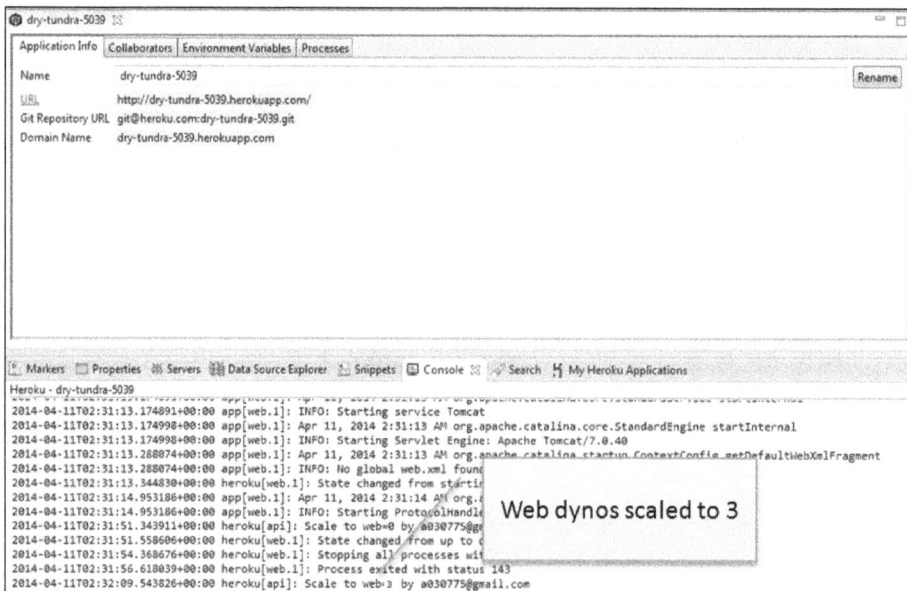

Restarting your web app

You can also restart a web application using the **Restart** button on the **Processes** tab of your web app. On clicking **Restart**, Heroku instantly restarts the dynos related to your web app. The following screenshot shows the dialog to confirm our choice to restart the **dry-tundra-5039** web app:

To verify what goes on behind the curtains of the Heroku platform, switch to the **Logs** view.

In this section, we learned how to use the different available options in Eclipse in order to manage Heroku apps. A few clicks can help you view, change, and expand your web app. Eclipse provides a very powerful abstraction over the Heroku command-line interface, which helps developers virtually perform every operation using a simple mouse click. This is what a developer really needs.

Summary

This chapter helped us experiment with what we learned in the earlier part of this book. We were able to build a web app using the Java toolset and demonstrated how easy it is to get up and running with the development of the Heroku cloud application in no time. Wasn't it easy?

Choose any programming language that Heroku supports and the ease of building apps would be no different. In that sense, Heroku does not reinvent the wheel for developers, but it creates the right platform, makes the right add-ons available, and helps you deploy web apps almost effortlessly. All that a developer needs to worry about is how to write the business logic of the app; no platform idiosyncrasies, no cumbersome installations of third-party software, and no sleepless nights managing new releases/deploys.

In the next chapter, we will look in detail at the software ecosystem surrounding Heroku. We will learn how to write web apps in a cloud IDE, giving you an end-to-end cloud-based development experience. We will introduce you to Heroku's support for the PostgreSQL database and then provide tips on how to make your app work with the PostgreSQL DB. We will review in detail the steps to manage the DNS for your apps. Finally, we will cover the newly introduced feature(s) for dynos in Heroku that helps to run the web apps faster and more efficiently. You don't want to miss it.

7
Heroku Best Practices

Well, here we are. So far, in this book, we have understood the basics of the platform, and we have delved into how Heroku works behind the scenes. We reviewed the underlying infrastructure that makes Heroku possible, whether it is the dyno process mechanism or the Logplex logging environment. We also looked at the list of supported tools on the Heroku platform that makes developing apps on the platform so easy. Heroku's add-on infrastructure further helps your applications to use the best-of-breed services to meet your application needs, whatever they might be. In this chapter, we will explore some of the best practices while developing apps on the Heroku platform.

We will cover the following topics in this chapter:

- **How to develop web apps on the cloud**: We will explore an interesting way of doing web development on a popular cloud-based IDE

- **Heroku's Postgres database support**: We will see how to set up the most popular Heroku data store, Postgres, and configure it for use in apps

- **Managing DNS within Heroku**: We will introduce DNS and then show how to use DNS with Heroku applications

- **Advanced features of the Heroku platform**: We will introduce the 2X dynos that help you supercharge your dyno memory and explore how you can keep your small Heroku apps live

The One Cloud development platform

In the development model discussed so far, we still needed to install a Heroku client or other client software (Ruby or Php interpreter) to build our web applications before pushing them to the Heroku platform for execution. While this model works well and is prevalent, another development model that holds equal promise is — develop and deploy on the cloud. In this model, the developer writes the code in a browser-based **integrated development environment** (IDE) and uses the supported tools in the IDE to build, deploy, and troubleshoot web applications. In this section, we introduce a very powerful cloud-based IDE called Cloud 9 that integrates seamlessly with the Heroku platform and lets you perform the same type of app-related operations that you would otherwise do using the Heroku CLI.

Introducing the Cloud 9 IDE

The Cloud 9 IDE (`https://c9.io`) was one of the first of its kind of cloud-based development IDEs that provided integration with the Heroku **Platform as a Service (PaaS)**. The Cloud 9 IDE platform provides built-in collaboration features that let a developer write, run, and debug web application code inside the web browser from anywhere. Like the Heroku platform, the Cloud 9 IDE also supports a variety of programming languages in the IDE environment: Java, Ruby, JavaScript, and Node. js to name a few.

The Cloud 9 IDE provides developers with easy accessibility to the code using secure protocols for data transfer between the IDE and the deployment platform. And there is more; teams can collaborate while writing applications, co-edit the applications, and efficiently consolidate the changes when they need to.

The Cloud 9 IDE makes code writing transparent to the developer. The developer writes code in a development environment just like Eclipse, and gets the same features such as code completion, Regex matching, file search, or adaptive themes in the online editor. It gets better. The Cloud 9 IDE offers additional key features such as code folding, multiple cursors, code section focus, and drag-and-drop out of the box, which improve developer productivity immensely. You can use the built-in Cloud 9 IDE command line to run various commands besides installing the required packages on demand. The Cloud 9 IDE also integrates with Git — the most prevalent distributed version control and social collaboration platform — besides supporting the Mercurial version control system.

In this section, we will briefly learn about the usage of the Cloud 9 IDE to deploy a sample application on the Heroku platform. In doing so, we will also review some of the common features of the Cloud 9 IDE. To create your account, visit `https://c9.io`.

The C9 user interface

The C9 dashboard provides rich development environment features. The following screenshot identifies the various sections of the C9 dashboard displayed on user login to the C9 environment:

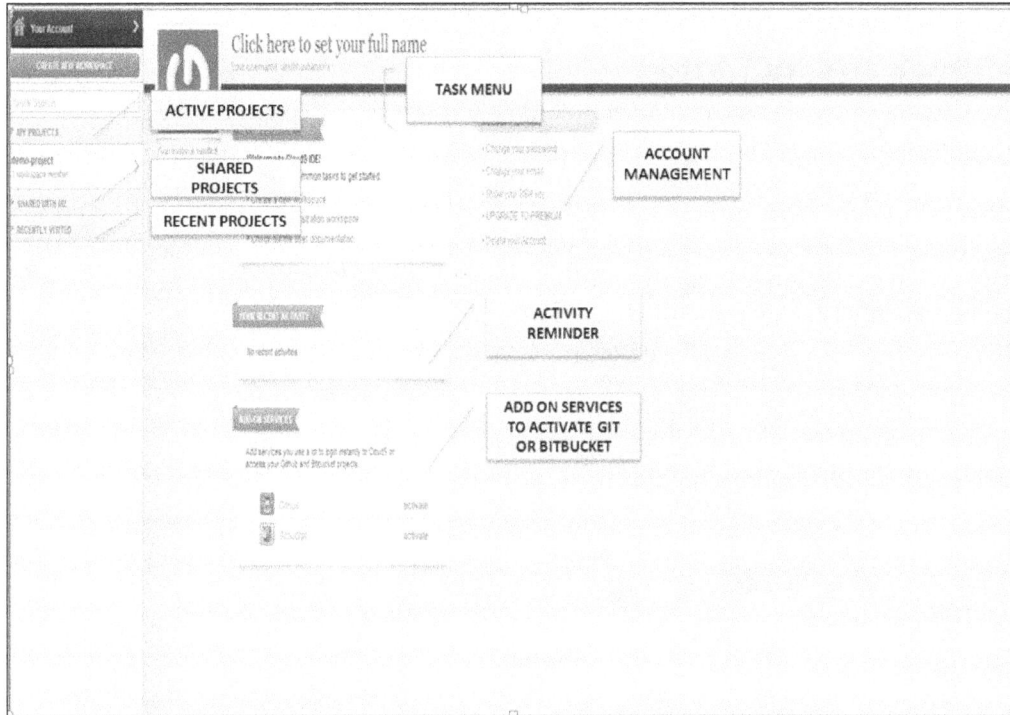

The C9 dashboard comprises the following components:

- **Task Menu**: This menu lists the available actions or tasks. It contains the most commonly used actions that a developer can initiate.
- **Account Management**: This menu allows you to manage your account, update e-mail details, or delete your account.
- **Active Projects**: This section lists your currently active projects. You can click on a specific project to start editing it.
- **Shared Projects**: This section lists projects that the developer is collaboratively working on with other users.
- **Recent Projects**: This section lists the last few projects worked on by the developer. Clicking on any of these projects lets the developer edit that project.

- **Add on services**: This option allows you to configure version control for your cloud application. Currently, it supports GitHub and Bitbucket as source code repositories for your application code.

- **Activity reminder**: This option logs the user activity in a chronological order for developer use.

The C9 project view

The C9 project view captures the actual look and feel of the code editor and other components of the C9 development environment. The C9 project view consists of the main menu including the application run and the debug buttons. Besides this, the C9 development environment is extremely flexible and provides a terminal window to type commands from a CLI, making it really easy to switch from a menu-driven application execution to a command-line-based execution environment. You can see the results of your execution in the output window as well. For web applications, the browser window on the right displays the output of the execution of your script or program. This serves developers very well in highlighting the issues present, then making changes to their applications, and running them instantly.

The following screenshot highlights the important sections of the C9 view:

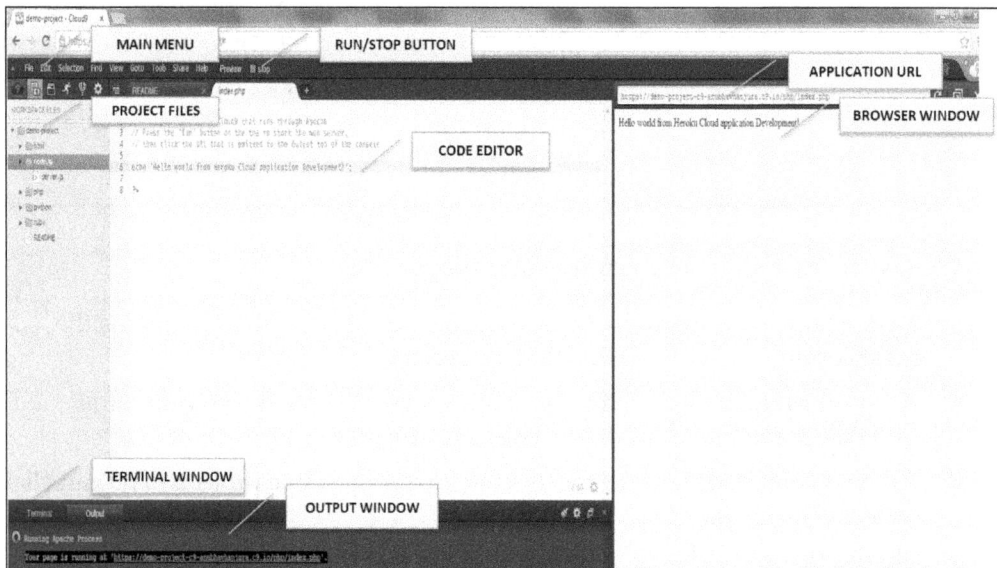

Setting up preferences in the C9 IDE environment

Developers can set specific editor preferences using the **Preferences** tab in the menu. The C9 development environment provides a rich set of the most common user preferences. The user preferences that are set become active with immediate effect, thereby improving the developer experience and overall productivity.

Deploying on Heroku

Now that we are familiar with the basic C9 IDE environment, let's write a simple application and deploy it to the Heroku platform. This feature of "code anywhere, deploy anywhere" is a powerful paradigm enabled by PaaS such as Heroku.

Perform the following steps to deploy a Cloud 9 based application on Heroku:

1. Write a simple web application.

2. Save the web application and click on the **Deploy** tab. This will show you a **+** sign in the section to the left as shown in the following screenshot:

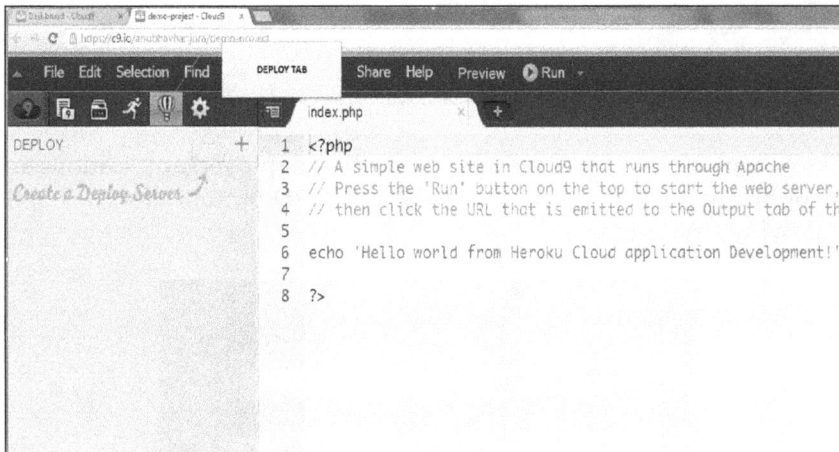

3. Click on the **+** sign. Choose the target deployment environment in **Add a deploy target** dialog as shown in the following screenshot:

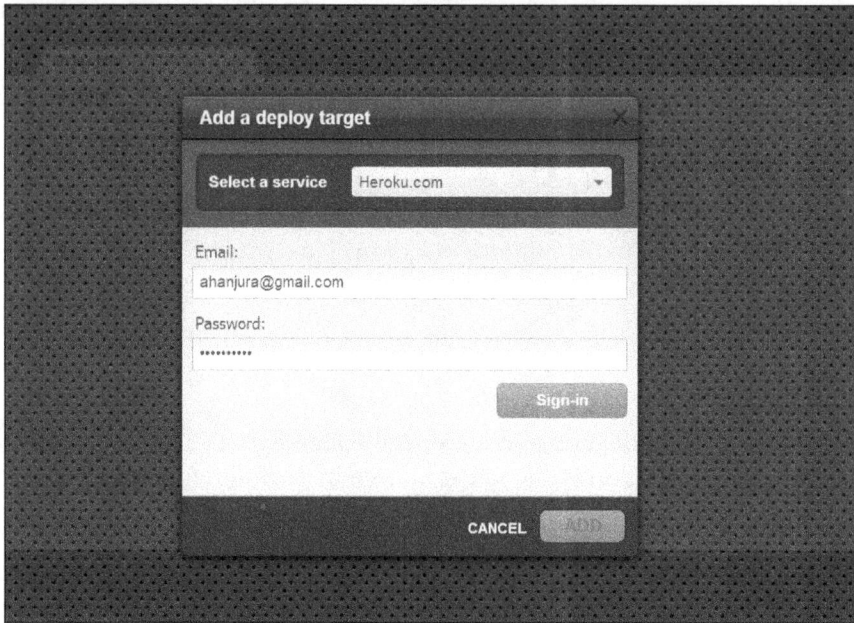

4. Once logged in, you will see a list of existing deployed applications and an option to create a new app. Choose the **ADD** button, as shown in the following screenshot:

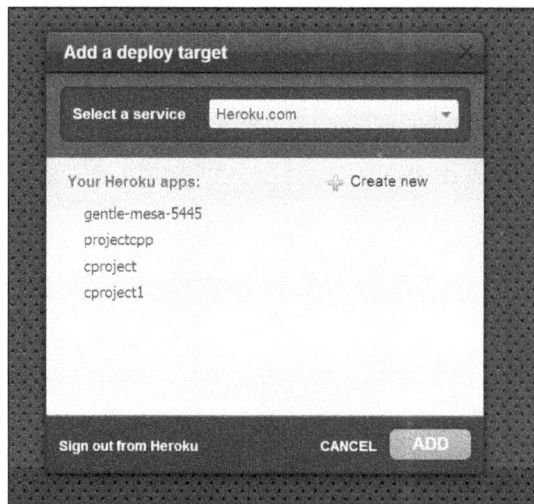

5. Choose the new app name, in this case, **simple-samurai-2660**, and click on **ADD**. A new application will be created for you as shown in the following screenshot:

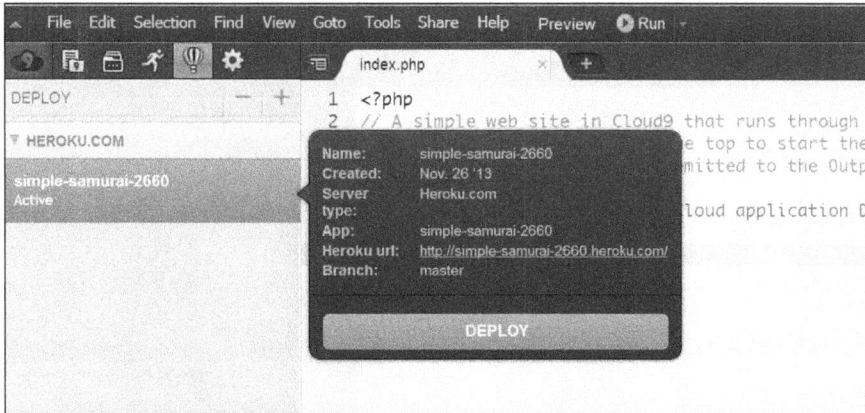

6. Click on the newly created app name. You will see a pop-up with an option to deploy the application. Click on **DEPLOY**, as shown in the following screenshot:

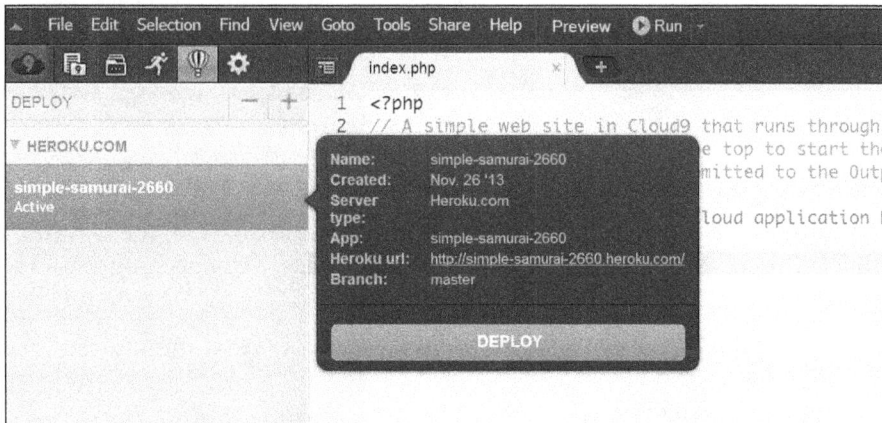

7. Review the deployment log in the **Output** window as shown in the following screenshot to check the progress of the deployment. If there are no errors in your application, it will be successfully deployed on the Heroku platform:

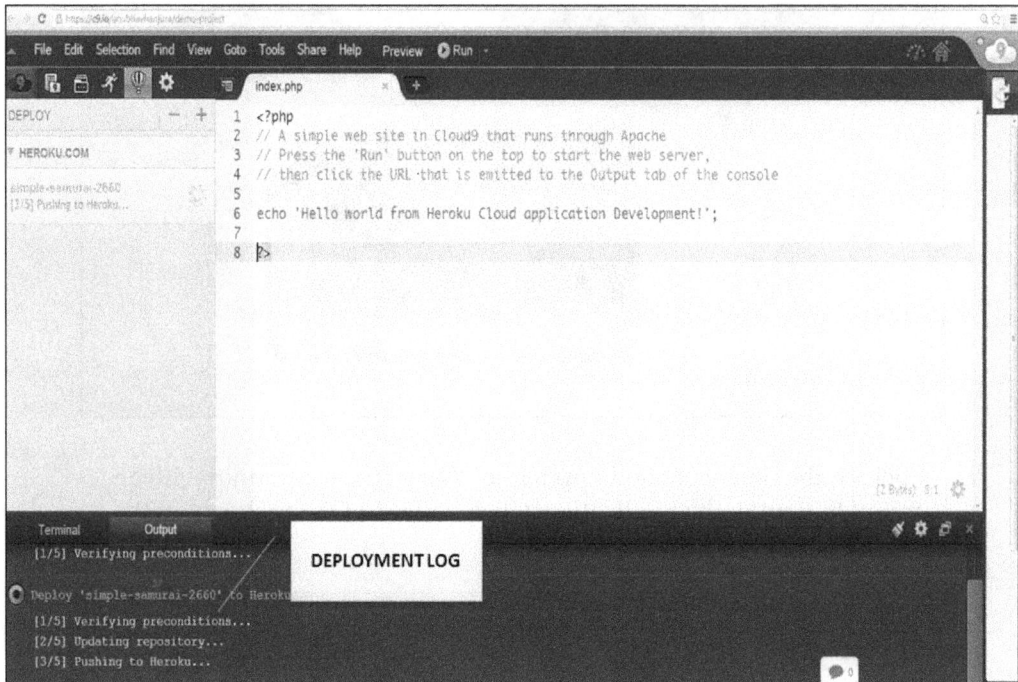

Performing Git operations using the C9 IDE

The C9 workspace allows a developer to integrate seamlessly with the GitHub and Bitbucket repositories. Checking out code from them and checking it back in is straightforward.

As an example, to clone a GitHub project, follow these steps:

1. Go to the C9 dashboard.

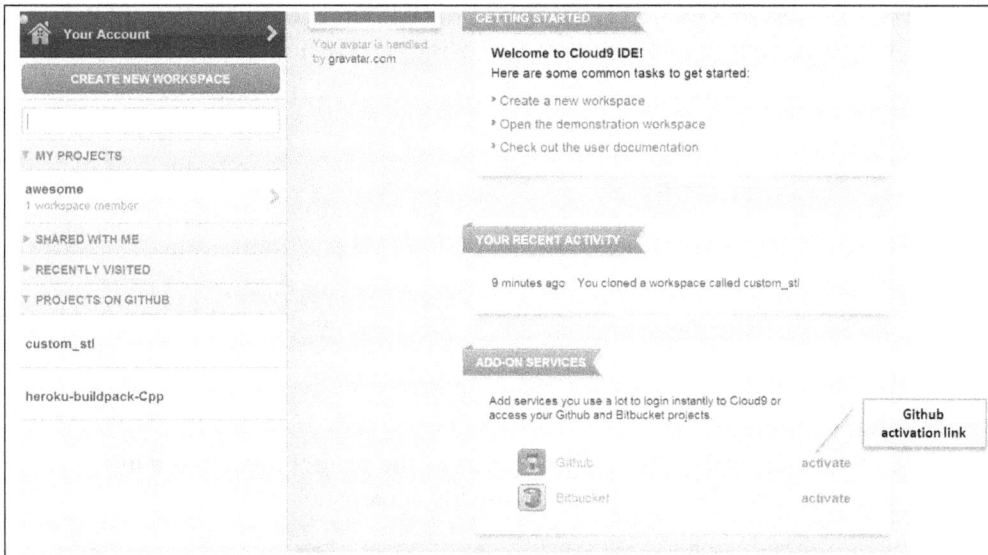

2. Click on the **Github** hyperlink in the **ADD-ON SERVICES** section as depicted in the preceding screenshot.

3. Enter the user credentials and sign in as shown in the following screenshot:

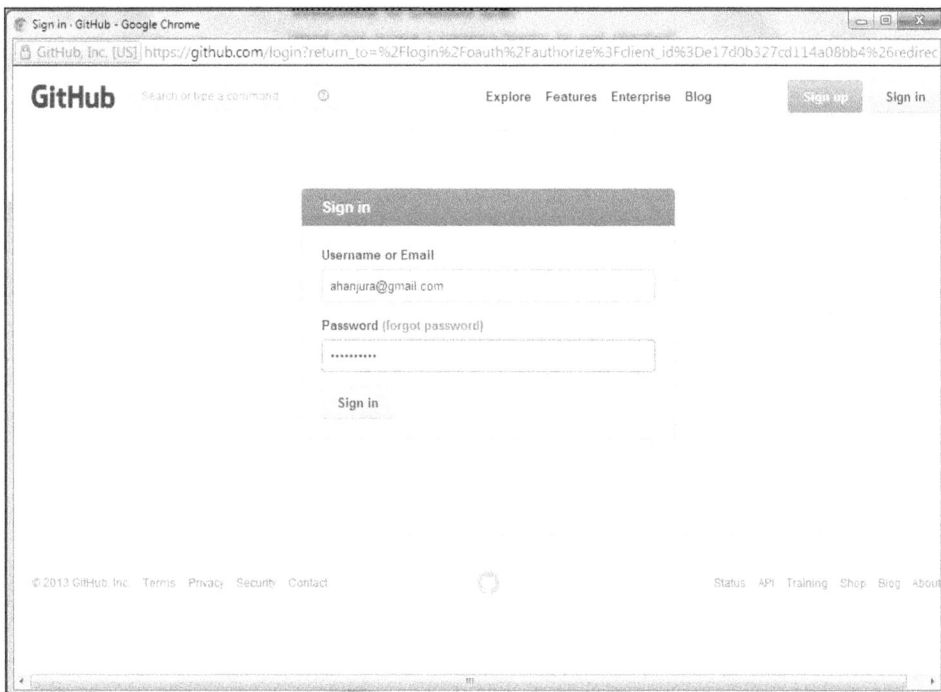

4. The **PROJECTS ON GITHUB** link in the left navigation bar lists all the GitHub projects as shown in the following screenshot:

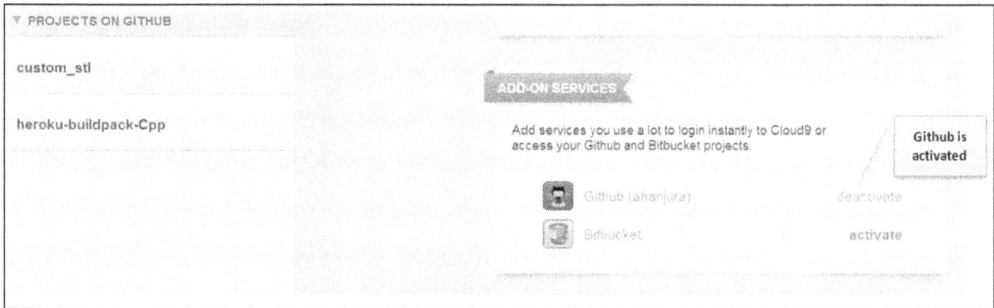

5. To clone a GitHub project, click on one of the project links in the left navigation bar as shown in the following screenshot:

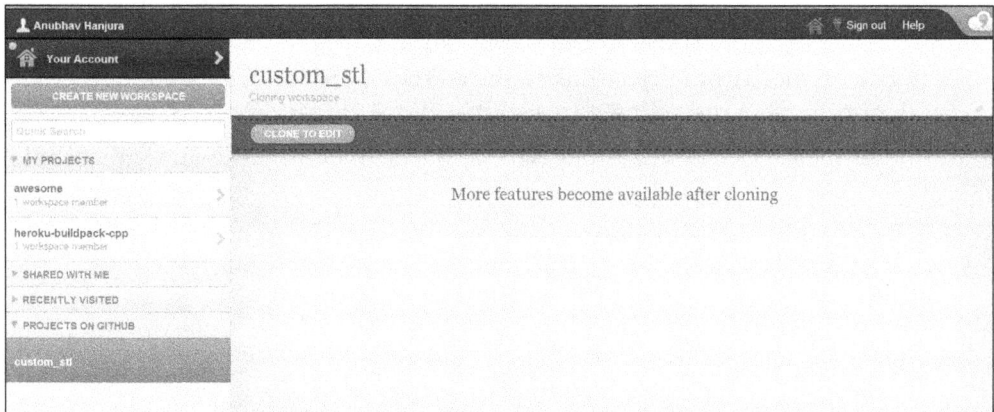

6. Click on the **CLONE TO EDIT** button shown in the previous screenshot. The options shown in the following screenshot are displayed:

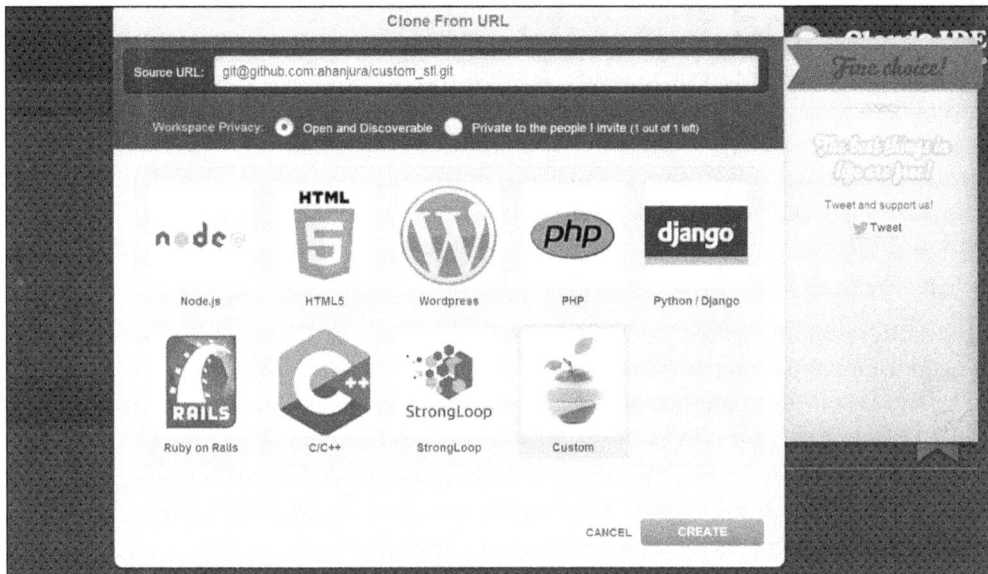

7. Click on **CREATE** and C9 will clone the GitHub project to the active workspace as shown in the following screenshot:

The C9 cloud development environment provides a great level of flexibility by providing out-of-the-box integration with GitHub and Bitbucket. Using your Git projects in C9 is very intuitive and as easy as managing code using a local development environment. The C9 development environment keeps the language runtime transparent to its user. The code is secure and backed up regularly.

Heroku and the data store

Most applications need to store data—temporary or permanent. This data store could take the shape of a full blown relational database or just a much smaller cache to store most frequently used application data. Your application might need to store complex data structures or much simpler name/value pairs. Any PaaS would need reasonable support for such data storage needs so that the applications written on the platform could easily talk to the data tier and perform the CRUD operations on the application data generated during the lifespan of the application.

Heroku offers the PostgreSQL database as a relational database service to meet the need for a robust, performant, scalable, and highly available database tier. The Postgres service is offered and managed as a Heroku add-on on the Heroku platform. Using the full power of Postgres is a matter of choosing the right plan based on the complexity of your deployment. Run a few commands either on the CLI or through the dashboard and voilà, you are up and running with the Heroku PostgreSQL service.

In this section, we will focus on how to get started with using the Heroku PostgreSQL service. We will understand how to create, change, and delete databases and how to create database replicas and monitor your databases. The Heroku Postgres service provides you with the failover and availability characteristics that meet the needs of your ever growing web applications.

Creating a Heroku Postgres database

If you are exploring the option of using a database service on Heroku, perform the following steps:

1. The first step is to go to `http://postgres.heroku.com` and log in to the site using your Heroku credentials:

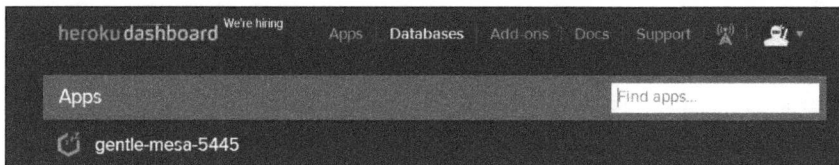

2. Once logged in, click on the **Databases** link on the top menu. You will see an option, **Create Database** and a list of the currently available databases:

3. Click on **Create Database** as shown in the following screenshot:

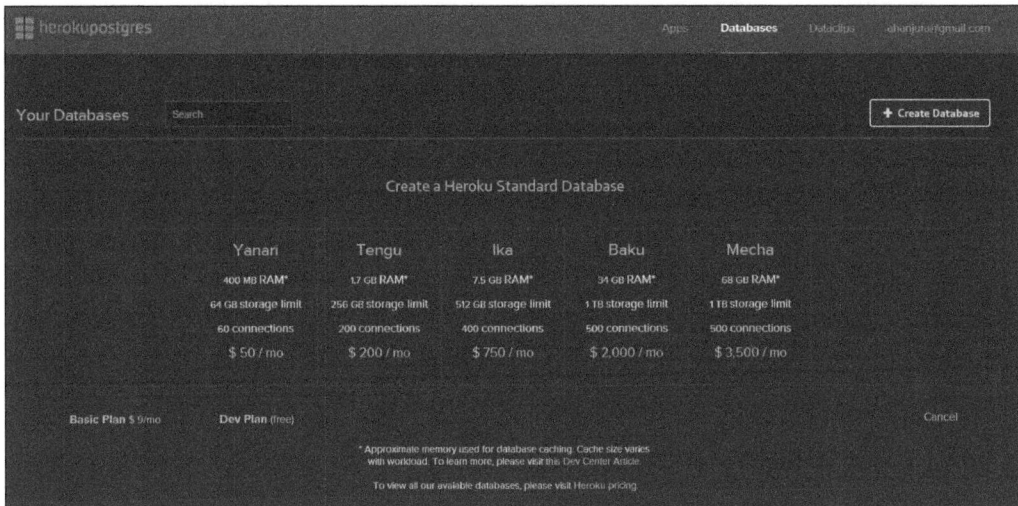

This page gives you a comparison of the available database configurations and their relative pricing. This is the most important choice you will make before using Heroku's PostgreSQL database service. You should take a good look at the available options and choose the one that fits your application's needs as well as your budget. Your choice will depend on the expected memory usage of your database, how much physical storage you need for the database, the number of database connections your application will need for optimal behavior, and of course how much you are willing to pay for the service. For hobbyists, using the free development plan suffices in most cases.

Once you have chosen the right plan, creating the database is easy. For example, if you choose the **Tengu** option for your application `sample-db-app`, use the following command to add the **Tengu** Heroku PostgreSQL configuration to your application:

```
$ heroku addons:add heroku-postgresql:tengu --app sample-db-app

Adding heroku-postgresql:tengu to sample-db-app... done, v2 ($200/mo)

Attached as HEROKU_POSTGRESQL_XXXXXX

The database should be available in 3-5 minutes

Use 'heroku pg:wait' to track status

heroku-postgresql:tengu documentation available at:

https://devcenter.heroku.com/articles/heroku-postgresql
```

You can run the `pg:wait` command after that to wait for your database creation to complete:

```
$ heroku pg:wait

Waiting for database ... available
```

Once the database is created and available, use the Heroku command line to verify the database details as follows:

```
$ heroku pg --app sample-db-app

=== HEROKU_POSTGRESQL_XXXXXX

Conn Info:

[Deprecated] Please use 'heroku pg:credentials HEROKU_POSTGRESQL_XXXXXX to

view connection info

Created: 2013-11-02 01:29 UTC

Data Size: 6.9 MB

Fork/Follow: Temporarily Unavailable

Maintenance: not required

PG Version: 9.x.x

Plan: Tengu

Status: available

Tables: 0
```

Logging in to the database

To verify the credentials of the database user, run the `pg:credentials` command as follows:

```
$ heroku pg:credentials HEROKU_POSTGRESQL_XXXXXX
Connection info string:
"dbname=database_name host=ec2-12-34-567-890.compute-1.amazonaws.com
port=3421
user=user_name password=database_password sslmode=require"
```

To set a given database to be the primary database for your app, `sample-db-app`, promote the given database to be the primary database using the `heroku pg:promote` command as follows:

```
$ heroku pg:promote HEROKU_POSTGRESQL_XXXXXX_URL --app sample-db-app
Promoting HEROKU_POSTGRESQL_XXXXXX_URL to DATABASE_URL... done
```

On successful promotion of the database, Heroku will set the database-related configuration variables, including `DATABASE_URL`, to point to the newly promoted database.

To review this configuration information, use the `heroku config` CLI command and pass the application name as follows:

```
$ heroku config --app sample-db-app
=== sample-db-app Config Vars
DATABASE_URL:
postgres://user_name :database_password@ec2-12-34-567-890.
compute-1.amazonaws.com:3421/database_name
HEROKU_POSTGRESQL_XXXXXX_URL:
postgres://user_name :database_password@ec2-12-34-567-890.
compute-1.amazonaws.com:3421/database_name
```

That's it. You have successfully created, verified, and reviewed the Heroku Postgres service for your application. You can also view the created database in the Heroku Postgres web console.

Heroku provides the facility to access a Postgres interactive terminal to the database over SSL via the CLI.

To connect to the Postgres database service, use the following command:

```
$ heroku pg:psql HEROKU_POSTGRESQL_XXXXXX
psql (9.x.x)
SSL connection (cipher: DHE-RSA-AES256-SHA, bits: 256)
Type "help" for help.
database_name=>
NOTE Using the psql terminal requires a local installation of the
PostgreSQL
(libpq) client. For platform-specific instructions for installing
Postgres, see
https://devcenter.heroku.com/articles/local-postgresql
```

Heroku provides an interesting set of database operations that one could use to fulfill typical data storage needs. How many times have you wanted to have a test database created for you similar to the customer's production database or perform load testing on different configurations of the database or experiment with the schema changes before opening it up to the broader set of users? Heroku PostgreSQL has an answer for this too. The answer is database forks. Heroku provides you with the ability to fork your database of choice and create an exact replica of it. However, Heroku restricts the ability to fork databases only to the paid production grade plans and not to the free developer plans.

Creating more databases – the fork

Sometimes, you may need a snapshot of an existing database, that is, you will need a database cut that contains all the data of the given database at a particular point in time. A typical example is when you want to test your app against a customer's database to isolate and troubleshoot an issue. You may want the customer to provide you with a snapshot of the data at a particular point in time. This is where database forks come in and provide you with the ability to create a database from a snapshot of another database. There are other use cases as well; for example, the operations team might want to test a database migration on a copy of the production before doing the actual migration, or the data security personnel may want to keep a copy of your production data at a point of time to secure critical customer data in case something were to go wrong with the production database. All these examples provide a compelling case for a utility that can create snapshots of a database. The database fork option does just that.

You can create a fork of your application's database using the `--fork` command-line parameter as shown in the following set of commands:

```
$ heroku addons:add heroku-postgresql:tengu --fork HEROKU_POSTGRESQL_
XXXXXX
Adding heroku-postgresql:tengu to test-db-app... done, v... ($200/mo)
Attached as HEROKU_POSTGRESQL_YYYYYY
Database will become available after it completes forking
Use 'heroku pg:wait' to track status
heroku-postgresql:tengu documentation available at:
https://devcenter.heroku.com/articles/heroku-postgresql
```

> Forking a database is different from following a database. In the case of follower databases, the data between the followed database and the follower database are kept in sync. Follower databases are better candidates for use as failover databases versus forked databases, which serve your need as a snapshot of your data at a particular point in time. For forked databases, data between the new and the original database is not kept in sync.

Synchronizing databases via database followers

These days, organizations have an enormous amount of data being generated by different software applications. The production database size and complexity seems to have multiplied exponentially. Database deployments have become more complicated. In larger deployments, different databases are used to handle requests from applications that only read, versus applications that constantly update the data as well. Organizations can no longer afford to let everyone query the production database even if it is just for reading a few records of a large table. To meet the specific needs of a distributed query load on sizable databases, Heroku supports the concept of database followers. If not for these database followers, your overall database system response might slow down significantly and cause unnecessary delay in serving requests.

Database followers are read-only copies of the source database that are updated with the latest changes to the source in near real time. The database follower meets the needs of most applications that need to run long running read-only queries or create reports based on data stored across various tables.

To create database followers, we can use the `--follow` command-line option as follows:

```
$ heroku addons:add heroku-postgresql:tengu --follow HEROKU_POSTGRESQL_
XXXXXX
Adding heroku-postgresql:tengu to test-db-app... done, v... ($200/mo)
Attached as HEROKU_POSTGRESQL_YYYYYY
Follower will become available for read-only queries when up-to-date
Use 'heroku pg:wait' to track status
heroku-postgresql:tengu documentation available at:
https://devcenter.heroku.com/articles/heroku-postgresql
```

If we want to reuse the follower database, we can run the `unfollow` command that will convert the read-only follower database to a read/write copy. This, in a way, is equivalent to forking the original database at that point in time.

To unfollow the given application database, run the following command:

```
$ heroku pg:unfollow HEROKU_POSTGRESQL_YYYYYY
! HEROKU_POSTGRESQL_YYYYYY will become writable and no longer
! follow HEROKU_POSTGRESQL_XXXXXX. This cannot be undone.
! WARNING: Destructive Action
! This command will affect the app: test-db-app
! To proceed, type "test-db-app" or re-run this command with --confirm
test-db-app
> test-db-app
Unfollowing heroku_postgresql_YYYYYY... done
```

Heroku recently started providing users with the ability to cancel queries that seem to be running for an undue amount of time and are eating up a lot of CPU, memory, or other resources. Earlier, canceling such queries would need the user to contact Heroku support who would then cancel the query.

To try canceling long running queries, start two terminal sessions. In the first terminal, log in to the Postgres service and run a potentially slow query, for example, `select * from processes;` (where `processes` is an existing table containing millions of records):

```
$ heroku pg:psql HEROKU_POSTGRESQL_XXXXXX
psql (9.x.x)
SSL connection (cipher: DHE-RSA-AES256-SHA, bits: 256)
Type "help" for help.
database_name=> select * from processes;
```

In the second terminal, use the following steps to cancel the potentially slow query:

```
$ heroku pg:psql HEROKU_POSTGRESQL_XXXXXX
psql (9.x.x)
SSL connection (cipher: DHE-RSA-AES256-SHA, bits: 256)
Type "help" for help.
database_name=> SELECT pg_cancel_backend(procpid) FROM pg_stat_activity
WHERE
current_query LIKE '%processes%';
ERROR:  canceling statement due to user request
```

The first terminal will also show the same message, indicating that the slow query was canceled.

One of the most critical needs for any database user, particularly the one managing the database, is the ability to monitor the database and operations running on the database. One obvious way of finding out what the database is doing is to look at database logs. In Heroku, the Heroku Postgres logs are located in the same location as the application logs.

Checking database logs

To view the database-specific log messages, use the `heroku logs` command and pass the `postgres` filter to the command as follows:

```
$ heroku logs --ps postgres
2013-11-05T03:45:12+00:00 app[postgres]: [17-1]   [XXXXXX] LOG:
checkpoint starting: time
2013-11-05T03:45:12+00:00 app[postgres]: [18-1]   [XXXXXX] LOG:
checkpoint complete: wrote 0 buffers (0.0%); 0 transaction log file(s) added,
0 removed, 0 recycled; write=0.000 s, sync=0.000 s, total=0.231 s; sync
files=0,
longest=0.000 s, average=0.000 s
[...]
```

Performance and the Heroku Postgres database

To measure your database's cache-hit ratios for tables, log in to the psql and execute the query as follows:

```
$ heroku pg:psql HEROKU_POSTGRESQL_XXXXXX
psql (9.x.x)
SSL connection (cipher: DHE-RSA-AES256-SHA, bits: 256)
Type "help" for help.
database_name=> SELECT
database_name-> sum(heap_blks_read) as heap_read,
database_name-> sum(heap_blks_hit) as heap_hit,
database_name-> (sum(heap_blks_hit) - sum(heap_blks_read)) /
sum(heap_blks_hit) as ratio
database_name--> FROM pg_statio_user_tables;
heap_read | heap_hit | ratio
----------+----------+------------------------
62351     | 81208    | 0.232206186582602
(1 row)
```

The results show that the cache-hit ratio is only 23 percent, meaning a larger cache size could improve the performance of the database queries.

A similar query for measuring cache-hit ratios for indexes is as follows:

```
database-name=> SELECT
database-name-> sum(idx_blks_read) as idx_read,
database-name-> sum(idx_blks_hit) as idx_hit,
database-name-> (sum(idx_blks_hit) - sum(idx_blks_read)) /
sum(idx_blks_hit) as ratio
database-name-> FROM
database-name-> pg_statio_user_indexes;
idx_read | idx_hit | ratio
---------+---------+------------------------
38       | 78      | 0.512820512820
(1 row)
```

Here, the cache-hit ratio of only 51 percent for your indexes also indicates that you could get a better hit ratio if you use a larger database cache.

Disaster recovery in Heroku PostgreSQL

The easiest way to recover your data is to keep frequent backups. Heroku provides a very convenient mechanism to back up your data through the free `pgbackups` add-on. Use this add-on to create data backups on demand.

To create a backup, you need to first add the `pgbackups` add-on to your account. To do so, use the following command:

```
$ heroku addons:add pgbackups

Adding pgbackups to test-db-app... done, v... (free)

You can now use "pgbackups" to backup your databases or import an
external backup.

pgbackups documentation available at:

https://devcenter.heroku.com/articles/pgbackups
```

There are multiple options available in the form of backup plans that you could use based on your business needs. Your decision to use a particular plan may depend on the level of automation needed, number of exports required, and the retention period of the backup. By default, the automated backup is performed on the database pointed to by the `DATABASE_URL` configuration parameter.

To create a manual backup, use the following command:

```
$ heroku pgbackups:capture HEROKU_POSTGRESQL_XXXXXX

HEROKU_POSTGRESQL_XXXXXX  ----backup---> b001

Capturing... done

Storing... done
```

Use the `--expirecommand` command to rotate your backups by automatically deleting the old backup before creating a new one.

To view a list of backups, use the following command:

```
$ heroku pgbackups
ID   | Backup Time          | Size  | Database
-----+----------------------+-------+------------------------
b001 | 2013/11/01 16:45.23  | 1.6KB | HEROKU_POSTGRESQL_XXXXXX
b001 | 2013/11/01 16:48.05  | 1.6KB | HEROKU_POSTGRESQL_XXXXXX
```

The b character in the ID denotes that it is a manual backup. If it was an automated one, an a would be prefixed to the ID instead.

If you need to access one of these databases, you can expose your backup file via a publicly available URL as follows:

```
$ heroku pgbackups:url b001
https://s3.amazonaws.com/hkpgbackups/smp405893@heroku.com/
b001.dump?AWSAccessKeyId=<...>&Expires=1234567890&Signature=tMuN1n65T
1gaNuEdR3
```

Accessing this URL (the URL is live for 10 minutes only) enables you to download a .dumpfile that contains a standard Postgres dump of your database, suitable for importing into a Heroku or non-Heroku Postgres database.

To destroy an old backup, use the following command:

```
$ heroku pgbackups:destroy b001
Destroying b001... done
$ heroku pgbackups
ID    | Backup Time          | Size   | Database
------+----------------------+--------+-------------------------
b001  | 2013/11/01 16:48.05  | 1.6KB  | HEROKU_POSTGRESQL_XXXXXX
```

To restore a backup from a previous version stored by pgbackups, use the restore command as follows:

```
$ heroku pgbackups:restore HEROKU_POSTGRESQL_XXXXXX b001
HEROKU_POSTGRESQL_XXXXXX  <---restore---  b001
HEROKU_POSTGRESQL_XXXXXX
2013/11/01 16:48.05
1.6KB
! WARNING: Destructive Action
! This command will affect the app: test-db-app
! To proceed, type "test-db-app" or re-run this command with --
confirm test-db-app
> test-db-app
Retrieving... done
Restoring... done
```

A few of the observations about the backups are as follows:

- Very large backups are split up into multiple URLs. Use a file concatenation utility such as the UNIX `cat` command to combine them together.

- When you restore a database backup, it overwrites the current database with the structure and contents of the previous backup. Hence, it is a good idea to create a backup of the current database before overwriting it through a restore.

- The number of backups available is determined by the `pgbackups` add-on you choose. You may need to delete your old backups to create new ones.

Importing data into Postgres

Often, you may need to import data from a customer's environment to reproduce an issue or migrate data from one database to another, or move to Heroku Postgres from some other database. Such use cases call for a mechanism to import data into Heroku Postgres. You can import a Heroku Postgres compatible dump format into Postgres, or use available tools to directly load your Postgres database from the source. In many cases, you would need to export data from your current database before it can be imported somewhere else. A good practice while exporting is to ensure that the dump file is compressed and that no access privilege and ownership scope information is saved inside the exported data.

There are two possibilities for importing data into the Heroku Postgres database:

- **Source database is a Postgres database**: In this case, you need to first create a Postgres dump of the source database before it can be imported into the destination Postgres database. To create a dump from your source Postgres database, use the following command:

  ```
  $ pg_dump -Fc --no-acl --no-owner old_pg_db_name > old_pg_db.dump
  ```

- **Source database is a non-Postgres database**: When the source database is non-Postgres, you need to convert the database to a Postgres dump format to enable it to be imported into the Postgres database.

If you are migrating away from MySQL, you can use the mysql2psql tool. It is an open source tool to convert the database and can load data directly from MySQL to the Heroku Postgres database.

There are multiple ways of importing data into Heroku Postgres:

- Through the `pgbackups` restore function
- Using the Postgres command line tool, `pg_restore`

Importing data with the pgbackups file requires that the database dump file be available via a public URL.

To import the database dump from a publicly available URL, use the `pgbackups:restore` command as follows:

```
$ heroku pgbackups:restore HEROKU_POSTGRESQL_XXXXXX
'https://myherokudump.s3.amazonaws.com/processes.dump'
HEROKU_POSTGRESQL_XXXXXX  <---restore---  processes.dump
! WARNING: Destructive Action
! This command will affect the app: test-db-app
! To proceed, type "test-db-app" or re-run this command with --confirm
test-db-app
> test-db-app
Retrieving... done
Restoring... done
ahan-ltr2:test-db-app ahan
```

Once restored, check that the data imported is correct by logging in to Heroku Postgres and verifying a few tables and their data:

```
$ heroku pg:psql HEROKU_POSTGRESQL_XXXXXX
psql (9.X.X)
SSL connection (cipher: DHE-RSA-AES256-SHA, bits: 256)
Type "help" for help.
database_name=> select * from processes limit 2;
```

id	start_date	proc_name	proc_desc	proc_type	end_date
10001	2013-09-02	Hiring	HRMSW	A	2013-09-23
10002	2013-10-09	LoanMgmt	BOALM	S	2013-10-21

To import directly from a database dump on your local filesystem, use the `pg_restore` command as follows:

```
$ pg_restore --verbose --clean --no-acl --no-owner

-h ec2-12-34-567-890.compute-1.amazonaws.com -U user_name -d database_
name

-p 3421 ~/Downloads/processes.dump
```

You can find about other command line options from `http://www.postgresql.org/docs/9.2/static/app-pgrestore.html`.

Deleting a Heroku Postgres database

Though rare, sometimes you may want to delete the database itself. This can be accomplished in the following two ways:

- By using the `addons:remove` command as follows:

  ```
  $ heroku addons:remove HEROKU_POSTGRESQL_YYYYYY

  ! WARNING: Destructive Action

  ! This command will affect the app: test-db-app

  ! To proceed, type "test-db-app" or re-run this command with
  --confirm test-db-app

  > test-db-app

  Removing HEROKU_POSTGRESQL_YYYYYY from test-db-app... done, v...
  ($700/mo)
  ```

  ° To simply reset the database to its initial empty form without destroying it completely, use the following command:

    ```
    $ heroku pg:reset HEROKU_POSTGRESQL_XXXXXX

    ! WARNING: Destructive Action

    ! This command will affect the app: test-db-app

    ! To proceed, type "test-db-app" or re-run this command with
    --confirm test-db-app

    > test-db-app

    Resetting HEROKU_POSTGRESQL_XXXXXX... done
    ```

This will delete all your data and remove any structure that was set up earlier.

- By using the Heroku dashboard as shown in the following screenshots. Perform the following tasks:
  - ○ Log in to the Heroku dashboard and select the application whose database needs to be deleted. We will delete the database of the **heroku-postgre-24015faa** application. Click on the **heroku-postgre-24015faa** application shown in the following screenshot:

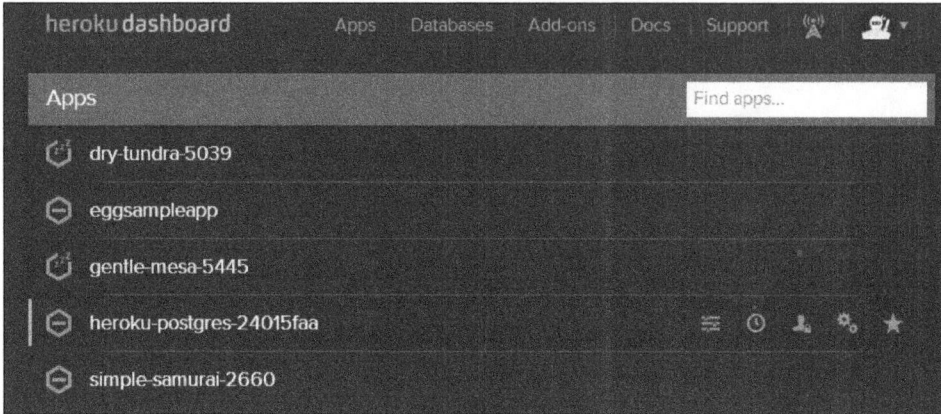

  - ○ This will direct the user to the application details page. Note that there is a Heroku **Postgres :: Pink** database plan associated with the app as shown in the following screenshot:

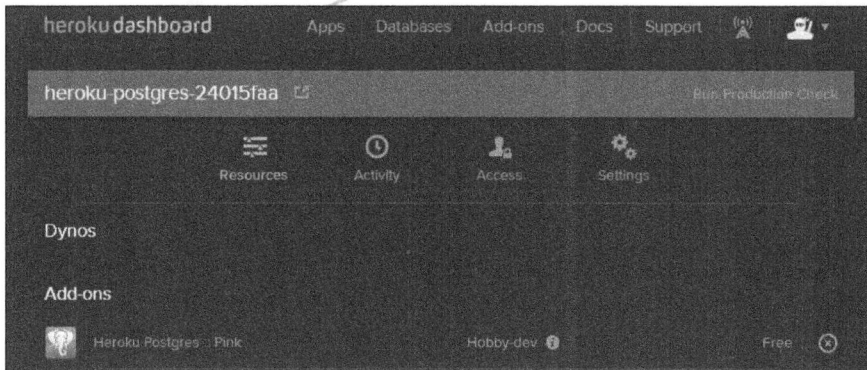

° Click on the database plan (Heroku **Postgres :: Pink**). This will direct the user to the database details page as shown in the following screenshot. Note that the menu list in the top right has a **Destroy Database** option. Click on the **Destroy Database** menu option:

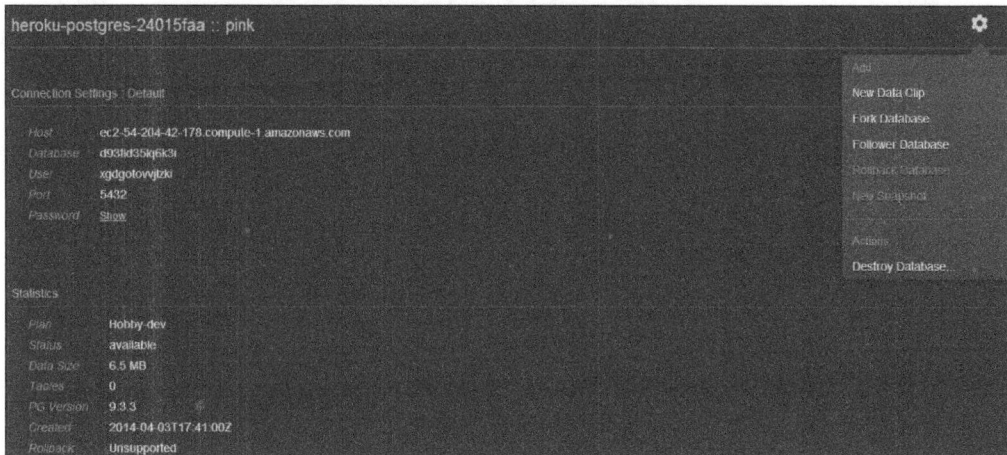

° Confirm the destroy database operation by entering DESTROY in the text area and clicking on the **DESTROY** button, as shown in the following screenshot:

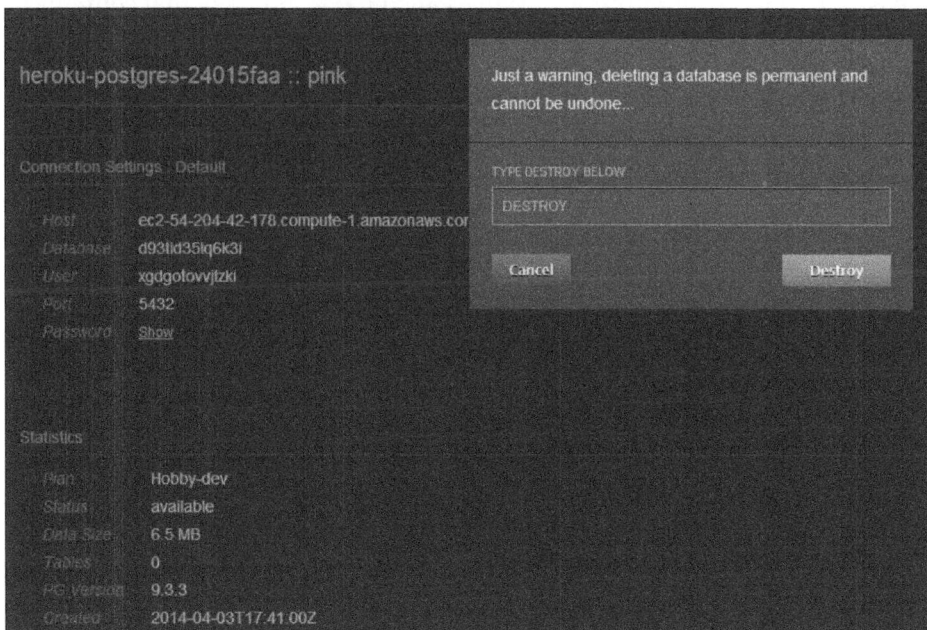

○ The **Heroku Postgres :: Pink** database of the **heroku-postgre-24015faa** application is successfully deleted as shown in the following screenshot:

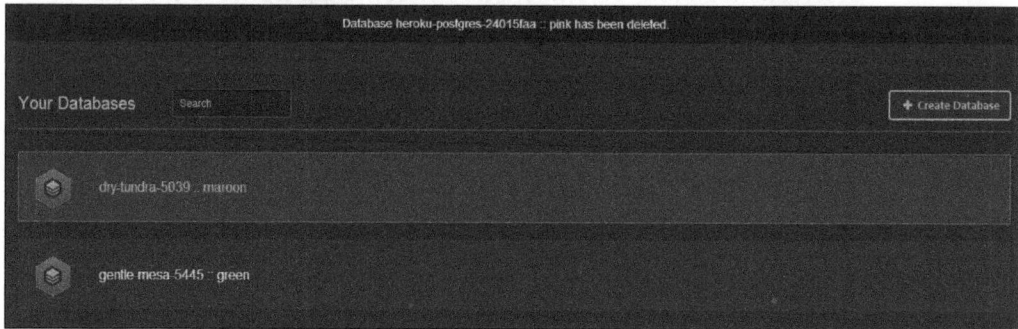

So, we learned a couple of ways to remove a database from an application and to remove the database altogether from the Heroku account. Now, let us look at how to access the Heroku PostgreSQL database service externally from a non-Heroku environment.

Accessing Heroku Postgres externally

Heroku Postgres databases are associated with a Heroku application. Usually you configure a Postgres database for a Heroku application. Heroku internally manages a database URL via a configuration variable called DATABASE_URL that contains the database details including the location and credentials.

Since the database credentials can change dynamically (as Heroku manages the database configuration parameter internally), it is recommended not to copy the credentials as is to another environment or inside your application code.

The DATABASE_URL variable, which is managed by Heroku, can change under the following conditions:

- **Unrecoverable database failure**: If the hardware on which your database is running fails, then your database might be recovered to a different database instance with the same database credentials

- **Security considerations**: The users can request a credentials change using a pg:credentials -reset command

- **Availability requirements**: Database failover can happen automatically for HA-enabled Postgres plans whenever Heroku determines a failover situation and switches over to a standby

Accessing the database credentials

The best practice is to fetch this configuration variable from the related Heroku application when the application starts. You should invoke your process as follows:

```
DATABASE_URL=$(heroku config:get DATABASE_URL -a app_name)
process_name
```

Connecting from outside of Heroku

If you want to access your Heroku Postgres database from outside the Heroku environment, your client or application must support SSL to connect to the Heroku PostgreSQL database.

To be sure that you always explicitly force an SSL connection from your application instead of relying on the default behavior of the client or application, you should use the `sslmode=require` parameter on the Heroku PostgreSQL connection string.

An example for connecting to Heroku PostgreSQL using the `sslmode` connection parameter is shown in the following command:

```
$ psql "host=<hostname or IP> port=<port no> user=<database user>
password=<database password> sslmode=require"
```

High availability Postgres

Heroku Postgres offers different tier plans for customers based on the desired level of functionality and database resilience, that is, failover and high availability. If your business needs are typical of an enterprise application or a large distributed system where failures and downtimes are expected but managed, you should consider premium or enterprise-tier plans.

Choosing the right plan

The enterprise and premium-tier plans come bundled with advanced features of high availability for the PostgreSQL database. What it means is that in case of an unexpected database failure, hardware or otherwise, your application database will switch over to a standby database that contains nearly the same data as your primary database. A switch over decreases the probability of a longer downtime and in turn avoids poor or no application response.

The **high availability (HA)** feature involves creating a standby database for your primary application database that can be used in case of an unexpected database failure. This standby is managed by the Heroku PostgreSQL staff, and is usually configured to be as close as possible to the primary database through scheduled data syncs with the primary database. When a database failure happens, it is possible for a small, but within limits, amount of most recently committed data to be lost. There is a threshold chosen as the acceptable delta of data difference between the primary and the secondary database to be used as a standby in case a failover occurs.

Ideally, a standby database should be an exact replica of the primary database. Only then can an application state be restored to what it was before the failover. However, in practical situations, there is potentially a small but negligible data loss possible during the failover. To minimize this loss, Heroku Postgres takes a few steps to define what is acceptable. For example, it doesn't attempt a failover to a standby if it is more than 10 database segments behind. Heroku also tries to apply any archived but not yet applied segments before bringing the standby out of the ready-only mode.

In case of HA database plans, the standby database is configured in a different **availability zone (AZ)** than the primary database to prevent data loss in case of failure of the entire AZ. The failed database instance is destroyed and the standby is reconstructed. Since the standby database is not visible to the application directly, you would need to create a follower database for the new database in case you need followers for your primary database to work after the switch over.

Another side effect of a database failover is that the value of the DATABASE_URL and HEROKU POSTGRES URL configuration variables is altered dynamically. Hence, it is recommended not to use the hardcoded values of these configuration parameters inside the application code or use the values in an outside application. The right way of using these configuration variables is discussed in the *Accessing the database credentials* section.

When does Heroku Postgres failover?

A database failure or slow response doesn't immediately trigger a database failover in the Heroku PostgreSQL database service. The Heroku PostgreSQL support ensures that the application database really needs a failover (as it involves some cost to switch to a new database instance and shut down the previous one), besides setting up new configuration and making the application live again on the new database. Heroku support runs a suite of tests to confirm that a failover is the only option. The tests are run for a given period of time, usually two minutes, across different application dynos to see a consistency in the database response behavior. Only when it is detected that the database is not responsive for all the requests for this period does the failover get initiated.

Effect of the failover

When a database failover takes place, the Heroku application is impacted in a few ways: The DATABASE URL and HEROKU POSTGRES URL variables change in their values and an attempt is made to restart the application with the new database credentials. Application performance might be affected for a while due to a cold database cache that is refreshed and re-populated over a period of time. A new standby database is automatically created for the new database and made available such that the standby meets the conditions required for a failover to be successful.

Checking the availability status after failover

Once the failover is completed, you can check the availability status of your newly created database by issuing a `heroku pg:info` command as follows:

```
$ heroku pg:info

...

HA status: Available

...
```

The HA status field's value Available shows that the database is ready for use. When the database is under preparation or not synced for failover yet, the HA status field will show the status Temporarily unavailable.

Configuring domains the right way

When we deploy a web application to Heroku, the application is accessible via the herokuapp.com app subdomain (in the cedar stack). For example, if your application is named myshoppingcart, the fully qualified Heroku URL for the application would be http://myshoppingcart.herokuapp.com. If you are an e-commerce site that wants to attract new users, you may want to use a more custom web URL for the site—for example, www.buyshoes.com or www.someecomsite.com. We can achieve this in Heroku by configuring the application to use a custom domain. Heroku provides the ability to map one or more custom domains to any application transparently. We start by getting a small introduction to the domain name system or DNS which is the foundational technology used for configuring domains.

Overview of DNS

The Internet is a large network of computers, each identified by an IP address such as 1.2.3.4. When users request resources (pages, images), they enter an easy-to-remember URL that gets translated to the physical IP address by the Internet service. The Internet service that helps resolve user-supplied, easy-to-remember URLs to the correct host IP is called the **Domain Name System** or **DNS** for short.

When the user requests a resource, the resource is identified by a specific URI (normally called URL). Part of the URL is the domain name, which could be simplified as an easy-to-remember textual alternative to the IP addresses of the machines where the resource is hosted.

When you request the URI, the DNS system makes it possible, via a resolver and DNS servers, to resolve your request into the IP that corresponds to the hostname part of the URI.

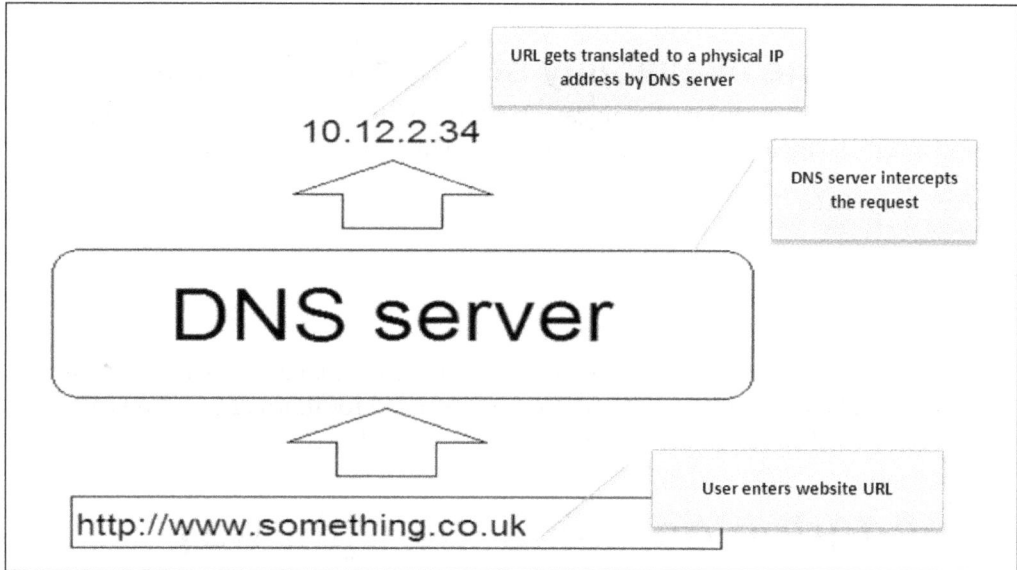

In a web URL such as www.google.com, the com part is what we represent as **top-level domain** (TLD). The top-level domain identifies the domains that belong to a specific country or category. For example, .gov belongs to the U.S. government and .edu represents most American educational institutes.

Each word and dot combination in a domain name before a top-level domain indicates a level in the domain structure. Each level refers to a server or a group of servers that manage that domain level. For example, heroku in www.heroku.com is a second-level domain of the com top level domain. Organizations can further use the concept of **subdomains** to organize their web presence, such as Citibank.co.in, which is Citibank's domain under CO, an additional level created by the domain name authority responsible for the **IN (India)** country code. A domain can contain a large number of machines, and since all of the names in a given domain need to be unique, the machine IP addresses need to be managed to guarantee uniqueness.

A domain registrar is an authority that does just that. It assigns domain names directly under one or more top-level domains and registers them with InterNIC, a service of Internet Corporation for Assigned Names and Numbers (ICANN), which enforces domain name uniqueness across internet devices including desktops, mobile devices and others. Each domain registration is part of a centralized domain database called the whois database. BigRock and GoDaddy.com are some of the companies that offer domain registration services.

A DNS server that manages a specific domain is called the **start of authority (SOA)** for that domain. In due course, the results from looking up hosts at the SOA for a domain propagate to other DNS servers across the Internet. **Root name servers** are a type of DNS server that start at the top of the domain hierarchy for a given top-level domain to locate SOA for a domain.

Now that we have understood common terms used in the DNS world, let us look at the tools used by the service providers to manage DNS.

There could be multiple domain configurations available to a web app namely subdomains (one or many) such as www.sampleapp.com, root domains such as sampleapp.com or wildcard domains such as *.sampleapp.com. There are widely available tools to manage the DNS settings for your domain to perform the following tasks:

- Add subdomains
- Redirect to fully qualified URLs
- Configure e-mail
- Other domain management services

When the DNS information for a domain is configured, the data is kept in a zone file on the DNS server. Several providers who offer DNS management services also provide a user-friendly web interface for editing this configuration.

Each new DNS configuration we add is called a record. The most common types of records configured for the DNS server are shown in the following table:

Record name	Notation	Description
Host	A	This is the basic mapping of an IP address to a hostname.
Canonical name	CNAME	This is the alias for the domain. Users accessing this alias get directed to the server indicated in the A record type.

Record name	Notation	Description
Name server	NS	This indicates the name server information for the zone. Configuring this lets your DNS server inform other DNS servers that your server is the ultimate SOA for the domain. This is important for DNS servers while caching lookup information on your domain from other DNS servers on the Internet.
Mail exchanger	MX	This maps e-mail traffic to a specific server. It could indicate another hostname or an IP address.
State of authority	SOA	This is one large record at the beginning of every zone file with the primary name server for the zone and additional information.

> DNS A record types can be used for configuring apex zone domains (also called bare/naked/root domains). However, they have critical availability implications when used on a platform such as Heroku (or cloud infrastructure services). Due to scalability considerations, applications should avoid using DNS A record types and instead use a DNS provider that supports CNAME for the apex zone domains.

Working with DNS in Heroku

In the context of Heroku, to use custom domains, it is very important to accurately configure your application's DNS information (a set of rules) to the right hostname. Once configured, the DNS information gets propagated to other parts of the Internet as the DNS servers run at multiple locations across the Internet to serve user requests from multiple geographies. Any further request to the updated URL ends up routing the user to the correct server hosting your application.

Configuring your domain

A single application can have any number of domains assigned to it with each domain belonging to one or more of the types described earlier.

To set up a domain, follow these steps:

1. Tell Heroku which custom domains are specific to your application.
2. Configure your application's DNS to point to Heroku.
3. Follow specific instructions for each configuration as detailed in the upcoming section.

Domain addition rules

Heroku ensures that domains claimed by one user aren't used by other users on different apps.

There are certain rules associated with adding a custom domain to your Heroku application:

- You can only add one domain to one application. For example, if `www.sampleapp.com` is added to the application, `sampleapp`, you are not allowed to add it to a different application, like `sampleapp2`. One application, however, can have multiple domains or subdomains assigned.

- You can add a wildcard domain if you own all existing applications already using a corresponding subdomain. For example, if an application is already using `www.sampleapp.com`, you must own it to add `*.sampleapp.com`.

- You can add a subdomain or an apex domain if you own the app assigned to the corresponding wildcard domain. For example, to add `www.sampleapp.com` or `sampleapp.com`, you must own the application with `*.sampleapp.com`, if such a custom domain exists.

Adding a custom domain to Heroku

To add a custom subdomain to your Heroku application, use the `heroku domains:add` CLI command from the command prompt:

```
$ heroku domains:add www.sampleapp.com
Adding www.sampleapp.com to sampleapp... done


$ heroku domains:add example.com
Adding example.com to sampleapp... done
```

Here, we added two different hostnames to the domain.

Configuring domain DNS

For each subdomain, configure your DNS with a CNAME record pointing the subdomain to your app's Heroku `herokuapp.com` hostname. The trailing `.` on the target domain may or may not be required, depending on your DNS provider.

The CNAME record shown here resolves `www.sampleapp.com` to the `sampleapp` app:

Record	Name	Target
CNAME	www	sampleapp.herokuapp.com

Checking DNS configuration

You can confirm that your DNS is configured correctly with the `host` command as follows:

```
$ host www.sampleapp.com
www.sampleapp.com is an alias for sampleapp.herokuapp.com.
```

The result of the `host` command shows that the hostname is either an alias or CNAME for `sampleapp.herokuapp.com`.

If you intend to use a root domain, for example, `sampleapp.com` or `sampleapp.co.in`, you must add it in addition to any custom subdomains as follows:

```
$ heroku domains:add sampleapp.com
Adding sampleapp.com to sampleapp... done
```

Zone apex domains (also called naked or root domains), for example, `sampleapp.com`, using DNS A records are not supported on Heroku, though there are alternative configurations possible that allow for root domains while still allowing the system to be resilient in a dynamic runtime environment.

There are some DNS hosting services that provide a way to get a CNAME-like functionality at the zone apex using a custom record type.

Two such record types are as listed in the following table:

Record type	Provider
ANAME	DNS made easy
ALIAS	DNSimple

To work around issues with the zone apex domains, you can set up the domain information as per the following steps (for most providers, the setup is very similar):

1. Point the ALIAS or ANAME entry for your apex domain to `sampleapp.herokuapp.com`, just as you would with a CNAME record.

2. Depending on the DNS provider, an empty or @ name value identifies the zone apex:

Record	Name	Target
ALIAS or ANAME	<empty> or @	`sampleapp.herokuapp.com.`

In case the DNS provider does not support such a record type, and you can't switch to one that does, use subdomain redirection to send root domain requests to your application on Heroku.

Most DNS service providers offer subdomain redirection that helps redirect all root domain requests to a specified subdomain using an HTTP 301 permanent redirect. `GoDaddy.com` is one such service provider that offers **domain forwarding** services for this very purpose. Using domain forwarding can however cause errors or warnings to show up in case a secure request to the root domain (`https://sampleapp.com`) is made. Otherwise, there will be no effect on your application if it is accessed securely in subdomain SSL form, for example, `https://www.sampleapp.com`, or if SSL isn't used at all.

A DNS configuration with domain forwarding would look similar to the data given in the following table:

Record	Name	Target
URL or forward	`sampleapp.com`	`www.sampleapp.com`
CNAME	`www`	`sampleapp.herokuapp.com`

> Note that the www subdomain is a CNAME record reference to `sampleapp.herokuapp.com`.

Use wildcard domains to map all subdomains to your application with a single record. An obvious use case for a wildcard domain is with applications that use a personalized subdomain for each user or account.

We can add a wildcard domain only if we own all existing apps already using the same top-level domain. For example, if an application is already using `www.sampleapp.com`, you must own it to add `*.sampleapp.com`.

To add the wildcard domain to your application, use the `*` wildcard subdomain notation as follows:

```
$ heroku domains:add *.sampleapp.com
Adding *.sampleapp.com to sampleapp... done
```

Use the * wildcard subdomain notation to add a CNAME record to `sampleapp.herokuapp.com` with your DNS provider as shown in the following table:

Record	Name	Target
CNAME	*	`sampleapp.herokuapp.com`

If one of the apps has a wildcard domain, we can still add specific subdomains of the same top-level domain to any of our other applications. Specific subdomains are evaluated before wildcard domains when routing requests.

Removing Heroku custom subdomains

To remove a custom subdomain associated with your Heroku application, use the `heroku domains:remove` CLI command from the prompt:

```
$ heroku domains:remove www.sampleapp.com
Removing www.sampleapp.com from example... done
```

When you destroy an application, any custom domains associated with it are automatically released. You can subsequently assign these domains to other applications.

Other domain-related considerations

Even if you set up a custom domain, the Heroku domain `sampleapp.herokuapp.com` will always remain active.

1. To direct users to the configured custom domain exclusively, your application should send HTTP status 301 (moved permanently) to instruct web browsers to use the custom domain.

2. The Host HTTP request header field will show which domain the user is requesting and redirect the user if that field's value is `sampleapp.herokuapp.com`.

3. Domain names may contain non-ASCII or accented characters. These domain names should be added only after converting the special characters using punycode. For instance, the `éso.com` domain name will be converted to `xn--so-91a.com` before passing to `heroku domains:add`:

   ```
   $ heroku domains:add xn--so-91a.com
   ```

Optimizing applications

There are few ways that can be leveraged by Heroku developers to get more out of their cloud apps on the Heroku platform. In this section, we discuss a few of these features that can be used to optimize the execution of your Heroku app when needed.

The 2X dyno effect

Heroku recently introduced the 2X dyno. The 2X dyno has twice the memory capacity when compared to the existing 1X dynos running on the Heroku platform. The 2X dyno comes with 1 GB of RAM and twice the CPU share for your processes to run faster and more efficiently. The 2X dyno costs more as well. It is interestingly priced at 0.10$/hr — exactly twice the price of a single 1X dyno.

Now, the questions that could come up are, "Why do I need the 2X dyno in the first place? I am already running my production app in an existing Heroku installation. Why should I switch to a 2X-dyno-based Heroku deployment if at all?" The answer depends on the use cases or scenarios specific to your application's needs. The following is a list of various scenarios:

- **Scenario 1**: Company A has a big data processing system that processes GBs of data through a distributed data processing application. One of the nodes that it runs uses 1X dyno and constantly encounters the R14 out of memory error. Moreover, you sometimes hit this issue across nodes. Well, the 2X dyno might just be the solution in this case. It might provide you with enough memory to run your distributed processing application without flooding the logs with hard-to-locate errors.

- **Scenario 2**: Company B uses a JVM-based language runtime and the critical applications are multi-threaded in nature. Though the JVM is designed on purpose to provide multithreaded concurrency, your application might be limited in the number of threads it can support or the size of memory each thread could use for processing data. The 2X dyno can come to the rescue in this case as well.

- **Scenario 3**: Company C has too many 1X dynos in their Heroku production system and this system seems to be experiencing a lot of out of memory issues. This is further resulting in delayed responses and poor overall performance for the end user. The 2X dyno might do the trick here as well. Replacing the plethora of 1X dynos by a smaller number of 2X dynos with a lot more memory per dyno and CPU share would improve the performance of each dyno. This results from the fact that applications tend to leverage the improved in-dyno queuing in a smaller number of dynos and provides an overall performance boost.

When do I need the 2X dynos?

The 2X dyno gives a tremendous performance boost to your app if your app happens to be computation or memory intensive. It can provide the necessary performance upgrade that your production app needs as it scales to support the increased user base. However, the 2X dyno may not be as effective if your application is more I/O bound as the app will be unable to leverage the benefit of twice the memory or CPU.

So, when do you decide to go for 2X dynos? Well, if you get a lot of R14 memory issues, that can be one hint, or if you want to utilize the improved ability of managing task queues within a 2X dyno versus splitting tasks between multiple 1X dynos. If you want to optimize the cost of your application, that is also a strong case for using 2X dynos. Using 2X dynos versus 1X dynos can often lead to decreasing the number of dynos required by more than a factor of two.

Checking whether you need 2X dynos

There are a few ways to determine if your Heroku application is hitting the ceiling in terms of memory usage and warrants increasing the memory for better performance. Heroku provides the following useful tools to determine the need for 2X dynos:

- **Log2viz**: This tool helps us understand how much memory and CPU is being used by the current application's dyno configuration. If the memory usage is hitting the upside limit of 512 MB on a regular basis, it might be time to upgrade your dyno configuration with 2X dynos. The upgrade is available at https://github.com/heroku/log2viz.

- **NewRelic**: The NewRelic application-monitoring tool is inarguably one of the best tools available for looking at web dyno behavior on an ongoing basis. The rich set of graphs, and data shown by NewRelic can help visualize the impact of high memory usage on a complex app configuration. Using 2X web dynos can help provide consistent queue times for the task and improve its processing time. To find out more about NewRelic, please visit http://www.newrelic.com.

What if I use 2X dynos?

2X dynos cost 0.10 dollars per hour and provide twice the memory per dyno (1 GB) and CPU when compared to 1X dynos. The 2X dynos provide the application with the ability to scale vertically. Deploying 2X dynos in place of 1X dynos can decrease the number of dynos needed for your application by a factor of two or more. Using 2X dynos also reduces the cost of operating the application besides improving the application performance of memory-intensive tasks significantly. Even users with the free subscription (free 750 dyno hours per month), can use 2X dynos and improve their app performance. The only thing to remember is that on migrating all the application web dynos to 2X, the number of free hours will also be reduced to 375 dyno hours per month. The Heroku scheduler also supports running one-off 2X dynos.

The following table illustrates the effect of using 2X dynos on your web app:

Dyno type	Memory/RAM available	CPU share	Price/dyno-hour
1X	512 MB	1X	0.05 dollars
2X	1024 MB	2X	0.10 dollars

Now some examples...

Once we determine that the application needs 2X dynos, resizing the application dyno count can be done simply by using the `ps:resize` command:

- To resize the dyno count, type:

```
$ heroku ps:resize web=2X worker=1X

Resizing dynos and restarting specified processes... done

web dynos now 2X ($0.10/dyno-hour)

worker dynos now 1X ($0.05/dyno-hour)
```

- To view the dyno size of a process type, use the `ps` command:

```
$ heroku ps

=== web (2X): `bundle exec unicorn -p $PORT -c ./config/unicorn.
rb`

web.1: up 2013/04/15 16:25:15 (~ 3h ago)

web.2: up 2013/04/15 16:46:23 (~ 3h ago)

web.3: up 2013/04/15 17:08:34 (~ 2h ago)


=== worker (1X): `bundle exec rake worker:job`
```

```
worker.1: up 2013/04/15 16:39:04 (~ 3h ago)
worker.2: up 2013/04/15 17:08:24 (~ 2h ago)
worker.3: up 2013/04/15 16:30:55 (~ 3h ago)
```

- To apply dyno size on a per process-type basis, set the dyno type for each process type as shown below:

```
$ heroku ps:resize web=2X worker=1X worker2=2X
```

- To configure one-off 2X dynos (for example, memory intensive jobs), enter the following command:

```
$ heroku run --size=2X rake heavy:job
```

Notes on 2X dynos

It is quite possible that running memory-hungry applications with 1X dynos can lead to constant swapping of your programs to the disk as the logs show a lot of R14 errors, and later Heroku has to forcibly kill the dyno if the memory requirement exceeds three times the dyno's memory limit. This leads to a lot of performance degradation eventually. It may so happen that no matter how many more 1X dynos you start, your application can't keep up with the surge in memory requirement and it swaps to disk very often. The solution in these cases is to leverage 2X dynos. You can write a script to detect the memory needs of the application and as soon as the memory crosses a predefined threshold (95 percent or more), the script can kill the dyno and start a resized 2X version of the dyno for the application. In this way, the application works seamlessly without causing performance bottlenecks for the consumers of the application.

Managing your app dynos

Heroku is a platform used by commercial product developers and hobbyists alike. It is an ideal platform to proof of concept ideas before building sophisticated web apps on it. There are many users who use Heroku for that very purpose. Usually, these users have a bare minimum Heroku configuration. Specifically, they have just one web dyno running their application on the Heroku platform. Imagine 10,000 of these users trying to use the Heroku platform to host an application that isn't run regularly or run for short bursts of time. Well, given that Heroku is a very popular PaaS that hosts an enormous number of real-world web apps and a host of equally numerous hobby apps, Heroku has a way to optimize its use of dyno resources. Heroku shuts down every single web dyno app after an hour of inactivity.

If you check the application logs when the app is not active, they might look like this:

```
2013-11-30T08:23:09+00:00 heroku[web.1]: Idling
2013-11-30T08:23:17+00:00 heroku[web.1]: Stopping process with
SIGTERM
```

Since Heroku manages the apps, the end user is unaware of this shutting down unless the user is closely monitoring the app. In such cases, whenever a new request comes for your web application, the router processing the request will notify the dyno manager and ask it to activate the web dyno. This would be reflected in the application log as follows:

```
2013-11-30T10:12:34+00:00 heroku[web.1]: Unidling
2013-11-30T10:12:34+00:00 heroku[web.1]: State changed from created
to starting
```

Since the app starts from scratch, the first few requests experience a few seconds of delay. The point to note is that if you are running more than one web dyno, your dynos won't be idled. Also, the worker dynos don't idle either.

A common way to work around Heroku's idling policy is to set up a script to send a ping once an hour to keep the web dyno alive.

There are a couple of ways to keep the web dyno alive:

- Using the Heroku scheduler
- Using a NewRelic add-on feature

Using the Heroku scheduler

It is easy to set up a keep-alive dyno ping using the Heroku scheduler. If you are a Ruby developer, you can create a rake task as follows, for an automated ping to your web dyno:

1. Write the following script:

```
desc "Pings YOUR_HEROKU_APP_URL to keep a dyno alive"
    task :wakeup_dyno do
      require "net/http"

      if ENV['YOUR_HEROKU_APP_URL']
        uri = URI(ENV['YOUR_HEROKU_APP_URL'])
        Net::HTTP.get_response(uri)
      end
    end
```

2. Add `YOUR_HEROKU_APP_URL` to your Heroku environment:

```
$ heroku config:add YOUR_HEROKU_APP_URL=https://yourherokuapp.
herokuapp.com
```

3. Now, set up the Heroku scheduler:

```
$ heroku addons:add scheduler:standard
```

```
$ heroku addons:open scheduler
```

That last command should open the scheduler interface in your browser.

4. Set up your `wakeup_dyno` task to run once an hour and run it:

```
$ rake wakeup_dyno
```

Using NewRelic to keep the dyno alive

NewRelic (`www.newrelic.com`) is a very popular web and mobile app monitoring service. It lets you monitor app up-time, down time, data stores, user behaviors, application performance, and more. It is also very easy to use on the Heroku platform. It supports virtually all web or mobile apps written in various programming languages such as Ruby and Java.

To set up an automated ping for your web app using NewRelic, follow the ensuing steps:

1. Add NewRelic to your Heroku account. The NewRelic standard package can be added to your account as follows:

```
$ heroku addons:add newrelic:standard
```

2. Open the NewRelic interface as follows:

```
$ heroku addons:open newrelic
```

3. Go to the **Reports** tab and locate the **Availability** menu option.

4. Add a URL to monitor and customize how often the check is made. Set the time to less than an hour to ping your web dyno frequently enough to keep it un-idled.

Summary

In this chapter, we reviewed tools and features that can add significantly to the way we develop Heroku web apps. We explored the Cloud 9 web-based IDE that supports most popular programming languages and provides a powerful development environment for writing cloud apps. We also delved into how the Heroku Postgres data service works and how you could use the most common database operations to support your web apps. We also introduced domain name resolution and how it works for Heroku when you configure custom domains. Finally, in the advanced features, we explored the power of 2X dynos that can power-up your web dynos to scale better and deliver superior performance. In the end, we looked at a few techniques to keep your small app web dynos active when they are not being used. All these tips can help you as a reference, as you maintain and enhance your applications on the Heroku platform.

In the next chapter, we will explore the security aspects of the Heroku platform and review tools to measure the security needs of you app and further secure your Heroku cloud app.

8
Heroku Security

We are almost near the end of our Heroku journey. In the previous chapter, we looked at the advanced uses of the Heroku platform for developing cloud apps. We explored the popular and feature-rich, cloud-based **integrated development environment (IDE)** called C9. We took a peek inside how to work with the Heroku PostgreSQL relational database and use the database to serve and store application data. Through a primer on the **domain name service (DNS)**, we understood the right way to configure DNS for your Heroku app. Last but not least, we were introduced to the world of 2X dynos—the faster counterpart of the traditional dyno process on Heroku. There is a key aspect of Heroku cloud application development that we will explore now: security.

Security has been one of the main concerns for enterprises and SMBs in accepting the cloud as a viable computing environment. The thought of executing applications and storing data on a hosted environment has made users think twice before moving their bread and butter applications to the hosted world. What if the data gets corrupted? What if data gets snooped while travelling the network? What if the application is hacked through a security hole? What if the application goes down while serving thousands of client requests? These and many more questions have prompted cloud service providers, and indirectly the underlying platform, and infrastructure providers to focus a lot of their effort on securing the cloud computing environment. Heroku is no exception.

Security on Heroku needs to be looked at in two dimensions:

- When a developer communicates from the local machine to the Heroku platform, it is important that the communication is secure and no software program is able to snoop on the contents of the communication. This is the first dimension of security with respect to working with Heroku.

- While working with Heroku, the second dimension of security is the security of Heroku and third-party servers in order to protect user applications and related data from unauthorized access. Both these dimensions are equally important for developers to build highly secure apps on the Heroku platform.

In this chapter, we focus on the following two dimensions of security on the Heroku platform:

- Communication between the developer's machine and the Heroku platform
- Continuous security of applications and data resident on Heroku and third-party servers

We also review a couple of useful application security tools such as wwwhisper and tinfoil, which are available for use from Heroku's add-on library.

Overview

Heroku's constant endeavor is to let developers focus on creating the apps, whereas Heroku provides everything from build, deployment, and scalability services to infrastructure management services. When it comes to security, Heroku applies best practices and manages platform security so that the customers can devote their energies entirely to building robust, highly available, and performant web apps on the Heroku platform.

The Heroku platform protects its customers from security threats — from physical to application, isolating user applications and related data — by enforcing tighter controls at every layer of the platform. Heroku's ability to rapidly deploy security updates without customer intervention or service interruption makes it a compelling PaaS environment to use for deploying applications of any scale.

If we break down the Heroku application development process into subparts, we'll see that any Heroku application's life cycle comprises the following:

- Application creation on a local environment (PC/Linux machine)
- Accessing a relational or key-value data store with available credentials
- Pushing the application code to the Heroku platform
- Deploying the application on the Heroku platform
- Running the app in production with potentially multiple data stores, caches, queues, and third-party software

When we look at Heroku from a security aspect, things can go wrong at any of these stages of an application's life cycle. Given that all Heroku applications run on Amazon's EC2 platform at the infrastructure layer means that Heroku platform security relies on the security of underlying hardware infrastructure services as well. Hence, securing the Heroku platform services requires securing each of these phases of a Heroku application's life cycle. This chapter describes how Heroku provides a solid, virtually bulletproof, secure environment for your applications to run securely and seamlessly.

Communication between the developer's machine and the Heroku platform

In this section, we will review the basic security concepts surrounding machine-to-machine communication. We will also review how a developer communicates with the Heroku server in a secure manner using a well-known communication protocol.

General concepts of security

A Heroku developer regularly interacts with the Heroku server/platform to make changes to the app, app configuration, or app data. In doing so, the developer repeatedly needs to connect to a remote system and authenticate user credentials before being accepted as a genuine user. In this section, we look at what makes the communication with a remote system possible for a Heroku developer and also briefly discuss the underlying algorithms used to secure access to the interaction between the developer and the remote system (in our case the Heroku server).

What the developer needs to communicate with the remote system (Heroku server) is as follows:

- Security of the communication; this means that no one should be able to read the message sent, and hence the message should be encrypted during the transfer

- Integrity of communication is important, that is, both the parties — client and server — should be able to check if the message was altered enroute

- The server and client should be able to identify each other to establish a secure authentication channel

To enable these developer needs, most apps use some form of cryptographic algorithms to secure the communication between different parties. The most common types of cryptographic algorithms for encryption and data security are as follows:

- **Public key cryptography algorithms**: This is also known as asymmetric cryptography. In these algorithms, a pair of keys is used. One of the keys called the private key is kept secret and not shared with any party. The other key known as the public key is not secret and can be shared with other parties. Data encrypted by one of the keys can only be decrypted and recovered using the other key. It is virtually impossible to derive the private key from the public key even though the two keys are mathematically related. A common example of the public key algorithm is the RSA algorithm. The Heroku SSH setup is one scenario where you can use the RSA algorithm (named after its founders) to enable secure communication between the developer's machine and the Heroku server.

- **Secret key cryptography algorithms**: This is also known as symmetric cryptography. In this mechanism, the key is a shared secret between the two communicating parties, and encryption and decryption both use the same key. Common examples of symmetric key algorithms are the **Data Encryption Standard (DES)** and the **Advanced Encryption Standard (AES)**.

Asymmetric cryptographic algorithms are slower than symmetric key algorithms. Hence, for most cases, apps use asymmetric algorithms to encrypt symmetric keys (to distribute keys) and hashes (to create digital signatures). The key and the cryptographic algorithm together transform the data. It is the key that controls access to the data and hence must be kept safe to protect the data. The algorithms are public knowledge and hence can be used by anyone.

Security of developer communication with Heroku

A developer using the Heroku platform can connect to the server using the secure shell protocol. The **Secure Socket Shell (SSH)** is a protocol for securely connecting to a remote computer. It is widely used by network administrators to manage web and other kinds of servers remotely. SSH commands are encrypted and secured in many ways. Both ends of the client/server connection are authenticated using a digital certificate, and passwords are protected by being encrypted.

SSH uses RSA public key cryptography for both connection and authentication. Encryption algorithms include DES, Blowfish, and IDEA (default). SSH2 is the latest version of the SSH protocol proposed as a set of standards for secure communication. SSH allows you to run both command-line and graphical programs, transfer files, and even create secure virtual private networks.

SSH provides both password-based and key-based authentication mechanisms. Though password-based authentication is also safe, using key-based authentication is recommended. There are additional features such as SSH tunneling and TCP port forwarding that are beyond the scope of our discussion. In this section, we will focus on the most relevant use case of how the client (developer's machine) communicates with the server (Heroku server) through SSH and the underlying semantics of this communication.

As we have seen in the *Setting up SSH* section in *Chapter 4, Deploying Heroku Applications*, working with the Heroku platform requires a secure channel of communication between the developer's local machine or environment and the Heroku platform to be established. The developer sets up the SSH client on the local development machine. The SSH server running on the Heroku platform accepts requests from the client machine to authenticate the client. The developer uses the `heroku login` command to connect to the Heroku server, and once authenticated, is allowed to perform various operations, such as creating or modifying web apps on the platform. All communication between the developer's local machine and the Heroku platform is encrypted during the course of interactions between the developer and the platform. The following link shows a comparison of various SSH clients available for developers to use: `http://en.wikipedia.org/wiki/Comparison_of_SSH_clients`. In the context of this book's examples, we have used the OpenSSH open source implementation to set up SSH.

A look inside the SSH protocol

The SSH protocol works by exchange and verification of information, using public and private keys, to identify clients and hosts. Once the communicating parties have been identified, SSH provides the encryption for the subsequent communication using public/private key cryptography.

The term client means a developer's workstation or PC, whereas the term server means a secondary remote workstation or PC that you wish to connect to for some work, such as a login session server. In the context of Heroku, the client is the machine where the developer types the `heroku login` command to try to connect to the Heroku platform. The host is the Heroku server that the client connects to after getting authenticated.

The Heroku developer generates an "identity" on the client machine by running the `ssh-keygen` program. This program creates a subdirectory `$HOME/.ssh` and creates two files named `identity` and `identity.pub`. These files contain the private and public keys for the developer's account on the developer's machine. The latter file can then be appended to a file named `<user home directory>/.ssh/authorized_keys`, which needs to be copied to any/all servers that the developer wants to connect to through SSH.

With SSH, the developer generates a public and private key pair for the local workstation using the `ssh-keygen` tool. As the keys exist on the developer's workstation itself and are protected (particularly the private key), the likelihood of a third party stealing the system's identity by various means such as manipulating DNS records or fudging IP addresses is minimal. The only way you can pretend to be an authorized user when you actually aren't is if you gain access to the user's private key on their local machine. That in itself is highly improbable.

The following client and server interaction shows how the client and server authenticate each other before sending encrypted data to each other using SSH. The following steps are performed for server authentication:

1. The client connects to the server and requests information. The server sends the supported protocol version and SSH server version running on the server.

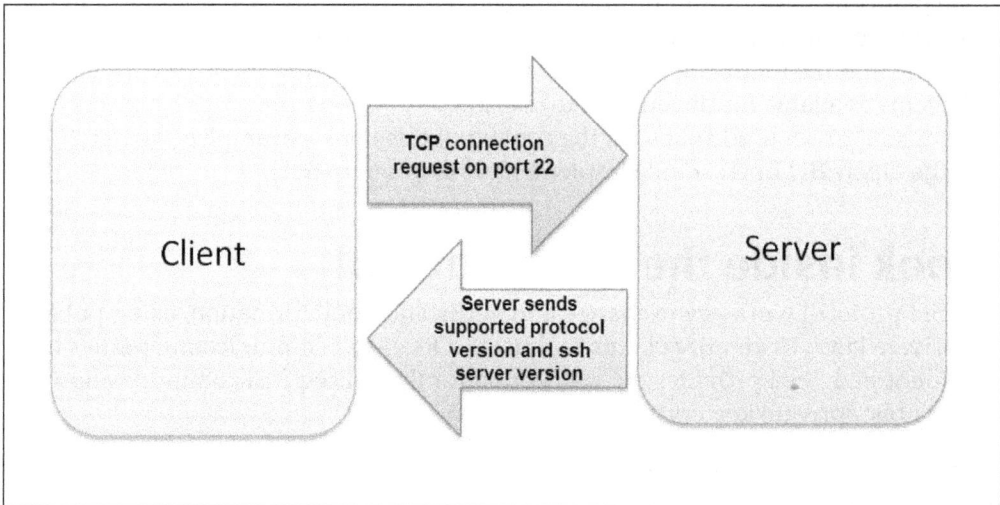

2. Based on the protocol version received, the client decides whether to continue the communication or not. If it does continue the communication, both the client and server switch to a **binary packet protocol** (**BPP**). In this the server sends the server identity, server key (not used in SSH2), checkbytes (the client sends these in the next reply as a handshake), and list of encryption and authentication methods that are supported.

BPP is responsible for the underlying symmetric encryption and authentication of all messages that are sent between two parties involved in an SSH connection.

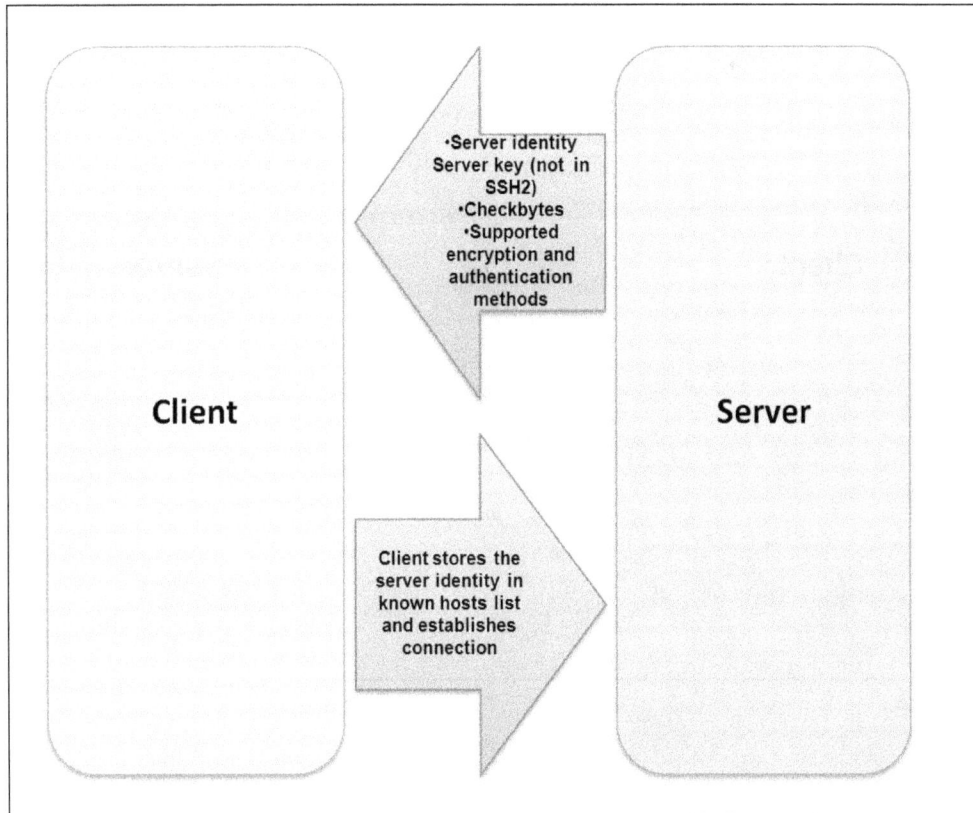

3. The client then chooses the encryption algorithm and creates a random symmetric key that it then sends to the server. The server replies with a confirmation message encrypted using the symmetric key sent earlier by the client. The client now receives the message and decrypts it using the key it already has and authenticates the server it was sent from.

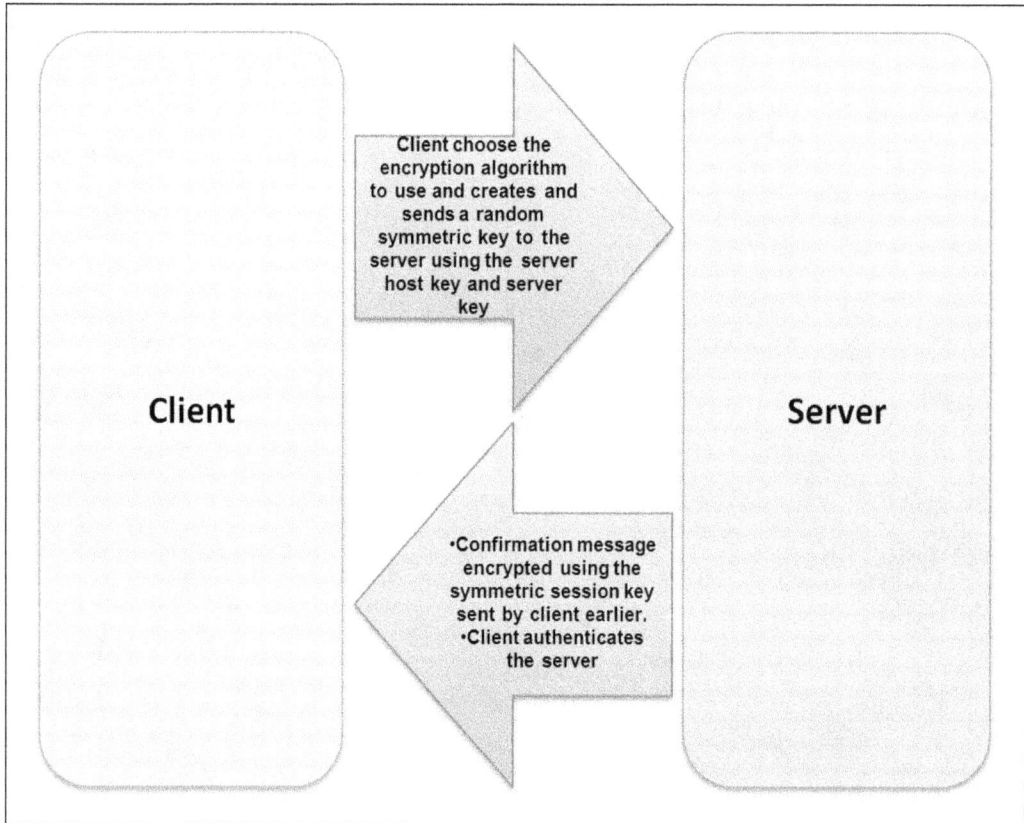

Client authentication

The following steps are performed for client authentication:

1. So far, the client just authenticated the server and a secret symmetric key was created. For client authentication, the client first selects the public key cryptography as the desired authentication mechanism and sends the cryptography used for this public key authentication. In the same step, the server creates a 256-bit string as a challenge for the client and encrypts it using the public key sent by the client earlier.

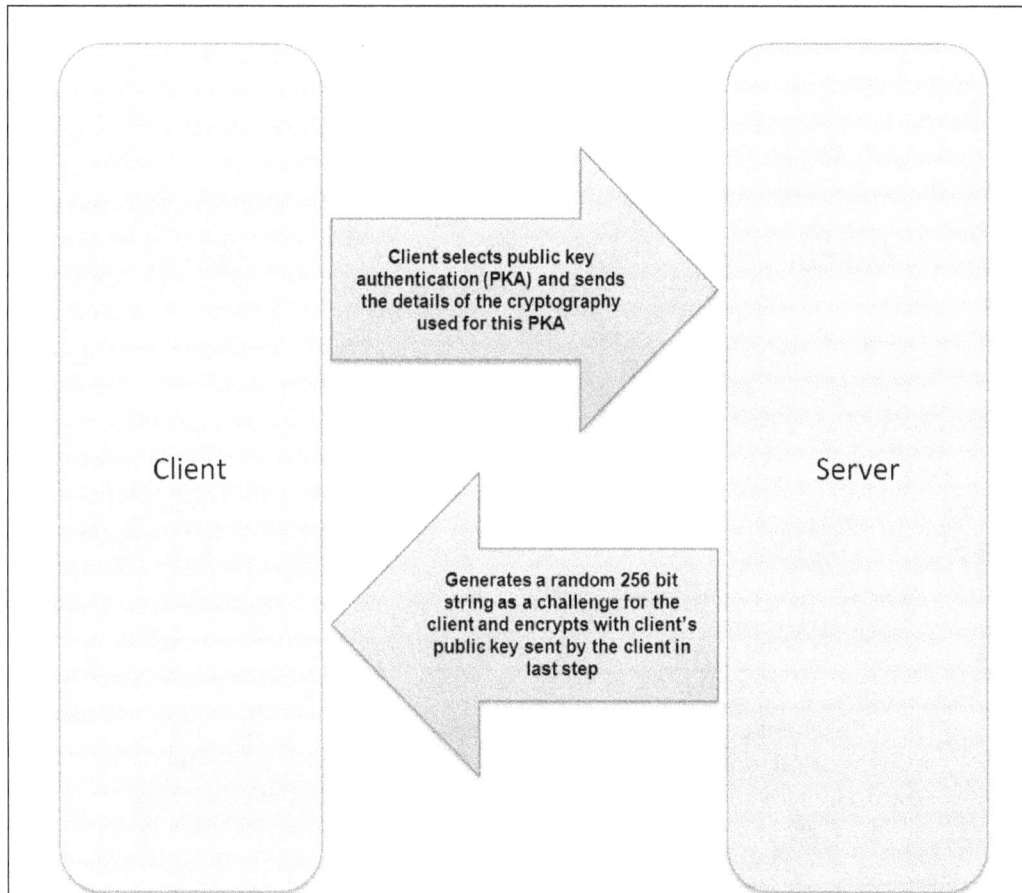

2. The client decrypts the server challenge with its private key and sends the decrypted message to the server in an encrypted form using the session key (the symmetric key created during server authentication). The server receives the md5 hash generated by the client, regenerates its own hash, and compares the two. If they match, the client is marked as authenticated.

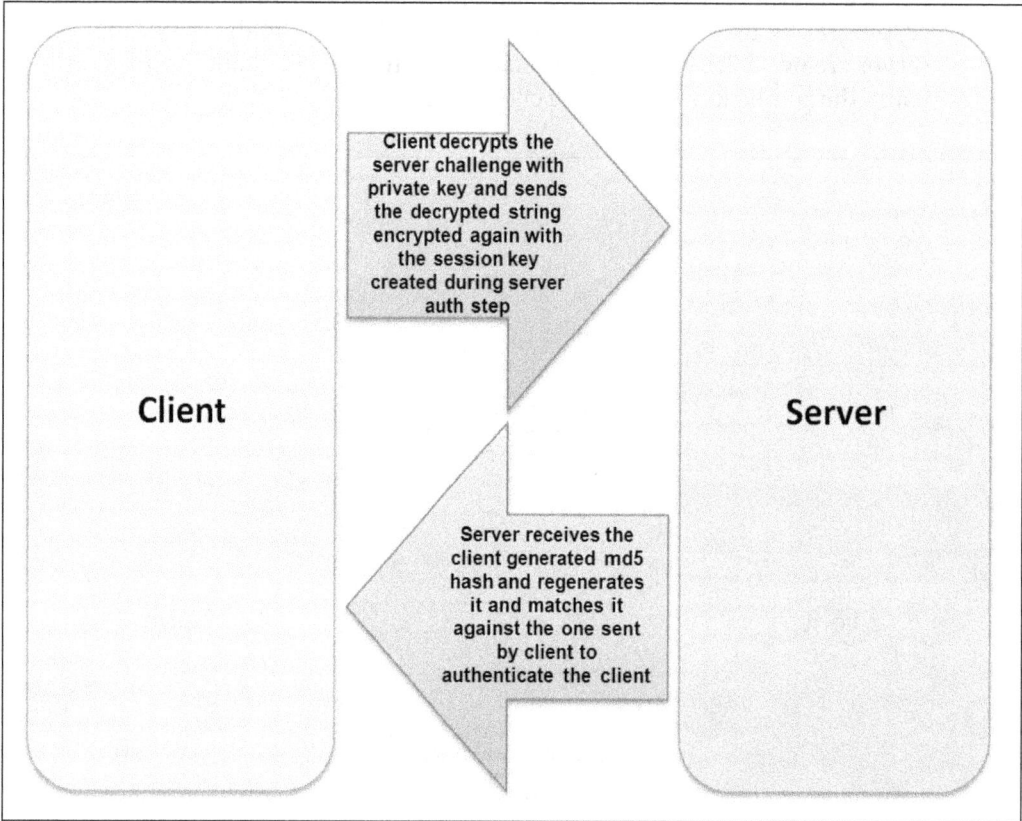

Client decrypts the server challenge with private key and sends the decrypted string encrypted again with the session key created during server auth step

Client

Server

Server receives the client generated md5 hash and regenerates it and matches it against the one sent by client to authenticate the client

Once the client and server have shared each other's identity and are authenticated, data transfer requests will be encrypted using the session key for the secure transfer of data between the two machines.

App security and the Heroku dashboard

There are some options available in the Heroku dashboard to manage certain aspects of application security. Though these options have been covered elsewhere too, it makes complete sense to discuss these options here to make the topic of app security complete.

Your Heroku account and the dashboard

Once you log in to your Heroku account and navigate to the Heroku dashboard, you can have a look at and change the account properties from the **Account** tab as shown in the following screenshot:

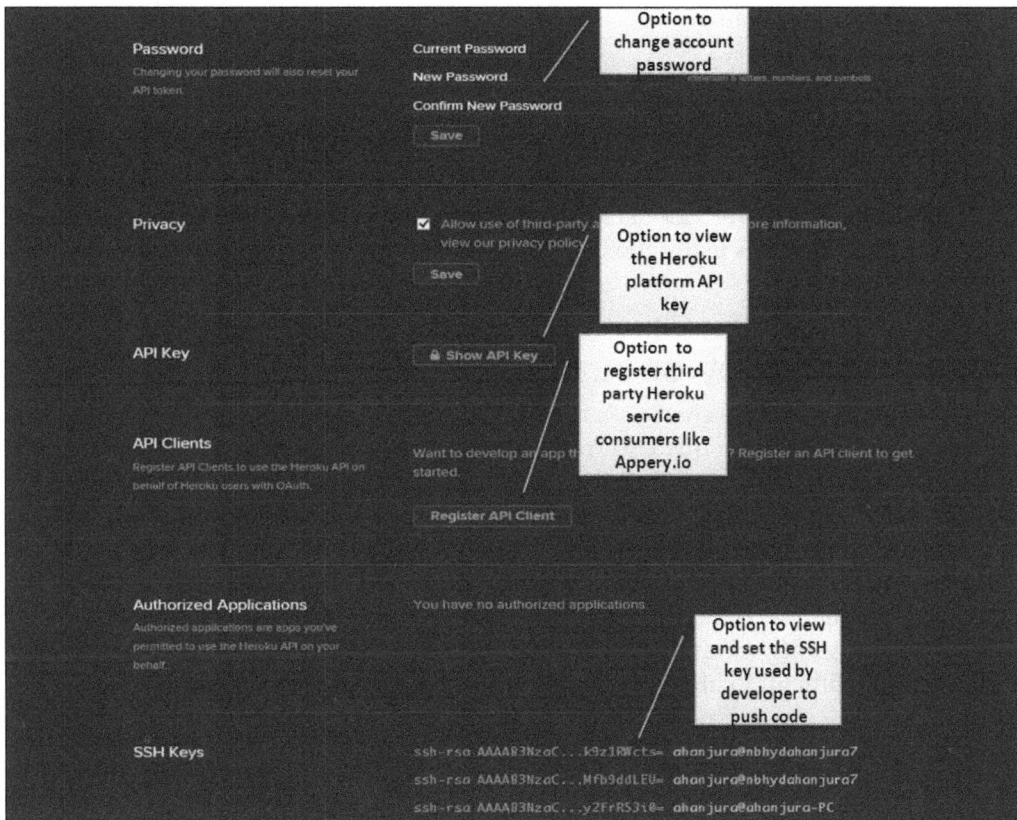

Security of applications and data resident on Heroku and third-party servers

In this section, we review the security practices followed by Heroku security to keep developers and data secure on Heroku servers. Heroku also provides a mechanism to securely access third-party servers that provide services to your apps.

Heroku security practices

Heroku employs various strategies to secure the platform and provide a seamless experience to the developer creating applications on the platform. With respect to data security, Heroku employs various measures to ensure that applications run in a seamless and secure manner.

Source code security

The Heroku developer needs to push the source code and other artifacts to the Heroku server, and hence it is required that no one is able to snoop on the source while in transit. The developer uses the SSH protocol, as described earlier, to encrypt the source code contents using the Git protocol as they are getting pushed to the Heroku environment.

Build and deploy security

The Heroku build process creates an executable (slug) by including code from trusted sources and provides a unique URL representing the built application. The likelihood of someone faking the URL and trying DoS attacks on the application is very limited, though there have been instances when hackers gained access to customer accounts by passing the encryption and were able to access account information using malicious HTTP requests. In another instance, customers' databases were deleted when their credentials were accidentally revealed. In spite of these challenges, Heroku has constantly strengthened the security cordon around the platform, making it increasingly difficult to break the methods used to access the platform.

Heroku follows the highest standards and best practices regarding the infrastructure hosting the application. Heroku uses Amazon's EC2 platform as its IaaS layer, which itself follows the strictest of infrastructure security standards. Heroku also leverages the security features of the specific application language or framework to secure deployed applications.

Heroku applications run within their own isolated environment and cannot interact with other applications or parts of the system. This scheme enables tighter security controls and more stable application environments.

Application security

Any application that runs on the Heroku platform is executed in the form of a dyno in a process execution environment called the dyno manifold. Dynos are executed in complete isolation from one another, meaning no two applications can see each other being executed — even when on the same physical infrastructure. These self-contained environments isolate processes, memory, and the filesystem. Each dyno has a predetermined resource limit that it can use. The dyno manager controls the behavior of each dyno in case of violation of the resource usage. This strategy provides protection from other application processes and system-level processes that consume all available resources.

Heroku restricts apps from making local network connections between hosts by having firewalls in place that are based on the host server. As part of the deployment process, apps hosted on the Heroku platform are also copied or backed on secure and redundant storage. Heroku uses these backups to deploy the applications across the platform and automatically bring them back online in the event of an outage. At the same time, Heroku's infrastructure is designed to scale seamlessly and be fault tolerant by automatically replacing failed application instances and reducing the necessity to restore the applications from a backup.

In general, Heroku takes several steps to protect the privacy of its customers and protect the application and data stored within the platform. The various types of protection enabled on the Heroku platform include user authentication, access control to resources, data encryption (in transit or in stored form), and HTTPS support for applications.

To assess the security of the Heroku platform, Heroku periodically undergoes system penetration tests, platform vulnerability assessments, and source code reviews. Heroku also participates in third-party security assessments that cover all the security areas in the platform, including testing for application vulnerabilities and verifying application isolation.

Data security

Customer data is certainly the most important asset for any organization. It is the basis of all business processes and applications built on top of them. Hence, it is critical that customer data be secured from any malicious attack, theft, or snooping.

Heroku enables customer data security by keeping customer data in access controlled databases. If the customer has more than one database, each of these databases has its unique username and password to access the data. Each application is usually associated with its own database to avoid any unauthorized cross-application intrusion that might lead to data corruption, though it is possible for multiple apps to refer to the same third-party resources. The developer, however, has the onus of designing the app correctly so that any type of contention is avoided and data consistency is maintained for the app. Postgres—the default database now available on the Heroku platform—requires SSL encryption to connect to applications to manipulate data.

Additionally, security requirements around customer data can be met by the application itself, by encrypting the data exchanged over the network or shared between multiple applications. During deployment, customer applications should use encrypted database connections to avoid snooping on the data being sent to the database server. Customer applications are also required to implement security mechanisms for data that they might use from custom caching solutions or receive from external systems.

Whenever data is changed, the corresponding change is recorded in write-ahead logs; these are in turn stored in highly available and durable storage systems in multiple data centers. If a disaster occurs, resulting in hardware failure or data corruption, the logs can be replayed to recover the data until the last checkpoint. You could also back up your database from time to time to meet your business needs for security and data retention.

Once you deprovision an application, associated data is retained for a period of seven days, after which the application and associated data is destroyed, making the data unrecoverable. Internally, Heroku can drop your database using the `pg:reset` command if you are using a shared database. The configuration can be deleted from the filesystem local to your app. Hardware deprovisioning is managed by Amazon, which provides the underlying infrastructure layer for the Heroku platform.

Unless requested, Heroku's internal staff doesn't access customer data or applications. Only if a customer request is received to troubleshoot a high-severity issue or a government order is in place to audit customer data, Heroku's staff will gain controlled access to customer data and application. Heroku staff keeps a record of the entire activity by keeping track of the support start and end times, the reason for accessing the resource, and the actions taken in the course of resolving the issue.

Configuration and metadata

The Heroku system also archives the configuration or metadata of your application periodically and archives it to the same highly available, durable, redundant infrastructure used to store database information. Using this archive, one can easily track the configuration changes undergone by the application from the time it was first deployed. The application developer can easily revert to an older configuration for a reference or verification of how the application in question has evolved over time.

Infrastructure security

When the underlying infrastructure changes, Heroku keeps the platform updated with the new changes. It maintains the system configuration and consistency through configuration management software, up-to-date system images, and the periodic replacement of systems with updated versions. New systems are deployed using latest images that contain the most recent configuration changes and security updates. When the new systems are deployed, existing systems are decommissioned. Since customer applications run in isolated environments, they are virtually unaffected by core system updates.

The access to underlying base operating systems is restricted to authorized Heroku staff using username and key authentication to gain access. Brute-force attacks, theft, and sharing are not possible because password authentication is disabled for users.

Heroku constantly engages with internal and external risk assessment agencies and gathers the potential vulnerabilities within the platform. The issues are prioritized based on how far reaching the impact is and how many users have been affected. Based on the risk involved, issues are resolved and sanity is restored to the overall platform.

Heroku uses the concept of component grouping to mitigate risk and create a higher level of security in the platform. It groups similar components into a unique network security group, providing access to specific resources (ports) and protocols for use. Components belonging to different security groups can't access each other's resources. For example, customer applications belong to a different network group than Heroku's internal management infrastructure; hence, customer applications can't access any resource belonging to Heroku's internal management infrastructure.

Security in add-ons

Heroku provides its customers with the ability to build additional features for their applications using add-ons that are third-party packages that solve specific application needs; for example, caching, security, and so on. These add-ons are offered and managed by third-party companies and implement their own security mechanisms. The application developers need to evaluate their application security needs while using these add-ons and check if they need to build an additional security framework to ensure the security of their application.

Securing the logging infrastructure

Logs tell us a lot about the state of the application. Depending on the level of logging enabled in the application, one can collect vital, in-depth information about the state of various application components. Logging serves a critical need for troubleshooting and resolving the application issues encountered from time to time. Hence, it is very critical that logs themselves are made secure.

It is very important that customer applications use encrypted database connections, mask critical data before logging (credit cards, addresses, and passwords), create periodic logs (not just one big log), and show transition points (switching from one module to another) clearly. These logging requirements keep your application data secure by logging only the relevant information and not disclosing data that might be a security risk for your customers.

The Heroku platform provides multiple options to interact with the system, application, and API logs. Someone troubleshooting the application can choose to receive these types of logfiles separately and then use an add-on to analyze log data or review the logs real time using the Heroku client. There are several add-ons available, for example, Loggly, to further analyze the application logfiles and derive useful insight into the problem encountered.

In general, Heroku takes steps to protect the privacy of its customers and protect data stored within the platform. The various types of protection enabled on the Heroku platform include authentication, access controls, data transport encryption, HTTPS support for customer applications, and the ability for customers to encrypt stored data.

Network security

The Heroku platform leverages firewalls to restrict access to systems from external networks and between systems internally. By default, all access is denied. Heroku groups similar components into a unique network security group, providing access to specific resources (ports) and protocols for use. This provides a type of isolation for the platform wherein components belonging to different platform functions can't interfere with each other.

The Heroku platform employs DDoS prevention techniques, such as TCP SYN cookies and connection rate limiting, besides maintaining multiple backbone connections and a large internal bandwidth capacity to meet the demands of application network traffic. Heroku uses managed firewalls to prevent any IP, MAC, or ARP spoofing on its network. It also uses advanced packet sniffing, including the hypervisor that prohibits traffic getting routed to the interface it isn't intended for. Heroku utilizes application isolation, operating system restrictions, and encrypted connections to further manage security requirements at each level.

Heroku strongly recommends that customer applications not engage in port scanning or other malicious security violation in any way. Port scanning is not allowed, and every reported instance is investigated and stopped, which results in access being blocked.

Security standards and compliance

To a large extent, the security of Heroku's underlying physical infrastructure relies on Amazon's physical infrastructure security policy. To that count, Amazon continuously manages risk and undergoes recurring assessments to ensure compliance with industry standards. Amazon's data center operations has several compliance certifications to its credit, including, but not restricted to, ISO 27001, SOC 1 and 2, SSAE 16/ISAW 3402, PCI, FISMA moderate, and SOX.

Heroku utilizes ISO 27001 and FISMA certified data centers managed by Amazon, which has many years of experience in managing large-scale data centers. AWS data centers are housed in nondescript facilities that contain critical facilities that have extensive setback and military grade perimeter control, besides other natural boundary protection. Physical access is strictly controlled using state-of-the-art security systems.

Securing web requests

When a user accesses a Heroku application, it could be for many reasons. The user could be registering with the application and entering key personal information, or they could be paying for a service using a credit card. A request from the user in either of these cases would require the browser to send personal information that ideally should have been hidden or encrypted during transmission. For such scenarios, the **Secure Sockets Layer** (**SSL**) cryptographic protocol comes to our rescue. SSL provides end-to-end data encryption and integrity capabilities for any web request. Any web request that transmits confidential or sensitive data should enable SSL for the secure transmission of sensitive data over the network.

Heroku also supports sending requests to your web application using SSL to secure the communication. Based on the type of URL supported in your application, you could use either the piggyback SSL or configure SSL capabilities for your custom domain application.

Piggyback SSL

If you are using `http://<yourappname>.herokuapp.com` as the URL for your application, you can "piggyback" on the SSL facility offered by default on the Heroku platform. You can access a URL related to your web application using an `https://` protocol specification, and Heroku will encrypt your request by default.

SSL for a custom domain

Heroku supports the SSL endpoint add-on to enable SSL for custom domains.

Configuring SSL for your custom domain is a slightly long-drawn procedure, and you will require third-party intervention to get it up and running. To get SSL working for your custom domain application, you will need to do the following:

1. Buy the SSL certificate from a provider:
    - **Self-signed SSL certificate**: One of the easiest and most inexpensive ways of securing your web application is to add SSL encryption through a self-signed SSL certificate. Typically, this certificate can be used to secure staging or non-production applications. A self-signed SSL certificate implements full encryption. However, when you use a self-signed SSL certificate with an application, the browser shows a warning about the untrustworthiness of the site.

- ° **Purchase SSL certificate from a vendor**: The Heroku developer can buy an SSL certificate from companies such as DNSimple or follow a series of steps to gain access to an SSL certificate. Typically, you can perform the following steps to acquire an SSL certificate:

   1. Generate a private key using openSSL.
   2. Create a **Certificate Signing Request** (**CSR**) using the private key generated from the first step.
   3. Submit the CSR created in the second step to the SSL provider.

2. Add the SSL endpoint Heroku add-on to your application:

   1. To use SSL for your Heroku application, you must configure the SSL endpoint add-on as follows:

      ```
      $ heroku addons:add ssl:endpoint

      Adding ssl:endpoint on sampleapp... done, v1 ($20/mo)
      ```

      The `ssl:endpoint` service is chargeable at $20 per month.

   2. Now, you can add the certificate, including any intermediate certificates and the private key to the SSL endpoint with the Heroku `certs:add` command:

      ```
      $ heroku certs:add server.crt bundle.pem server.key

      Adding SSL Endpoint to sampleapp... done

      sampleapp now served by nanking-1234.herokussl.com.

      Certificate details:

      Expires At: 2013-10-31 09:30:00 GMT

      Issuer: C=US; ST=CA; L=SF; O=Heroku; CN=www.sampleapp.com

      Starts At: 2012-11-01 09:30:00 GMT

      ...
      ```

      The endpoint URL assigned to your application in this example is `nanking-1234.herokussl.com`.

3. The details of the SSL endpoint configuration can be reviewed with the `heroku:certs` command as follows:

```
$ heroku certs

Endpoint                          Common Name          Expires
Trusted

-------------------        ----------------       ----------------
-------        -------

nanking-1234.herokussl.com     www.sampleapp.com    2013-10-
31 09:30:00GMT     False
```

4. Detailed information about an SSL certificate can be retrieved using the `certs:info` command as follows:

```
$ heroku certs:info

Fetching SSL Endpoint nanking-1234.herokussl.com info for
sampleapp... done

Certificate details:

Expires At: 2013-10-31 09:30:00GMT

Issuer: C=US; ST=CA; L=SF; O=Heroku; CN=www.sampleapp.com

Starts At: 2012-11-01 09:30:00GMT

Subject: C=US; ST=CA; L=SF; O=Heroku; CN=www.sampleapp.com
```

For a `herokussl.com` endpoint URL, visit it via `https`, for example, `https://nanking-1234.herokussl.com`.

3. Upload the SSL certificate to Heroku.

4. Modify the application's DNS settings to reference the new SSL endpoint URL.

   After the SSL endpoint is provisioned and the SSL certificate confirmed, you need to configure the DNS for your custom domain to enable routing to your application.

Once SSL is configured for your custom domain, user requests for resources are encrypted during the communication between the browser and the web app.

Application security tools

There are a few security tools that can help developers identify security issues in their web apps. In this section, we explore two such tools—the wwwhisper and tinfoil security tools supported as add-ons on the Heroku platform.

wwwhisper

As an application developer, you can use an add-on such as wwwhisper to authorize access to RoR or other Rack-based Heroku applications. The administrator of the application can use a web interface to specify the e-mail addresses of those users who are allowed access to your application. wwwhisper provides smooth and seamless access control to your Heroku applications.

wwwhisper utilizes Persona—a cross-browser login system for the Web (supported on all modern browsers)—which eliminates the need for site-specific passwords to establish the ownership of a particular e-mail address.

The Rack middleware provides integration with the wwwhisper security service. As a result, the integration cost is kept to a minimum, and there is no need to make any application code changes or call any wwwhisper API.

A sample wwwhisper app

There is a sample wwwhisper application available at `wwwhisper-demo.herokuapp.com` that demonstrates the use of this add-on. Though everyone can access this site by default, you still need to sign in to access the application.

To access the app, visit the mentioned URL. You will see the following on your screen:

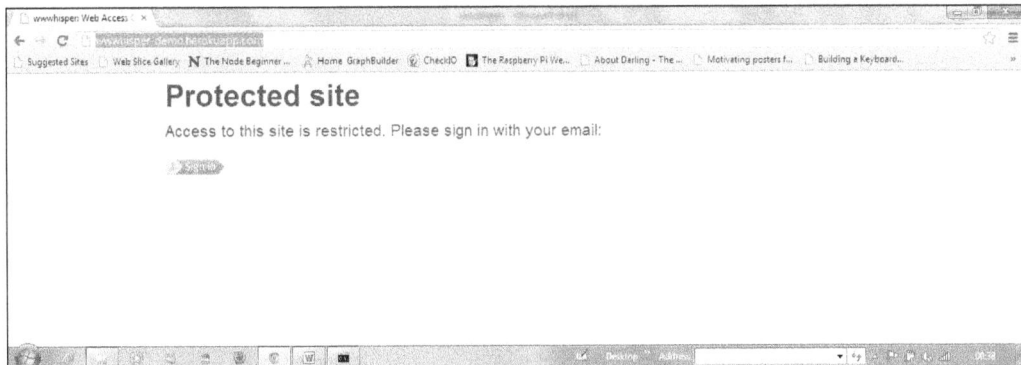

Now, perform the following steps:

1. Click on **Sign in** to get routed to the **Persona** login page, as shown in the following screenshot:

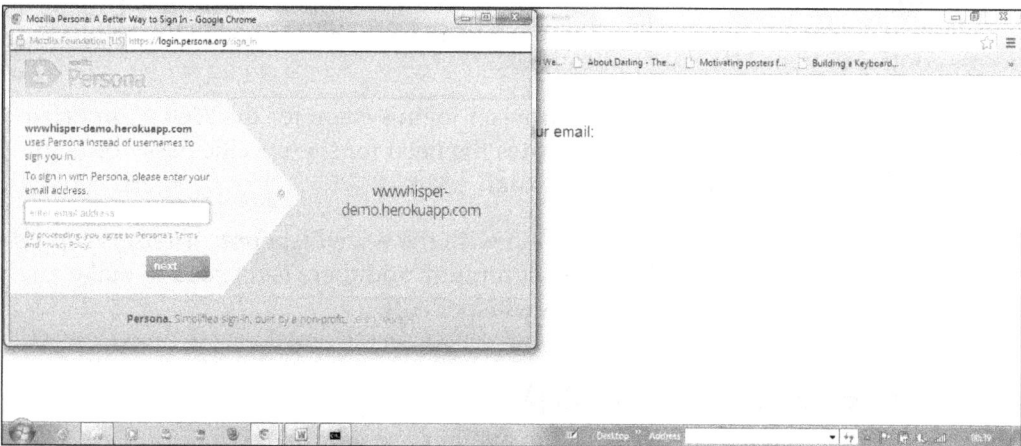

2. If you already have an account with Persona, enter the e-mail address as shown in the following screenshot:

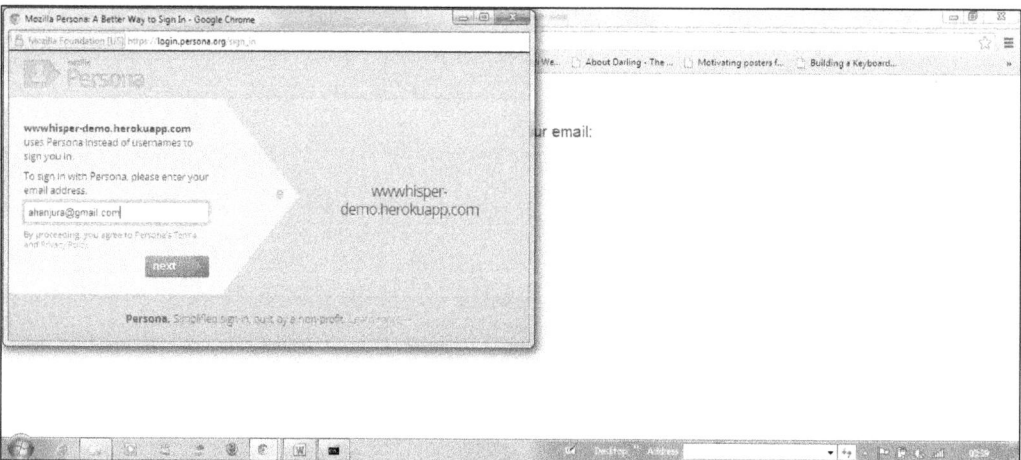

3. Enter the password for the Persona account as shown in the following screenshot:

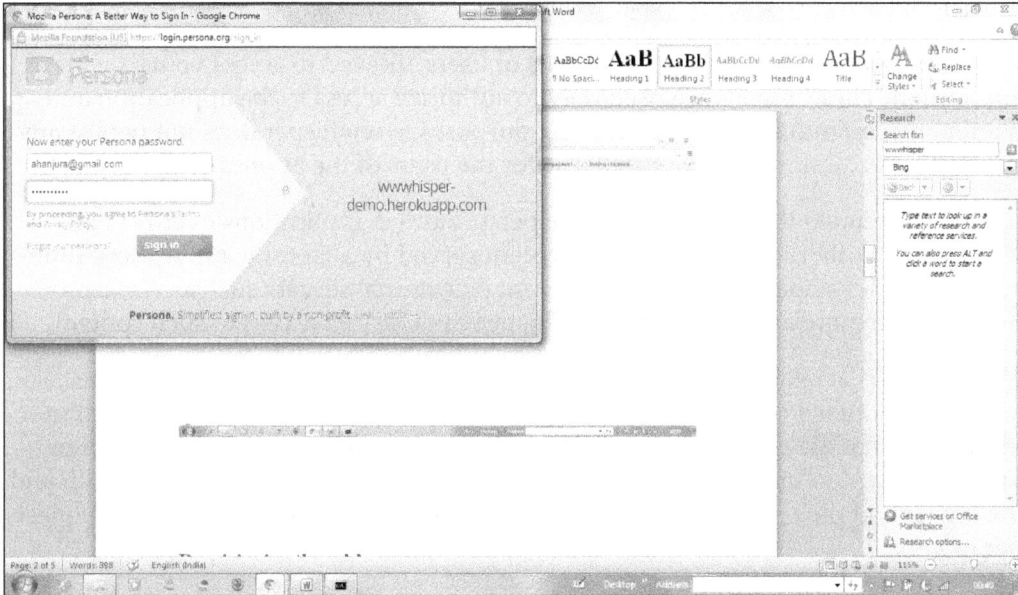

4. You will be routed to the demo wwwhisper application. The currently logged-in user is shown in the bottom-right corner of the screen:

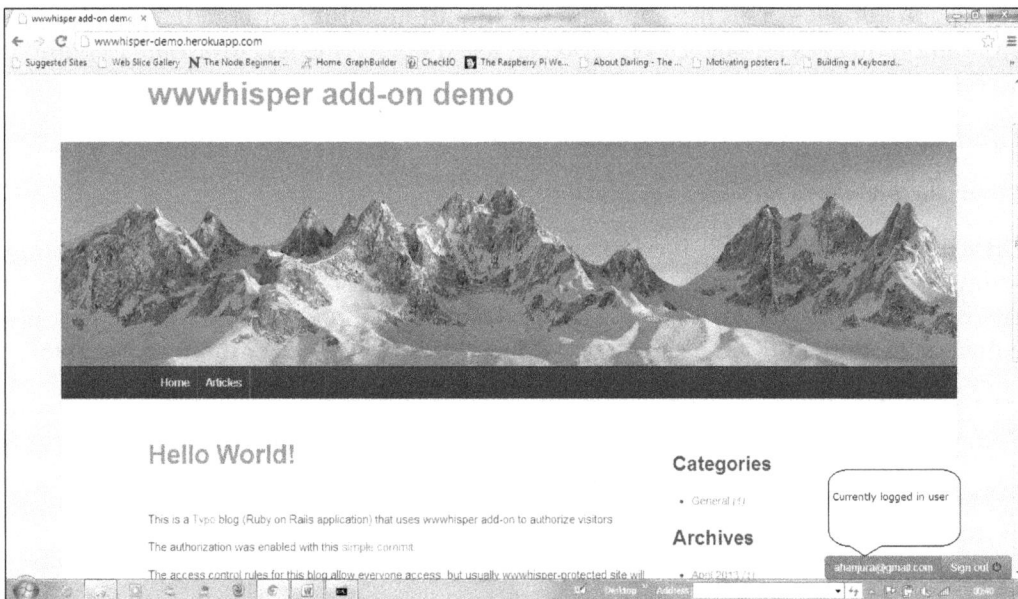

Getting wwwhisper

You can download wwwhisper to a Heroku application via the Heroku CLI. To review the detailed features of wwwhisper, visit `https://addons.heroku.com/wwwhisper`.

The wwwhisper service stores the e-mails of users allowed to access your application. These e-mails are used only to authorize access to the application and not for any communication or marketing purposes. wwwhisper does not persist any application browsing history or patterns for the users of the application.

It is recommended that you use wwwhisper-protected applications over HTTPS. wwwhisper authorizes access only to content served by a Heroku application. If the application developer puts sensitive content on external servers such as Amazon S3 that do not require authorization, wwwhisper can't restrict access to such content.

wwwhisper is available in three plans—starter, basic, and plus. You can choose any one plan based on your business requirements. With the free, single-user starter kit, you can handle up to 10,000 authorization requests per month. The basic plan provides access to up to 10 users and 1 million authorization requests per month and the higher end plus plan allows up to 100 users and 10 million authorization requests per month.

To add wwwhisper, type the following:

```
$ heroku addons:add wwwhisper [--admin=your_email]
```

The `--admin` parameter is an optional parameter that specifies who should be allowed to initially access the application. Without the admin option, the Heroku application owner's e-mail is used. You can use the wwwhisper admin site to grant access to other users.

To add a specific wwwhisper plan, type the following:

```
$ heroku addons:add wwwhisper:plus
```

Once the add-on has been added to your application, a `WWWHISPER_URL` configuration setting will be available in the application configuration. This URL can be used to communicate with the wwwhisper service. While developing an application, the e-mail of an authenticated user can be retrieved from a Rack environment variable named `REMOTE_USER`.

You can verify this using the following Heroku `config:get` command:

```
$ heroku config:get WWWHISPER_URL
https://user:password@domain
```

Removing wwwhisper

You can remove wwwhisper via the CLI. This will destroy related data. Consider the following command line:

```
$ heroku addons:remove wwwhisper
```

Enabling wwwhisper in your application

The developer needs to include the wwwhisper security tool in the configuration to enable its use by the app. The steps to enable the tool in various types of apps are as follows.

For Ruby applications, we need to execute the following steps:

1. Add the following entry into the Gemfile of a Ruby application:

    ```
    gem 'rack-wwwhisper', '~> 1.0'
    ```

2. Update application dependencies with bundler using the following command:

    ```
    $ bundle install
    ```

Place the following line at the end of `config/environments/production.rb` for a Rails application:

```
config.middleware.insert 0, "Rack::WWWhisper"
```

This line will make wwwhisper the first middleware in the Rack middleware chain.

For other Rack-based applications

For Rack-based applications, add the following two lines to `config.ru`:

```
require 'rack/wwwhisper'
use Rack::WWWhisper
```

Post wwwhisper enablement

Once wwwhisper is enabled in your application, you can verify if it actually works by entering the URL `https://yourapp-name.herokuapp.com/` in your browser. You should be presented with a login page. Sign in with your e-mail and then visit `https://yourapp-name.herokuapp.com/wwwhisper/admin/` to specify the locations that can be accessed by visitors and those (if any) that should be open to everyone.

Local setup for wwwhisper

You can enable or disable wwwhisper for local development on your development machine.

Using wwwhisper locally

If you want to use the wwwhisper service locally, copy the WWWHISPER_URL variable from the Heroku configuration. If you use Foreman, execute the following:

```
$ echo WWWHISPER_URL=`heroku config:get WWWHISPER_URL` >> .env
```

Credentials and other sensitive configuration values should not be committed to source control. In Git, exclude the .env file with `echo .env >> .gitignore`.

If you don't use Foreman, execute the following:

```
$ export WWWHISPER_URL=`heroku config:get WWWHISPER_URL`
```

Disabling wwwhisper in a local environment

It is usually convenient to disable wwwhisper authorization for a local development environment. If your application uses a separate configuration file for development (for example, `config/environments/development.rb` in the case of Rails), you don't need to do anything; otherwise, you need to set the WWWHISPER_DISABLE=1 environment variable.

If you used Foreman to start a local server, execute the following command in the application directory:

```
$ echo WWWHISPER_DISABLE=1 >> .env
```

If you didn't use Foreman, execute the following:

```
$ export WWWHISPER_DISABLE=1
```

Tinfoil website security scanner

Another important tool that a Heroku practitioner can use to check the security vulnerabilities in the application is the Tinfoil website security scanner. You can add this tool as an add-on and scan your application for potential security vulnerabilities. Try this tool free of cost at `https://www.tinfoilsecurity.com/` and have the results of the scan sent to a chosen e-mail address.

The Tinfoil website scanner is like a security agent that crawls through the pages of your web application and detects potential security threats and analyzes them. It further recommends possible changes in your application that could improve the security of your app. To use this tool for your Heroku application, you would need to pay a low monthly fee. The security scanner will send actionable items to your e-mail after scanning the application. The Tinfoil security scanner doesn't need any special configuration, libraries, or installation to get started.

The first step in using the Tinfoil security scanner is to add it to your application as an add-on.

Go to the Heroku CLI and enter the following command:

```
$ heroku addons:add tinfoilsecurity
-----> Adding tinfoilsecurity to smoky-hill-1245... done, v18 ($59)
```

The Heroku add-on system responds by including the add-on with your application, `smoky-hill-1245`, and shows the version and price for the tool. Since using this tool in production incurs a charge, you should ensure that you have paid for it by visiting the accounting and billing section of your application.

Upgrading the add-on

You might want to remove the test version of this add-on and configure a production version.

There are two ways to do this:

1. Remove the test version and then configure the production version:

    o   To remove this add-on via the CLI, type the following command:

        ```
        $ heroku addons:remove tinfoilsecurity:test
        -----> Removing tinfoilsecurity from smoky-hill-1245...
        done, v20 (free)
        ```

    o   To add the new version, type the following command:

        ```
        $ heroku addons:add tinfoilsecurity
        -----> Adding tinfoilsecurity to smoky-hill-1245... done,
        v18 ($59)
        ```

2. Upgrade your add-on price plan using the `addons:upgrade` command as follows:

    ```
    $ heroku addons:upgrade tinfoilsecurity:standard
    -----> Upgrading tinfoilsecurity:newplan to smoky-hill-1245...
    done, v18 ($199/mo)
    ```

    As a user of this add-on, you should be careful about the timing of the upgrade to ensure proper functioning of the application during the upgrade. The upgrade done during another scan will come into effect only from the next scan.

The TINFOILSECURITY_SCAN_SCHEDULE configuration parameter

Once the Tinfoil security scanner is installed, your application configuration will make TINFOILSECURITY_SCAN_SCHEDULE available. The initial value of this configuration parameter is set to Pending while the application is being configured. This parameter contains the proposed scanning schedule for your application and can be set accordingly. You can change this schedule via the Tinfoil security dashboard.

If you want to view the current scanning schedule, use the config:get command as follows:

```
$ heroku config:get TINFOILSECURITY_SCAN_SCHEDULE
Weekly on Mondays
```

The Tinfoil security scanner dashboard

The Tinfoil security website scanner dashboard allows you to do the following:

- **View all the statistics and the current state of the information**: The details of the scan requests can be reviewed and necessary actions can be taken based on the recommendations of the scanner.

- **Run manual scans**: You can run manual scans from the dashboard. Based on the chosen plan, there is a limit to the number of full scans you can run in a month. If you want to run more scans than currently available to your application, you can upgrade your plan.

- **Cancel scans**: You can log in to the Tinfoil security dashboard, then select **View Progress** and **Cancel** to immediately stop the scan.

- **Verify successful vulnerability fixes**: To verify that a vulnerability fix has been applied, hit the rescan button on the Tinfoil security dashboard. The scanner will quickly check to make sure that the issue is fixed and then mark the issue as complete.

The dashboard can be accessed via the CLI using the following command:

```
$ heroku addons:open tinfoilsecurity
Opening tinfoilsecurity for smoky-hill-1245...
```

Alternatively, you can log in to the Heroku website and choose the Tinfoil security add-on from https://addsons.heroku.com.

The scanning process

The Tinfoil security scanner runs according to the schedule configured for your application in the Tinfoil security scanner dashboard. Once the scan is completed, the results and recommendations are sent via e-mail. You can then take the necessary steps to modify the application, including the best practices suggested by the scanner results.

You can either scan automatically (scheduled) or configure a manual scan for your application URL. The URL for the scan is automatically determined from the Heroku configuration and cannot be altered. In case the application uses a Heroku Custom Domain, the scanner will attempt to scan the first listed domain.

Automatic scans are run as per US Pacific Standard Time. The request rate determines the maximum requests per second that the scanner uses to scan the web app. A higher request rate implies faster finish time for the scans but more use of dynos to support additional traffic generated as a result of the scanning process. The scanner is intelligent enough to customize the request rate in case the application has slowed down significantly due to the scan.

The Tinfoil security scanner works on many web frameworks and programming languages. Usually, it is recommended that you provide information about what software is run and what languages are used on the website.

Summary

In this chapter, we reviewed how security is handled under Heroku. We understood in detail how security is ensured when the developer pushes code to the Heroku platform by encrypting the source code using SSH. We looked at different parts of the Heroku application life cycle and reviewed how security is enforced in each of them to ensure that the Heroku platform and the applications running on the platform are secured at all times. Finally, we learned how to use two of the many popular security tools available on the Heroku platform as add-ons to search for various security gaps and for ways to close them. In the next chapter, we will learn various techniques to take the development of apps on the Heroku platform to the next level by using several newly introduced features.

Troubleshooting Heroku Applications

9

In the last few chapters, we learned how to build, deploy, and run Heroku apps. We also explored how to test your apps locally using foreman and once that was done, how to successfully deploy your app to the Heroku platform. We have also looked at the various options available to run and manage our apps through the Heroku dashboard—a one stop shop for many app management needs. Now, we are at a point where the application is up and running. Suddenly the app stops working or starts throwing errors at you. It is time to troubleshoot what went wrong. This chapter covers this very important aspect of deploying an app on Heroku, that is, troubleshooting the app when it starts misbehaving.

In this chapter, we will cover the following topics on troubleshooting in Heroku:

- Using Heroku's logging infrastructure to troubleshoot your app
- Troubleshooting the Heroku app using available tools and techniques
- Learning how to troubleshoot the app downtime
- Understanding the most commonly encountered issues and ways to address them
- Leveraging the production check feature to identify issues before they surface
- Using the recommended configuration for your app
- Managing maintenance windows
- Understanding Heroku errors and how to address them using custom error pages

The need for troubleshooting

Heroku is one of the most formidable platforms for developing applications on the cloud today. It offers a unique blend of platform services from application deployment to monitoring, and from routing web requests to logging a trail of all that happens in the application. Heroku is highly available and scalable and ideally suited for deployment of web applications of any complexity. It also offers developers a wide variety of choices in terms of programming languages to use for writing web apps.

However, like any other robust computing environment, Heroku sometimes encounters operational or application-related issues that cause your production or development app to behave erratically. A problem could originate from any of the following aspects of your Heroku app:

- Operational issues
  - Configuration issues
  - Database issues
  - Request queuing issues
  - Scalability troubles
  - DNS issues
  - Missing libraries
- Memory-related issues
- Language- or framework-specific problems
- Access control issues and security vulnerabilities
- Deployment issues
- Communication problems

The most common way for Heroku to tell you that there is a problem is through the Heroku logs. Typically, Heroku adds custom error information to your logs to help you troubleshoot problems. It collects logs from various sources and shows you a consolidated view of the app behavior. You can filter the specific areas of the log that you find relevant to your troubleshooting. Some of the other useful facilities Heroku offers for troubleshooting problems are process monitoring and automatic process restart commands, application checks, and more. There are several techniques one could use to troubleshoot the issue at hand and resolve nagging issues quickly. More often than not, Heroku error codes in the application logfiles add immensely valuable information to enable effective troubleshooting. Heroku's erosion resistance property helps you run your applications with no downtime coupled with effective use of the resources and transparent scaling of services.

Your window to the running app – the logs

Logs are files on your disk (or data in memory) that apps write to when executing. Writing logfiles is enabled by the use of various logging frameworks in your application (for example, `log4j` for Java) and also the operating system's own system logs that track various system events. Databases, queuing systems, and pretty much every component of the app has logs. Anything your application writes to the standard error or output stream is usually captured in application logs.

Logging is arguably the most widely known resource for troubleshooting applications in any deployment. Logs are more often than not the first and most critical resource used to understand the status of the application when it crashes or starts behaving erratically. Logs are designed to collect information from disparate elements of your application and provide a time ordered view of how an application executes in real time and a log traces the events as they happen.

A little more about Logplex – Heroku's logging system

The Logplex system forms the foundation of the Heroku logging infrastructure. It collates and distributes log messages from the application and other parts of the Heroku infrastructure. The developer can trace the application flow using these log messages and narrow down the scope of the encountered error to a subset of the entire app's code. On the Heroku system, these log entries are made available through a public API and the Heroku command-line tool. Due to the distributed nature of the Heroku platform, trying to manually access log messages across different application components and making sense out of those is practically impossible. You cannot get a unified view of the entire system behavior if you collate these messages manually and try to troubleshoot problems. The Logplex integrated logging system provides a powerful alternative in this case.

Sources and drains

The Logplex system acts like a conduit that routes messages from log entry sources, that is, a producer of the log messages (for example, an application running on the dyno, the Heroku platform itself) to log entry drains, that is, consumers of log messages (for example, archival systems or post processors doing mining of information).

The message limit

The Logplex system does not provide storage for the entire generated log data, but keeps only the most recent data that is good enough to extract relevant information from the application run. Typically, the size of this data is about 1,500 consolidated log messages. If you have a business need to store more than the predefined limit, you would need to choose alternative storage services, for example, syslog drains to archive all messages. Besides, the Heroku add-ons ecosystem allows you to work with more sophisticated logging tools to store, analyze, and create intelligent log-driven apps to alert you in exceptional/error conditions.

Retrieving Heroku logs

Heroku log messages can be reviewed by typing the `heroku logs` command on the prompt (after you have logged in to Heroku). Consider the following code snippet:

```
$ heroku logs
2013-04-26T15:23:21.278990+00:00 app[web.1]: Rendered includes/_header (0.1ms)
2013-04-26T15:23:21.298234+00:00 app[web.1]: Completed in 74ms (View: 31, DB: 40) | 200 OK
[http://xxx.heroku.com/]
2013-04-26T15:13:46.723498+00:00 heroku[router]: at=info method=GET path=/posts
host=xxx.herokuapp.com fwd="x.x.x.x" dyno=web.1 connect=1ms service=18ms status=200 bytes=975
2013-04-26T15:13:47.893472+00:00 app[worker.1]: 2 jobs processed at 16.6761 j/s, 0 failed ...
```

The preceding log output includes log entries from one of the application's web dynos, the Heroku router, and one of the application's worker dynos. The `logs` command retrieves 100 log entries by default.

Getting last 'n' log messages

To retrieve a specific number of log messages, use the `--num` or `-n` command-line option. For example, to retrieve the last 300 lines of log data, type `$ heroku logs -n 300` or `$ heroku logs --num 300`.

Getting live log messages

If you need to observe the live application and troubleshoot issues as they happen, using Heroku's `tail` command is a good idea. The `tail` command provides a real-time view of log messages from the application and helps you get a closer look at events as they occur. To view the log messages as they are generated, type `$ heroku logs --tail` or `$ heroku logs -t`.

[💡 Use *Ctrl* + *C* to terminate the real-time logging trail.]

Some frameworks allow log buffering, that is, collecting a set of log messages before sending it out to a standard output for display. If you don't need this behavior and want to see logs being shown in real time without buffering, you would need to configure your application to disable buffering. Different frameworks have different ways to do it; for example, in Ruby, you need to add the following code snippet to your `config.ru` file to disable buffering and allow logs to show up in real time:

```
$stdout.sync = true
```

Also, it is important to understand that many frameworks have their log messages routed to destinations other than the standard output of their system. In such cases, it is easy to get confused and start looking for log messages where there are none. If you want to change the default behavior, you would need to configure the correct logging destination for your application.

Setting up logging levels

By default, the logging level on the Heroku platform is set to INFO. If you want the DEBUG level logging, you will need to manually set the level to DEBUG as follows:

```
heroku config:add LOG_LEVEL=DEBUG
heroku addons:upgrade logging:expanded
heroku logs --tail
```

Then, run your app and get ready to hit the page with an error. You should be able to see the errors in your console.

Dissecting the Heroku log message

It is important that you understand what each component of the log message means. This will help you narrow down your analysis to the right segment of the log and understand the log message completely and quickly.

The Heroku log message format is as follows:

```
timestamp source [dyno identifier]: log message
```

An example log message is as follows:

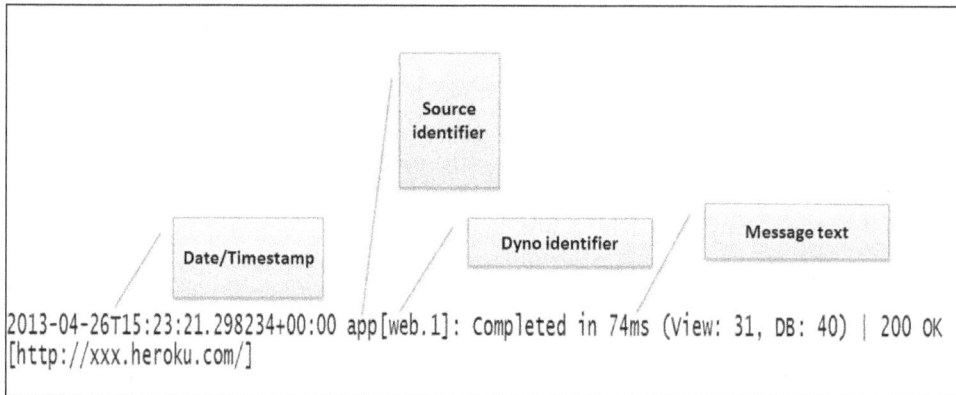

The description of the preceding syntax is as follows:

- The timestamp contains the date and time when the log message was generated by a component. The time shown has microsecond precision.

- The source identifier shows which part of the Heroku infrastructure the log message originates from. It could be the app if it originates from any of the application dynos, or it could be Heroku if it originates from the underlying Heroku infrastructure components such as the Heroku request router.

- The dyno identifier represents the specific dyno name or process that generated this log message.

- The actual log message contains the information written by the application or Heroku or other components of the system. A log message could be up to 1024 bytes in size. Longer messages are truncated.

Log message types

Logs in Heroku can come from many sources in the Heroku platform:

- **Application-generated log messages**: These log messages typically come from within your application and servers, plus libraries used by the application. These are typically the top-level messages and are closer to the user. These types of messages provide high-level information about the code flow of your application.

- **Heroku-generated system logs**: These are messages generated by the Heroku infrastructure. Typically, these messages are about actions taken by the platform on behalf of your application. The types of messages that would be classified under this type are dyno reboot messages or system error messages thrown by the underlying Heroku infrastructure.

- **Application Programming Interface (API) logs**: Log messages under this category include those related to some administrative steps taken by developers while working on the application, for example, deploying an application or scaling the web workers.

Log filters

The Heroku logging system collects and distributes log messages from disparate sources. It provides a unified view of the log events generated in the entire Heroku infrastructure and your application. Often, for troubleshooting issues, only certain types of messages are of importance. In such situations, the log filters provided by the Heroku logging system come to the rescue.

To fetch logs with a specific source or a particular dyno or both, Heroku provides the `--source` (`-s`) and `--ps` (`-p`) filtering arguments.

Examples of log filtering

Let us look at the following few examples of supported log filters in Heroku:

- To extract messages that contain `router` component-related information, type the following command:

```
$ heroku logs --ps router
```

```
2013-05-07T06:12:06.209875+00:00 heroku[router]: at=info
method=GET path=/articles/css/sample.css host=sampleapp.herokuapp.
com fwd="207.207.207.207" dyno=web.2 connect=1ms service=12ms
status=200 bytes=12
```

```
2013-05-07T06:12:06.209875+00:00 heroku[router]: at=info
method=GET path=/articles/install host=sampleapp.herokuapp.
com fwd="207.207.207.207" dyno=web.3 connect=1ms service=12ms
status=200 bytes=1403
```

- To extract messages sent by the `app` source, type the following command:

```
$ heroku logs --source app
```

```
2013-05-07T02:12:47.209875+00:00 app[web.1]: Rendered common/_
search.html.erb (1.0ms)
```

```
2013-05-07T02:12:47.209875+00:00 app[web.1]: Completed 200 OK in
48ms (Views: 23.7ms | ActiveRecord: 24.3ms)
```

```
2013-05-07T02:12:47.209875+00:00 app[worker.1]:
[Worker(host:465bf64e-61c8-46d3-b480-362bfd4ecff9 pid:1)] 1 jobs
processed at 33.0330 j/s, 0 failed ...

2013-05-07T02:13:01.209875+00:00 app[web.6]: Started GET "/
articles/install" for 4.1.81.209 at 2013-05-07 02:13:01 +0000
```

- To extract messages sent by app, but originating from a specific dyno, type the following command:

```
$ heroku logs --source app --ps worker
```

```
2013-05-07T02:13:59.239875+00:00 app[worker.1]:
[Worker(host:260bf64e-61c8-46d3-b480-362bfd4ecff9 pid:1)]
Article#show_results completed after 0.0421

2013-05-07T02:13:59.239875+00:00 app[worker.1]:
[Worker(host:260cf64e-61c8-46d3-b480-362bfd4ecff9 pid:1)] 3 jobs
processed at 21.6842 j/s, 0 failed ...
```

- To get a real-time stream of filtered output, you can use the --tail command-line argument; type the following command:

```
$ heroku logs --source heroku --tail
```

This command will filter messages for the Heroku system and show a continuous stream of system log messages as the application continues to run.

Getting more from logging – other logging tools

Heroku provides a rich set of add-ons for providing advanced log management and analytics services for your app. You could use one or more of the available add-ons and create superior app monitoring capabilities for your app. A few of these services are as follows:

- **Papertrail**: This is a killer real-time log management service that lets you troubleshoot app errors, create monitoring alerts, and track service tickets and lost e-mails. Papertrail provides easy access through command-line tools, the API, or the web browser. It also integrates with powerful tools such as Elastic Mapreduce, S3, and Campire besides having the ability to search an ever increasing database of app alerts and events for deriving critical information about the app.

- **Logentries**: This is another powerhouse log management system that lets users get notified about critical Heroku errors including mobile notifications. Logentries provides visualization for easy debugging of consolidated Heroku logs, pointing specifically at critical errors, besides providing an ability to export/download logs to your own machine.

- **Loggly**: This is a solid online log management service used by over 3,000 customers, that needs no configuration, has a rich REST API for building custom apps based on logging information, and allows searching (including wildcard searches) your entire Heroku deployment for specific issues. Loggly provides awesome application analytic capabilities to measure performance besides having real-time application debugging support to troubleshoot issues as they happen. Through a rich set of tools such as dashboards and charts, Loggly helps you narrow down the erring section of your app quite easily.

- **Flydata**: This is another useful log storage service for your Heroku app that lets you back up your entire Heroku logs to Amazon's S3 storage, at the same time enabling the analysis of log data on Amazon's Redshift platform. It also sends you an e-mail notifying you of the critical Heroku errors it found in your logfiles.

- **Keen IO**: Keen IO is a scalable and analytics-driven platform that provides the ability to track specific events in the lifecycle of your app whether it is the purchase transactions or new user registrations or the critical Heroku errors thrown by your app. Keen IO uses JSON to store your app's event data and provides an extremely user-friendly query API to find the information you need. Keen IO lets you extract and port your app data easily as well as providing embeddable metrics and charts you can see within your app.

> If any of these external tools or services are unable to consume messages generated by Logplex, they can lose some of these messages. However, Logplex does insert a warning entry anytime it has to drop messages due to the consuming service downtime.

Techniques for troubleshooting your app

There are various types of errors you could encounter on the Heroku platform while working on your app. This section describes the different types of issues one could face and how to address them using the available time-tested techniques and tools.

Troubleshooting application downtime

No matter how available your application is, downtime is a reality of production applications. Applications could stop working due to many reasons. You could have a bad design leading to stuck requests or not enough storage, or a slower network leading to poor application performance. Often, it is not that bad and you may have to restart the application to use a new version of your application or a new database. All these situations could lead to application downtime. When the downtime is a planned one, things are better, but what if the downtime is unwarranted and accidental.

As indicated earlier, the errors could be from the application or the Heroku platform underneath. Application-related errors could mean logical or runtime errors in the source code or it could be one of Heroku's platform errors. For the latter case, Heroku error code that appears in the application logs can help you troubleshoot the particular issue. If the logs show one of Heroku's error codes, the error code documentation at `https://devcenter.heroku.com/articles/error-codes` is a very good resource to look at.

Another way to figure out the error is to try replicating the error scenario by restarting the application and running a tail command on it to trace the log messages generated due to continuous user actions on the application in real time.

You can restart the application by typing the following command line:

```
$ heroku restart
```

In general, it makes a lot of sense to review the status of the Heroku environment before deploying your application. You can visit the Heroku status page at `http://status.heroku.com` to get a view of the most recent issues encountered on the production and development environments on Heroku.

The following screenshot shows the Heroku status page that contains information about the various environments and reports about encountered errors:

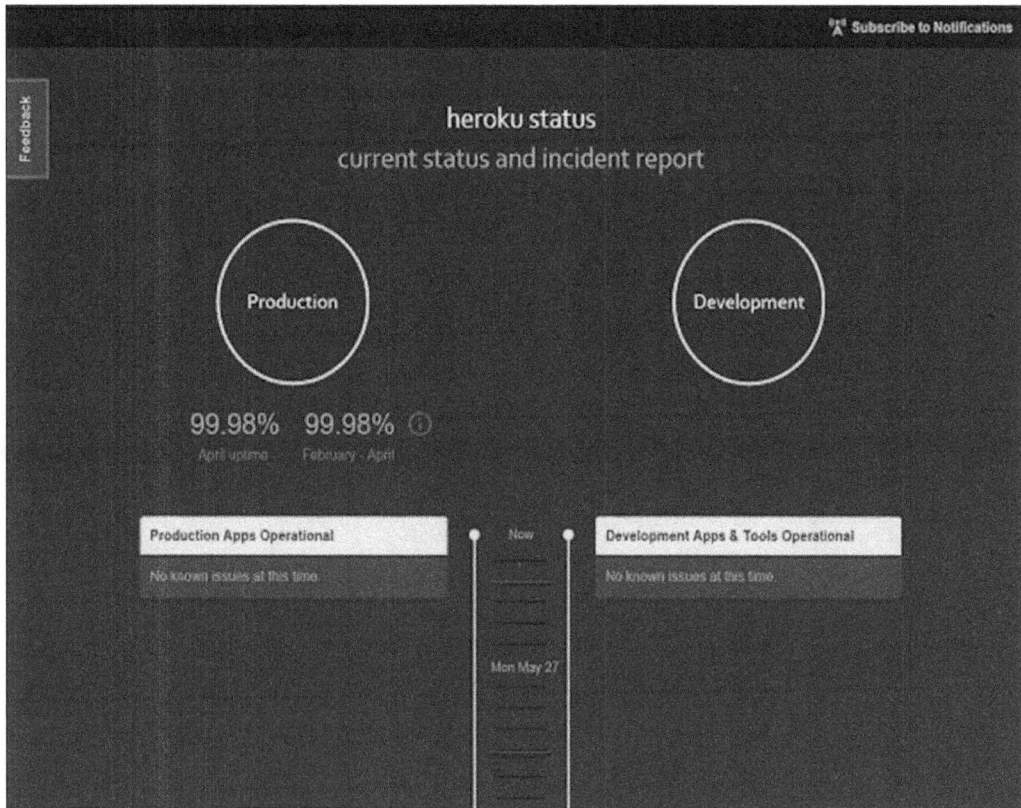

Heroku provides a lot of interesting features that help you limit app downtime during planned maintenance windows:

- Lot of troubleshooting is done for you by the platform itself in situations where manual intervention would have been needed otherwise. For example, unlike most server-based platforms, Heroku's dyno manager keeps your application running irrespective of intermittent failures. Heroku restarts your crashed dynos automatically and ships your dynos to other hosts transparently and instantly whenever a failure in the underlying hardware occurs.

- Heroku internally manages any upgrades or patches required for its operating environment without any impact on the running dynos except for a restart when needed.

- Databases running on the PostgreSQL database are fully managed and monitored by the Heroku platform team and any hardware failures are handled completely by the Heroku's database team. No intervention is required from the application developer.

Debugging HTTP requests and APIs

If you are unable to make HTTP requests to some URL, there can be many reasons for its failure. One easy way to get a detailed view of the HTTP response from the server and why the requested page cannot be served is to use the **hurl** web-based tool. Hurl makes HTTP requests, optionally letting you set header information and gets you the response details. You can use this tool to test even your APIs that make HTTP requests to some server expecting the server to serve some data back.

You can also use **curl**—a command-line tool for the same purpose. Consider the following screenshot:

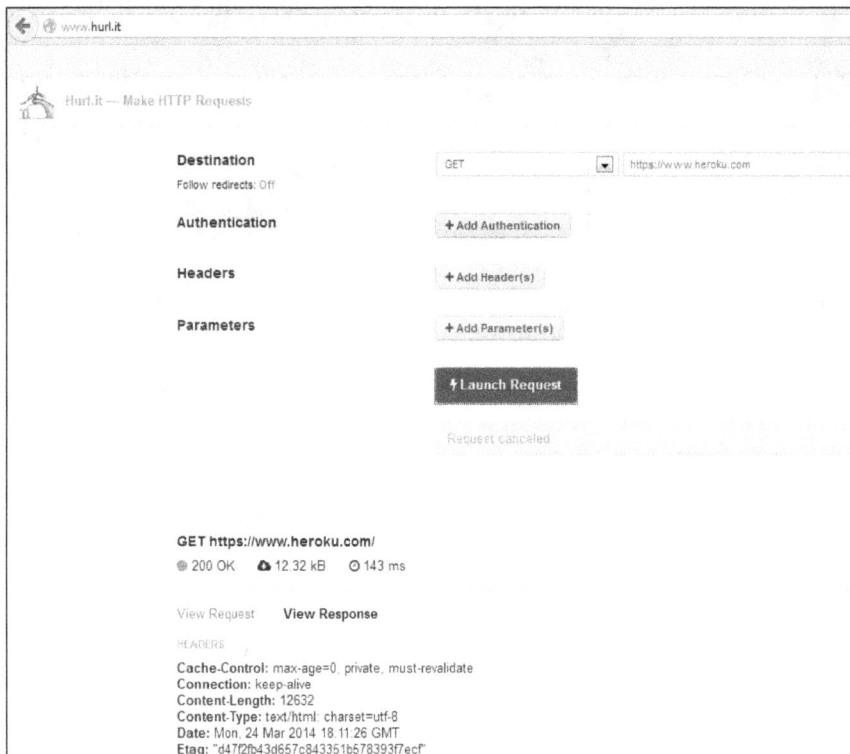

To use curl after you have installed it, type the following command line:

```
$ curl -v http://helloworld.herokuapp.com/
```

In this case, you can easily tell whether the issue is with your application or with your configuration of the custom domain.

There are many other ways to handle erring HTTP requests in Heroku. You can drop long running requests by configuring the timeout for the request or moving them to background jobs, for example, uploading or downloading a large word document or creating multiple queues sitting behind a load balancer where one queue is for slow moving requests and another for fast requests.

Validating your process formation

Sometimes, the application response seems to be very slow due to the existing dynos getting overwhelmed by too many requests. As a result, the requests are queued waiting for dyno time. The problem could be circumvented by adjusting the dyno formation by increasing the dyno count handling your application on the fly by using the following heroku scale command:

```
$ heroku scale web=2
```

This command creates two more instances of the web dyno to handle your additional requests.

Checking your database

If you suspect that the database of your app is the erring party causing the slow response times, you can view the query status for your app using the heroku pg:ps command. This command will list all the queries currently being run against your app database.

If you are encountering memory-related issues, try to find queries that are idle or have the same structure even though they have different where clauses. These queries might be the ones causing the Heroku PostgreSQL out-of-memory error. Examine the query plan for those queries by executing EXPLAIN on the suspected query. If you find that the query is very expensive, that is, it could be doing full table scans or joining multiple tables, you can try to tune it. To get over the existing error and further confirming that the query is indeed the culprit, kill the query using the Heroku Postgres extra command as follows:

```
$ heroku pg:kill <process id>
```

When everything else fails

It is not uncommon to encounter situations when a new release of your application does not work as intended and you want to go back to the previous version as an interim measure. To do it on the fly is another question. Here lies the magic of the `heroku rollback` command. It lets you revert to a previous version of your application.

To check the history of your application releases, you can type the following:

```
$ heroku releases
=== gentle-mesa-5445 Releases
v2   Enable Logplex    ahanjura@gmail.com   2012/12/03 03:39:37
v1   Initial release   ahanjura@gmail.com   2012/12/03 03:39:36
```

You can also issue the following command:

```
$ heroku rollback
Rolling back gentle-mesa-5445... done, v2
 !    Warning: rollback affects code and config vars; it doesn't add or
remove addons. To undo, run: heroku rollback v3
```

Alternatively, you can be specific and issue the following:

```
$ heroku rollback <version name>
```

Production check

Heroku recently introduced the concept of a production check—a live health check for your application. You can use it by logging in to the Heroku dashboard.

Perform the following steps in order to do a production check:

1. Log in to your Heroku account by visiting `https://www.heroku.com`.

2. Click on the specific app you want to run a production check on:

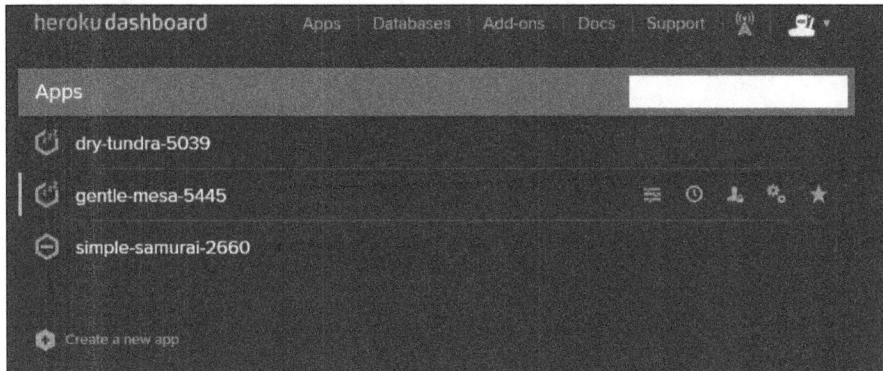

3. Click on the **Run Production Check** link in the top-right corner of the application's dashboard page:

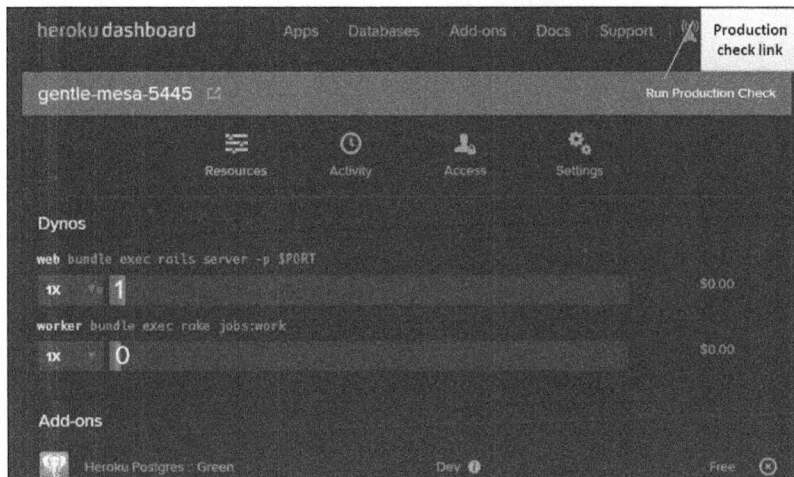

4. Review the current production status of different parts of your app. Clicking on a specific section will provide details about the errors in that component. Consider the following screenshot:

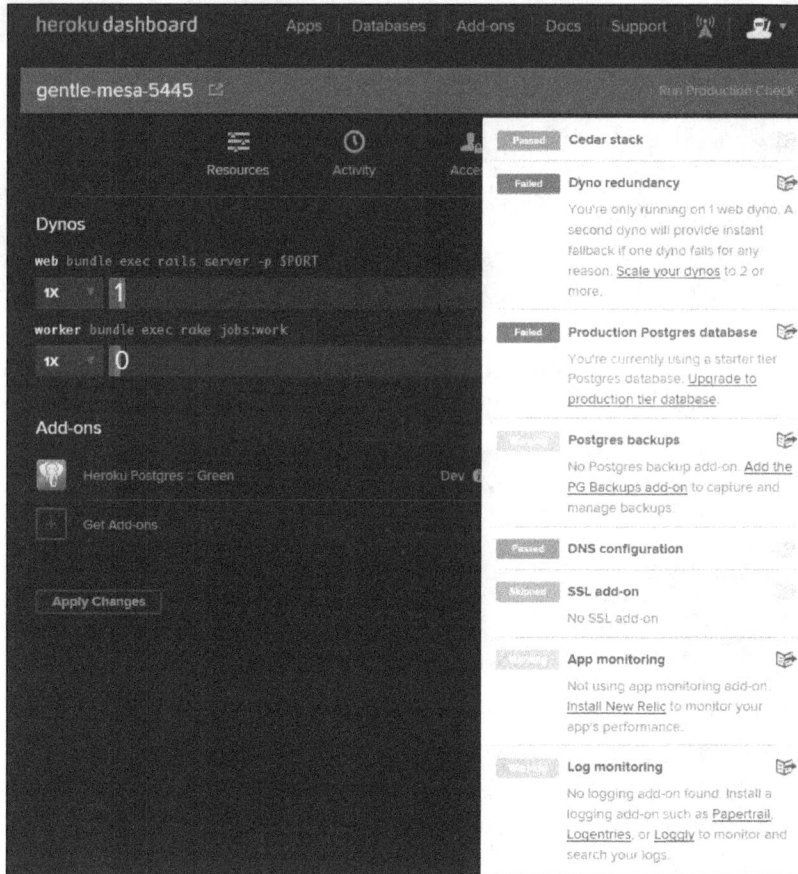

A production check will run a series of tests on the application and indicate the run status for each of the components of your application. Once it points out the failing component, you can isolate the relevant component and delve deeper into the root cause by looking further at the logs and potentially employing other techniques described in this section.

The recently introduced production check feature tests the target application against a set of well defined and highly recommended criteria. This benchmark criteria is chosen by Heroku to ensure high availability for the application. It also validates that you have the necessary software tools at your disposal to monitor the parameters required for system availability. It is recommended that you utilize the production check feature from time to time, for example, when your application user base is expected to rise drastically or you have launched a new product feature that can potentially strain your existing infrastructure as the application starts handling significantly larger volume of requests in the production environment.

Now that we have looked at the available techniques to troubleshoot your apps on the Heroku platform, let us try to understand how to use a Heroku-recommended configuration for running your applications in the most performant, robust, and scalable way.

A recommended Heroku configuration

The stack

The Heroku Cedar stack is the current and most performant Heroku platform stack in place. It is based on Ubuntu 11 as the base operating system and delivers a scalable and highly available, fault-tolerant platform for running your Heroku applications.

If your application runs on older Heroku stacks or you are migrating to Heroku, make sure you are using the Cedar stack for your applications. The link at `https://devcenter.heroku.com/articles/cedar-migration` provides detailed information about how to migrate your app to the Cedar stack to get the best performance and features. If you are running on the older stacks, it makes sense to migrate to the Cedar stack and harness the full power of the Heroku platform.

If you are already on Heroku, you can check the current stack used by your application by logging in to Heroku and going to the specific application folder and typing the following `heroku stack` command. The * indicates the currently used stack.

```
$ heroku stack -a sampleapp
=== sampleapp Available Stacks
  bamboo-mri-1.9.2
  bamboo-ree-1.8.7
* cedar
```

The process formation

You can build availability into your application by running multiple dynos. For example, if you run at least two dynos for your web application, these dynos are likely to be executed on different machines, thereby increasing the redundancy of your mission critical app. It is recommended that you use two or more web dynos for your app to enable continuous availability of services to your users. By running app dynos on different machines, Heroku ensures that at least some dynos are available for servicing user requests when a few dynos encounter issues and have to be restarted. You should also consider scaling your application according to your needs to ensure that your system can keep up with the increased requests during peak times. Having enough redundancy is critical to your system's efficiency in handling requests.

Sometimes, you may want to monitor the running web dynos and see if they are making progress serving user requests. To check the current status of your process formation, use the `heroku ps` command as follows:

```
$ heroku ps -a sampleapp
=== web:
web.1: up for 37m
```

Often, a sudden increase in the user request load can bring disaster to your app if the app doesn't scale automatically due to increased load. For example, imagine running a Heroku-based e-commerce app that sells gifts for friends and family and guess what, you see a sporadic increase in the request volume due to users buying gifts for Christmas. Before the request load hits your app's threshold, you should consider adding additional web processes to handle this potentially large workload. You may need to scale up your background processes and other jobs as well, depending on the current formation running on the platform.

Doing so in Heroku is simple. Type the `heroku ps:scale` command as follows. This command starts 3 more dynos for handling HTTP requests for the app.

```
$ heroku ps:scale web+3
Scaling web processes... done, now running 4
```

Database service

Heroku offers a reliable and powerful database as a service on PostgreSQL. You can use Heroku PostgreSQL for your app's data storage needs in development as well as production environments. For serious production grade applications, you could buy one of the eight available PostgreSQL add-on plans provided on the Heroku platform. Heroku also supports several other data store architectures such as in-memory databases (Memcached), nonrelational data stores (CouchDB), and document-oriented data stores (MongoDB) to provide highly available data storage.

Certain advantages of using Heroku PostgreSQL include:

- Support on multiple hardware and OS platforms.

- A straightforward API to connect from various programming languages and frameworks and the ability to generate configuration strings for these languages automatically.

- Range of available data storage add-on plans — as of today, the entry level production tier plan called Crane provides up to 410 MB RAM, whereas the high-end Mecha plan, suitable for large database deployments, provides up to 16 GB RAM. The current pricing of these production tier plans range from 50$ per month to 6,400$ per month.

- Also, as your application needs increase and you need to support a larger user base, you can scale your PostgreSQL database horizontally by adding read-only followers that stay up to date with the master database. Additionally, some of the advanced PostgreSQL plans provide the following features:
  - Expected uptime of 99.95 percent
  - Connection limit of up to 500 database connections
  - Unlimited rows
  - Daily automatic snapshots with a one month retention check
  - Automated health checks
  - Data clips database followers
  - Database forks
  - Direct `psql`/`libpq` access
  - A fully managed database service
  - Postgres 9.2, unmodified for guaranteed compatibility
  - Postgres extensions (`hstore`)
  - Write-ahead logs backed up every 60 seconds

To add the PostgreSQL add-on to your application, you can type the following:

```
$ heroku addons:add heroku-postgresql
```

To check your current database configuration, use the `heroku pg:info` command as follows. The command displays the plan you have subscribed to, the availability status of the database, the database size and the version of the database besides other details.

```
$ heroku pg:info -a sampleapp
=== HEROKU_POSTGRESQL_RED
Plan:        Ronin
Status:      available
Data Size:   7.3 MB
Tables:      0
PG Version:  9.1.4
Fork/Follow: Available
Created:     2013-05-13 11:23 UTC
Maintenance: not required
```

Domain and security considerations

If you are using custom domain names, you should validate beforehand if the application URL is correctly configured and would resolve to the correct address during the DNS lookup. Often, an incorrect configuration would land you on a "no website found" error page.

Another key aspect of DNS resolution is the fact that if you are using the **Secure Sockets Layer (SSL)** to secure browser communication with the server, your DNS configuration should correctly point the user to the SSL endpoint. On the Heroku platform, the same would look like `endpoint-name.herokussl.com`. You should see an alias mapping `www.sampleapp.com` to either `app-name.herokuapp.com` or `endpoint-name.herokussl.com`.

You should use a standard way to access different types of domains. Bare, root, and naked domains should not be configured using A-records. You should configure your domains appropriately using the CNAME-like functionality or subdomain redirection.

Also, Heroku by default lets the user access any of its sites such as `https://status.heroku.com` using `https` to further secure the communication with your application.

To check if DNS records are properly configured for your application, use the following host command-line utility:

```
$ host www.sampleapp.com

www.sampleapp.com is an alias for dora-1234.herokussl.com.

dora-1234.herokussl.com is an alias for xxxx-xxxx.us-east-1.elb.
amazonaws.com.

xxxx-xxxx.us-east-1.elb.amazonaws.com has address x.x.x.x â€¦
```

The output of this command provides details about our web app's actual server location.

Proactive health monitoring

Designers and users of cloud applications expect failures at some point. Hence, most cloud service providers plan for disaster-like situations upfront when deploying their services. Heroku provides an excellent add-on called New Relic (http://www.newrelic.com) that helps monitor your application's health in a proactive manner. New Relic helps you monitor web/mobile applications and servers with no configuration required. It aids in identifying bottlenecks before they start affecting your application performance negatively. You can take measures and modify your application as required to circumvent these problems.

Heroku recommends that you use this configuration and related tools to reduce the likelihood of problems for your web app.

When your web app starts misbehaving or needs an upgrade due to a new feature being introduced, you might want to redirect your app user to an informational page while you fix the problem or complete the upgrade. This is where custom error pages come in handy, especially during the planned downtime, also called the maintenance window.

Maintenance windows

During application maintenance or migrations, you can display a custom web page to the user of your application. Heroku serves a static page whenever a user tries to access the application during a maintenance window.

Checking the maintenance status

If you need to check the current status of the maintenance window for your application, you can use the `heroku maintenance` command. This command will show the current status of the maintenance window, that is, on if maintenance is in progress and off if the application is running in the regular production/development mode:

```
$ heroku maintenance
Off
```

Enabling the maintenance mode

To enable the maintenance mode for your application, you can use the following command from the Heroku client interface (CLI):

```
$ heroku maintenance:on
Enabling maintenance mode for sampleapp... done
```

Disabling the maintenance mode

To disable the maintenance mode for your application, you can use the following command from the Heroku client interface (CLI):

```
$ heroku maintenance:off
Disabling maintenance mode for sampleapp... done
```

The maintenance window – behind the scenes

During the maintenance window, the web or worker dynos already running on the Heroku platform don't stop. Instead, the HTTP router blocks any requests from reaching these dynos. You can choose to decrease the scale of dynos running on the Heroku platform during the maintenance window since you will not receive many requests anyway. However, be sure to scale back up once the maintenance window is over and the application starts operating at a normal rate.

Customizing site content

To customize the content to be used for display during the maintenance window, you can use the `MAINTENANCE_PAGE_URL` configuration parameter.

For example, to set the maintenance page URL, you can type the following:

```
$ heroku config:set MAINTENANCE_PAGE_URL=http://s3.amazonaws.com/johndoe/
maintenance_pagehtml
```

In the preceding example, johndoe is the specific bucket name of the user owning the storage on AWS.

Customizing error pages

You can also customize the content displayed when your application throws an error. This can be achieved using the ERROR_PAGE_URL configuration parameter.

To set ERROR_PAGE_URL, type the following:

```
$ heroku config:set ERROR_PAGE_URL=http://s3.amazonaws.com/johndoe/error_
page.html
```

You need to make sure the resources (html/images/css/others) you need to use for displaying the page are readable by everyone.

Testing custom maintenance and error pages

To test that the maintenance page works as designed, enable the maintenance mode of the application and then use the following heroku open command:

```
$ heroku maintenance:on

Enabling maintenance mode for sampleapp... done


$ heroku open
```

The custom page will be served and application logs will show the H80 Heroku error code for that web request indicating that a maintenance page was served to the user.

```
$ heroku logs -p router -n 1

2013-05-08T14:44:12-06:03 heroku[router]: at=info code=H80
desc="Maintenance mode" method=GET
```

To test if the error page configuration works, you can create a request for the application that times out. The application returns the H12 request time error. You can check the logs while making this request and the logs will look like the following:

```
$ heroku logs --tail

2013-05-08T18:04:40-07:00 app[web.1]: Sleeping 35 seconds before I serve
this page

2013-05-08T18:05:10-07:00 heroku[router]: at=error code=H12 desc="Request
timeout" method=GET path=/ host=sampleapp.herokuapp.com fwd=X.X.X.X
dyno=web.1 connect=3ms service=30001ms status=503 bytes=0

2013-05-08T18:05:15-07:00 app[web.1]: Done sleeping
```

The custom error page is displayed in your browser. Only system-level errors such as no response or a malformed response result in the display of the Heroku error page described earlier. Application errors will display the application's error page and not the Heroku error page.

When requests time out

One of the reasons for requests timing out is the queuing of client requests for a dyno, resulting in the sequential execution of requests. In this case, any request currently in the queue has to wait for the earlier one currently getting executed to finish. The time taken to execute requests is proportional to the position of the request in the queue. The further away the request, the longer it takes to execute. This scenario is typical of languages that support single-threaded request handling. Such problems could be mitigated (at least to some extent) by doing the following:

- Sharing a dyno between processes. You could use alternative web servers such as Unicorn that help share dyno queues between processes. This helps clear the request backlog quickly and create a better response throughput.

- Running more dyno processes to increase the concurrency. This particularly reduces the likelihood of request queuing as described earlier.

- Tuning your application, especially the areas that take the most time or need synchronization.

Error classification in Heroku

Troubleshooting a distributed application could be a major concern for most developers. Distributed logs, multiple jobs, and more than one user interface can cause sleepless nights for someone trying to troubleshoot an application. So, it becomes very important that the execution environment of your application provides enough clues about the potential cause of an error or fatal situation. Heroku application errors usually appear as error pages for the user when a web request is made. Heroku will return a standard error page with the HTTP status code 503. On top of that, Heroku adds custom error information to the application log.

The Heroku platform uses the following conventions to classify various types of these errors:

Error code prefix	Error type
H	HTTP error
R	Runtime error
L	Logging error

For example, the following is an excerpt from a crashed web process. The error code is indicated in a different shade.

```
2013-03-04T11:25:10-07:00 heroku[web.1]: Process exited
2013-03-04T11:25:12-07:00 heroku[router]: at=error code=H10 desc="App crashed" method=GET
```

Currently supported HTTP errors are shown in the following table:

Error code	Error message	Resolution
H10	App crashed	Troubleshoot and restart.
H11	Backlog too deep	Run more dynos, tune database, or make the code faster.
H12	Request timeout	Set application timer or push long duration jobs to the background.
H13	Connection closed without response	Avoid timeouts.
H14	No web processes running	Boot dynos or scale web process using the heroku ps:scale command.
H15	Idle connection	Usually due to connection inactivity, no particular resolution.
H16	Redirect to herokuapp.com	This is not really an error but an information message indicating that a request made to a Cedar stack application using the old heroku.com domain will get redirected to herokuapp.com.
H17	Poorly formatted HTTP response	No particular resolution. The error indicates an invalid or malformed HTTP response from the dyno handling the request.
H18	Request interrupted	Caused due to either the closure of the client or server socket. No particular resolution except retrying the request.
H19	Backend connection timeout	Usually caused due to more requests made than the dynos can handle. Typically resolved by running more dynos.
H20	App boot timeout	Occurs if web dynos cannot reach a "booted" or "up" state within 75 seconds of request enqueuing by the router. No particular resolution.

Error code	Error message	Resolution
H21	Backend connection refused	Usually a symptom of the app being overwhelmed and unable to accept new connections. Run more dynos.
H22	Connection limit reached	Caused due to a surge in HTTP client connections to the application resulting in an overload. No particular resolution.
H80	Maintenance mode	This is not an error but an indication that the application is running in the maintenance mode.
H99	Platform error	Logged due to an internal Heroku platform error. It can be an intermittent error or a serious issue. Typically resolved by trying again later, checking the Heroku status site for Heroku-wide issues, or raising a ticket with Heroku.

Currently supported runtime errors are shown in the following table:

Error code	Error message	Resolution
R10	Boot timeout	Caused when a web process fails to bind to the designated port. Usually resolved by reducing dependency on external systems or re-engineering code to reduce its size or dependency on time taking computations such as external queries.
R11	Bad bind	Now deprecated. Usually happened when the process tried binding to a non-designated port.
R12	Exit timeout	Occurs when a process doesn't stop after `SIGTERM` is sent to it. Can be resolved by forcibly killing the process using `SIGKILL`.
R13	Attach error	Generated when a process started with `heroku run` fails to attach to the invoking client. Can be resolved by retrying.
R14	Memory quota exceeded	Occurs when a dyno crosses its predesignated limit of 512 MB of memory usage. The application can continue to run, but its performance will degrade over time. Potential resolution is to use 2X memory sized dynos, create more dynos, and share them.
R15	Memory quota vastly exceeded	Results when a dyno uses an excessively large amount of RAM against its allocated 512 MB. Usually ends up killing the erring process. Typical resolution is to reboot multiple dynos to share the request load.

Error code	Error message	Resolution
R16	Detached	Occurs when an attached process continues to run even after being sent SIGHUP when its external connection was closed. If this error occurs and you want the process to exit, you can forcibly clean it.

Currently supported logging errors are shown in the following table:

Error code	Error message	Resolution
L10	Drain buffer overflow	A surge in log messages generated by dynos, resulting in the Logplex system dropping some of them to keep up. Resolution could be code instrumentation to reduce emitted number of log messages or fixing a buggy loop, for example.
L11	Tail buffer overflow	Similar to the preceding error, the difference being that the tail session being run by you is unable to keep up with the volume of logs generated by the application. You may need to reduce the logging volume emitted by the application or get a better bandwidth to accept more log messages in the same time delta.

> You can refer to a detailed description for each of the error codes at
> `https://devcenter.heroku.com/articles/error-codes`.

Summary

In this chapter, we reviewed various ways of troubleshooting Heroku applications. We looked at how logging works in Heroku and how to leverage the Heroku CLI utility to review application logs and troubleshoot specific problems. We also reviewed the available techniques to troubleshoot app downtime, debug HTTP requests, and process the formation of your app. We also found how you could roll back your app to a prior working condition when every other troubleshooting technique fails. We discovered a recommended app configuration that helps the app avoid errors and downtime. We learned how to handle maintenance windows and avoid timeouts. Finally, we delved deep into Heroku's error code system—the error-naming convention and the error code catalog of Heroku.

In the next chapter, we will learn the advanced features of the Heroku platform and how to leverage those features to build and deploy feature rich, performant, scalable, and production-ready web apps.

10
Advanced Heroku Usage

We are at the end of our journey with Heroku. In this book, we have learned that Heroku is fun and easy to work with. Through this journey, we have learned how to build, deploy, and troubleshoot Heroku apps using a wide variety of available add-ons and tools. Our focus was on the Heroku platform, that is, what it offers to developers in terms of services, and how developers can leverage the services and roll out apps built on top of the Heroku stack. During our journey, we also learned about how the Heroku platform is secured for developers to build reliable apps for the end user. By demonstrating various techniques, we also learned how to use the Heroku platform more effectively, be it the configuration of DNS for your app, usage of 2X dyno configurations, or setting up and managing data stores such as Heroku PostgreSQL.

In this chapter, we will look at some useful and advanced aspects of the Heroku platform:

- We review some really useful experimental features provided by Heroku Labs, specifically for building, deploying, and monitoring your app.

- We will go through a primer on the Websockets technology and its use in Heroku that helps developers build high-performance real-time web apps

- We will learn how to leverage the Heroku Platform API to programmatically perform any app-related operation on the Heroku environment, a feature that helps you build and sell services built on top of the Heroku cloud environment

- Finally, we will learn an often ignored yet very important aspect of cloud based app development, that is, collaborative development, and understand how to share your app with others for higher productivity

So, let's get started.

Experimenting with Heroku Labs

While we have focused on various key features of the Heroku platform in earlier chapters, we still have a very powerful aspect of the Heroku platform to uncover: the Heroku Labs. As the name suggests, Heroku Labs is an experimental environment - an advanced computing environment for researching and experimenting with potential features being considered for the Heroku feature set.

Heroku Labs provides an open ground for you to experiment with new capabilities and also test alternatives built to address fixes to the known limitations on the Heroku platform. For example, Heroku recently started supporting Websockets on Heroku (currently this feature is in public beta) for building performant real-time web apps on the Heroku platform. This is a completely new capability for the Heroku platform.

Earlier in this book, we learned and experimented with the currently available feature set of the Heroku platform. In this section, we will take a step further and look at the Heroku Labs offerings. You can try these features with your app and build faster, portable, and well behaved real-time web apps.

Using Heroku Labs features

Heroku Labs is an advanced experimental environment that provides a bunch of useful features for developers to experiment with. In this section, we explore some of the prominent features available in the Heroku Labs environment that come in handy while developing or maintaining web apps on the Heroku platform.

Seamless deployment using pipelines

Most operations teams have mastered the art of creating a step-by-step code promotion methodology to facilitate appropriate levels of testing before the software is exposed to the end users in production. The usual process flow is that developer's code is promoted to the quality testbed where it is built and tested and from there the product is promoted to user acceptance and customer acceptance before reaching the end users. Most delivery workflows are a minor variation of this process flow. However, most teams still find it quite difficult to create a consistent deployment workflow between these environments.

More often than not, application owners have to manually manage all the important workflows and ensure that only the desired components or modules are promoted along the delivery pipeline. As soon as we create a dependency on manual intervention for these deployment processes, we make the code promotion process vulnerable to human errors such as pushing the wrong code or promoting the code to the wrong test bed. This isn't just an overhead for the operations team, but it is also a bottleneck for the goal of providing the ability of continuous and seamless deployment of your web application software.

Heroku Labs offers a key experimental feature to circumvent a large chunk of these issues. This feature called **pipelines** helps you define the rules of the deployment workflow that is, with this feature, you can define your app deployment guidelines or rules. The Heroku pipelines feature carries out your app deployment instructions automatically, thereby reducing the probability of most common human errors. Pipelines help you dictate the rules for moving your code from one environment to another.

Some common use case scenarios appropriate for the use of Heroku pipelines are as follows:

1. The **Operations (OPS)** team promoting code from a single test environment to another.

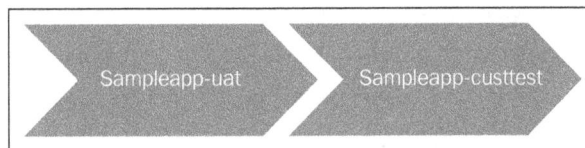

   In this case, the OPS team promotes the **sampleapp-uat** (user acceptance test) code to the **sampleapp-custtest** (customer test bed) environment through a pipeline. In this example, the **custtest** environment is considered as the downstream end of the **uat** environment.

2. Code changes from multiple developers get merged and are promoted to the **quality assurance (QA)** environment.

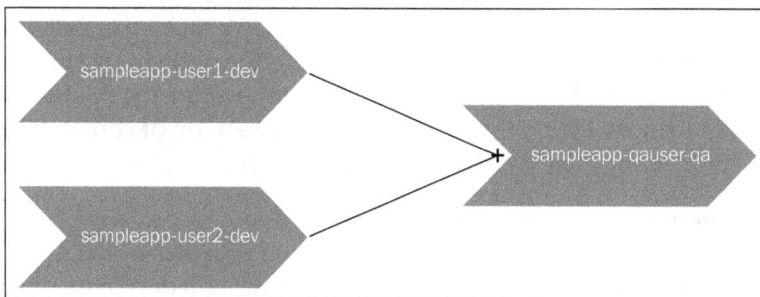

Here, the ops team promotes code from two development environments to the QA environment. In this example, the **qauser-qa** environment is considered to be the downstream of the **user1-dev** and **user2-dev** environments.

Enabling the pipelines feature

Using the pipelines feature of Heroku Labs is straightforward:

1. Enable the Pipelines feature using the `labs:enable` command as follows:

   ```
   $ heroku labs:enable pipelines

   Enabling pipelines for name@company.com... done

   WARNING: This feature is experimental and may change or be
   removed without notice....
   ```

   > For more information, see `https://devcenter.heroku.com/articles/using-pipelines-to-deploy-between-applications`.

2. Install the Heroku CLI plugin for pipelines as shown in the following command:

   ```
   $ heroku plugins:install git://github.com/heroku/heroku-pipeline.git
   ```

3. Use the `heroku pipeline:add` command to associate a downstream application with your current application:

   ```
   $ heroku pipeline:add sampleapp-custtest

   Added downstream app: sampleapp-custtest
   ```

   In this example, `sampleapp` is the downstream application associated with your current application.

4. To check the downstream application for your current application, use the `heroku pipeline` command:

```
$ heroku pipeline

Pipeline: sampleapp-uat ---> sampleapp-custtest
```

In this example, `sampleapp-uat` has the downstream application `sampleapp-custtest` associated with it.

5. Once the pipeline has been defined, you can use the `pipeline:promote` command to execute the code promotion instructions and copy your application's slug to the defined downstream application as a new version or release using the following command:

```
$ heroku pipeline:promote

Promoting sampleapp-uat to sampleapp-custtest...done, v3
```

6. You can find the difference between the upstream and downstream applications by using the `heroku pipeline:diff` command as follows:

```
$ heroku pipeline:diff

Comparing sampleapp-uat to sampleapp-custtest...done,
sampleapp-uat ahead by 1 commit:

31cd650  2013-11-27  Fixed overflow condition  (user1)
```

> Using the Pipelines feature does not imply the automatic promotion of your Git repo, configuration variables, installed add-ons, and environment-related dependencies. These aspects of your web app need to be managed separately from the promotion of your code.

Performance monitoring

Heroku is awesome. Not only does it let you build, deploy, and troubleshoot your apps with utmost ease, it also provides you with tools that you can enable (for example, Heroku Labs features) or configure (add-ons) and then utilize the new capability instantly. One of the key abilities you would need to work with your web app is the ability to monitor the performance of your web dynos. As a developer, you need to know how well your web dynos are performing. What are the bottlenecks - increased CPU load, very high memory usage, or something else.

Heroku Labs provides an experimental feature called **log runtime metrics** that does just that; it lets you measure the CPU and memory (real and swap) for your web app's dynos.

Once you enable the feature, the data about memory and swap use besides the CPU load of the dyno is emitted into the application's log stream. Metrics are logged optimally every 20 seconds.

You can use the Heroku logs command to review these statistics or feed the log to an add-on that can consume logs.

Switching on monitoring

You can start using the log runtime metrics feature by using the `heroku labs:enable` command as follows:

```
$ heroku labs:enable log-runtime-metrics

Enabling log-runtime-metrics for sampleapp... done
```

Once you enable the feature, run the `heroku restart` command as shown in the following command-line to activate it for your apps:

```
$ heroku restart
```

Log snapshot

The following diagram shows the format of the generated log metrics describing various parts of the message:

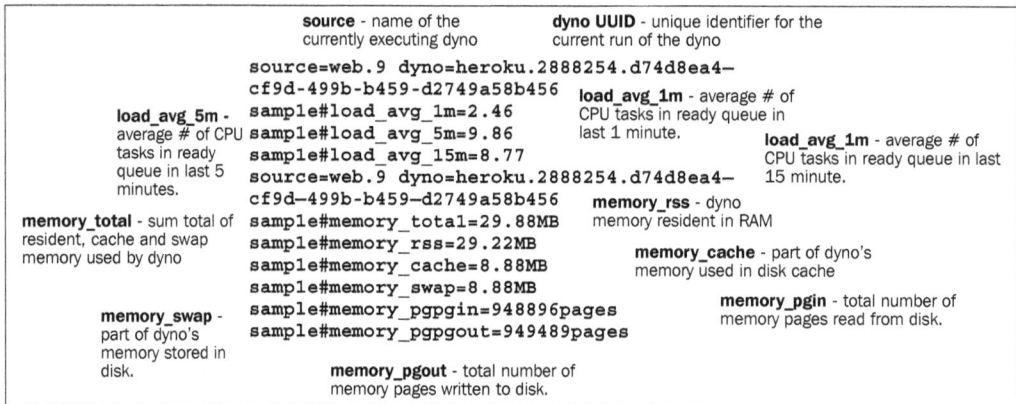

Dynos do not consider tasks blocked on I/O operations when calculating load averages. The article http://www.linuxjournal.com/article/9001 provides an overview of the concept of load averages.

Watching your app closely using the Request ID

Given the size and complexity of modern day web applications, logging plays an important part in troubleshooting issues encountered during the handling of your client requests. Even then, you might find it hard to locate the specific thread that got blocked or terminated due to an error somewhere in the system. Troubleshooting such an issue can often be a bother. Fortunately, Heroku Labs provides a really useful feature that allows you to correlate log events at the router level with the log events at the web dyno level. This feature, called **Request ID**, is an experimental feature that helps you trace your web request to the web dyno log and understand the root cause of runtime issues.

Supporting the Request ID

Heroku supports the concept of Request ID by providing an additional functionality at the Heroku router level. Whenever a web request comes to the Heroku router, the router generates a unique request identifier — the request_id — and associates it with the incoming request. This request_id is logged in the router logs, and the router stores it in the HTTP header before sending the HTTP request to the web dyno. The field request_id in the HTTP header can be retrieved by the application and logged for tracking the specific web request.

You can enable this feature by using the `labs:enable` command as follows:

```
$ heroku labs:enable http-request-id

Enabling http-request-id for sampleapp... done
```

Once this feature is enabled, your router log will create a unique request ID and attach the identifier with the web request before forwarding it:

```
2013-12-10T07:53:10+00:00 heroku[router]: at=info method=GET path=/
host=sampleapp.herokuapp.com
request_id=6d1410f3cfc85a8af9bac12bfd0930e3 fwd="209.87.1.23"
dyno=web.3 connect=0ms service=47ms status=200 bytes=1132
```

With access to the request ID field, troubleshooting a web request becomes much easier. All you have to do is the following:

1. Look up the router log and locate the specific error (H13) and the request ID (6d1410f3cfc85a8af9bac12bfd0930e3), for example:

   ```
   2013-12-16T11:25:12-03:00 heroku[router]: at=error code=H13
   desc="Connection closed without response" method=GET path=/
   host=sampleapp.herokuapp.com
   request_id=6d1410f3cfc85a8af9bac12bfd0930e3 fwd="209.87.1.23"
   dyno=web.1 connect=1234ms service=4567ms status=503 bytes=0
   ```

2. Look up the web dyno logs and search for the specific request ID you retrieved in the first step:

```
2013-12-16T11:25:12-03:00 heroku[web.1]:
request_id=6d1410f3cfc85a8af9bac12bfd0930e3
```

```
2013-12-16T11:25:12-03:00 heroku[web.1]: /lib/fft/calc.rb:27:
[BUG] Segmentation fault
```

As you can see, there was a segmentation fault at line 27 in the `calc.rb` file. You can now easily refer to the specific source code and investigate the possible reasons for the error.

Introducing Websockets

The **Websocket (WS)** protocol is a new protocol that supports a bidirectional channel for communication between a server and a client. This protocol overcomes several serious shortcomings of the earlier HTTP communication method. It includes a full duplex, bidirectional communication channel between a server and client over TCP. The RFC 6455 (`http://tools.ietf.org/html/rfc6455`) provides a detailed specification of this protocol. The Websocket protocol was standardized about two years ago by **Internet Engineering Task Force (IETF)** and since then has found several uses in real-time web apps (games, real-time chat, and more).

Websocket versus HTTP

The Websocket protocol also has some distinct advantages over HTTP, especially when it comes to bidirectional notifications between the server and the client. Once the Websocket connection is established between the client and host server, data can flow in both directions simultaneously over TCP. This circumvents the communication techniques that are employed using HTTP for simulating real-time event notifications, be it polling, long polling, or comet. These old techniques bore a large overhead. This is because for smaller HTTP requests, the overhead of using HTTP seemed to cause unnecessary performance concerns as compared to using Websockets, where the overhead might be just a few bytes per frame. The Websocket protocol is an ideal candidate for low-latency real-time web apps.

Websocket is not HTTP

The Websocket protocol is a lightweight protocol layered on top of TCP directly. Other than the fact that HTTP helps set up a Websocket connection by an HTTP upgrade request (generic upgrade, not specific to Websockets), HTTP and Websockets are two completely different protocols.

Websocket use cases

One could broadly classify most of the use cases for Websockets into the following categories:

- Real-time push notification
- Real-time interactive user experience
- Server-sent events

Typical apps using Websockets

Some of the common applications using Websockets are as follows:

- Multiplayer games
- Collaborative editing of documents / source code
- Social feeds
- Online multimedia chat
- Real-time financial data (for example, stock tickers)
- Location-based apps

Supporting Websockets in your app

If you find a web application where you could use Websockets, the first question to ask may be this: can I use Websockets with my desktop or mobile device browser? The following website provides a compatibility matrix for various browsers that support / don't support the Websocket protocol at this point in time:

```
http://caniuse.com/Websockets
```

Establishing a Websocket connection

To establish a Websocket connection, a client can initiate a client handshake request. An HTTP upgrade request is used to initiate a Websocket connection as shown in the following example:

```
GET /chat HTTP/1.1
HOST: server.sampleapp.com
Upgrade: websocket
Connection: Upgrade
Sec-WebSocket-Key: gRfTgYJhYRBGfDRHJuYKW==
```

```
Origin: http://sampleapp.com
Sec-WebSocket-Protocol: chat, superchat
Sec-WebSocket-Version: 13
```

If the server accepts the request (otherwise, an HTTP 500 is sent back), the server handshake will be returned as follows:

```
HTTP/1.1 101 Switching Protocols
Upgrade: websocket
Connection: Upgrade
Sec-WebSocket-Accept: j8pUytRNy8UyUjILoHrTHjLo+xOo=
```

On a successful handshake between the client and server, the TCP connection used to create the initial HTTP request is upgraded to a Websocket connection. Both the server and client can now send messages simultaneously.

Disadvantages of using Websockets

While Websockets are really suited for real-time, bidirectional event notifications between the client and the host, it too has its own disadvantages. Since Websockets require a persistent connection between the client and the server and the server needs to manage some sort of a state, the protocol consumes a lot of resources. However, for the type of apps we just saw, the gains far outweigh the pains. Also, the older HTTP and more recent REST APIs do have their own credibility in specific use cases for web communication; they should be considered while deciding on the desired mode of communication between your server and client.

Heroku and Websockets

Heroku provides Websocket support to the `herokuapp.com` domain, custom domains, and custom SSL endpoints through the experimental Heroku Labs Websockets feature.

One major caveat though is that to provision custom SSL endpoints with Websocket support, the Websockets feature should be enabled *before* the endpoint is provisioned. If you enable the Websockets feature for an app with an existing custom SSL endpoint, Heroku throws an error about the SSL endpoint being in use as shown in the following command line:

```
$ heroku labs:enable Websockets
Enabling Websockets for sampleapp... failed
!    Can not add Websockets feature when ssl-endpoint is in use.
```

The right way of working with existing SSL endpoints is to remove them first using the `heroku addons:remove ssl:endpoint` command, add the Websockets support for the app and then provision the SSL endpoint back again. It goes without saying that you will need to update the DNS records for related custom domains to point to the new hostname derived during the endpoint provisioning process.

Switching on Websocket support

Heroku lets you use the experimental Websocket support using the `labs:enable` command on the Heroku CLI. To enable Websocket support for your application, type the following command:

```
$ heroku labs:enable Websockets -a sampleapp

Enabling Websockets for sampleapp... done

WARNING: This feature is experimental and may change or be removed
without notice.
```

Once the feature is enabled for your application, the DNS record for your `herokuapp.com` domain is automatically updated to point to a Websocket-capable endpoint. When it comes to the use of custom domains, they should be configured correctly to ensure there is consistent Websocket support on all related domains.

Turning Websockets off

Disabling Websocket support for your Heroku app is straightforward. Just use the `labs:disable` command as follows to discontinue supporting Websockets:

```
$ heroku labs:disable websockets -a sampleapp

Disabling websockets for sampleapp... done
```

The Websockets example

The following Websockets example shows minimal client and server code written in JavaScript. In the code, a simple timer application opens the Websocket to the server and receives a timestamp from the server every second, which is then displayed on the page.

The server code

The server is written in server-side JavaScript as a Node.js application. In this application, when the server connects to a client, it creates a method that runs every 10,000 ms, sending a timestamp to the browser over the Websocket as shown in the following screenshot:

```
1  var server = http.createServer(timerapp);
2  server.listen(port);
3
4  var wsserver = new WebSocketServer({server: server});
5  console.log('websocket server created');
6  wsserver.on('connection', function(ws) {
7    var id = setInterval(function() {
8      ws.send(JSON.stringify(new Date()), function() { });
9    }, 10000);
10
11    console.log('websocket connectio
12
13    ws.on('close', function() {
14      console.log                      ction close');
15      clearInterval(id);
16    });
17  });
18
19
```

The client code

Assuming that the browser supports the Websockets feature, the client establishes a connection with the server. The following client code written in JavaScript parses the server event and appends it to a HTML list element which is then displayed on the browser:

```
1
2                                           Use ws instead of http
        Create a websocket
             client
3   var host = location.origin.replace(/^http/, 'ws')
4   var wsc = new WebSocket(host);
                                            Create a list HTML
5   wsc.onmessage = function (event) {        element

6     var li = ent.createElement('li');    Parse event
        Append each                         received from
7     li.inner timestamp to JSON.parse(event.data);  server
        the HTML list
8     document.querySelector('#pings').appendChild(li);
9   };
10
11
```

The client and server example is just a plain vanilla example of what the usage of Websockets API looks like. You can use these examples as the foundation for developing more complex use cases.

This completes our review of some of the prominent Heroku Labs features. Next, we will look at the Heroku Platform API—a powerful way to build, deploy, and manage a Heroku app programmatically. For a brief overview of the Heroku Platform API, please refer to *Chapter 2, Inside Heroku*. In the current chapter, we will understand the facilities available in the Heroku platform API to write and maintain Heroku apps. We will also review a few samples of how a developer can call the platform API to perform various operations related to the Heroku web application.

Your first Heroku Platform API call

Several client libraries are already available for making Heroku Platform API calls. Heroku natively supports the Heroics client library for Ruby. At the time of writing this text, there are client libraries available for Node.js, Scale, and Go.

Since the API clients use HTTP for interacting with the Heroku Platform API, all we need to create API support for a new programming language is an HTTP library with the required methods to send and receive requests to or from the platform API. Alternatively, we can use the curl tool to demonstrate the usage of the platform API. Armed with a Heroku account and an installed version of the curl tool, we will now experiment with a sample set of Heroku Platform APIs and show how one can easily and intuitively build Heroku apps programmatically. This is the third way of creating Heroku apps besides the Heroku CLI and the Heroku dashboard.

Before we get started

Well, before you can access the platform API, your client should be authenticated. The authentication token is then used in the future calls made to the platform to verify the client's access.

The API key is available in the **Account** section of your Heroku dashboard. You can also use the `heroku auth:token` command to retrieve this token:

```
$ heoku auth:token
0123456-89ab-cdef-0123-456789abcdef
```

You can also derive the authorization key from this command for a script by accessing the key using the `heroku auth:token` command and converting it to a base-64 value. If you use curl along with the Heroku toolbelt, curl can handle authentication details by reading the `netrc` file.

Supported API methods

The client can access several Heroku Platform API methods to manipulate the app depending on the needs of the caller. The list of methods available for the client is shown in the following table:

Method	Purpose
POST	Creates new objects
GET	Retrieves an object or a list of objects
PUT	Replaces existing objects
DELETE	Deletes existing objects
HEAD	Retrieves metadata about existing objects
PATCH	Updates existing objects

If the client doesn't support a particular method, it can override the request header by using the POST method and set the X-Http-Method-Override header to the intended method. For example, to perform a PATCH invocation, the client can perform a POST invocation with the Http-Method-Header set to PATCH in the client request.

Sample uses of the platform API

You can do pretty much everything that you can with the Heroku CLI or the dashboard by using the platform API. The key advantage of using the platform API is that it allows the developer to have complete control over the entire lifecycle of the Heroku app. Developers can perform any app-related operation from the comfort of the code snippet.

In the following examples, we will create an application, list information about the app, update the app information, and finally delete the application using the platform API. In the process, we will review the typical request and response content of the platform API's call. We will use the curl tool to demonstrate the use of the Heroku Platform API in these examples.

Creating an application

To create a Heroku app, use the following `curl` command. The following diagram shows different components of the `curl` command that are required to create an app:

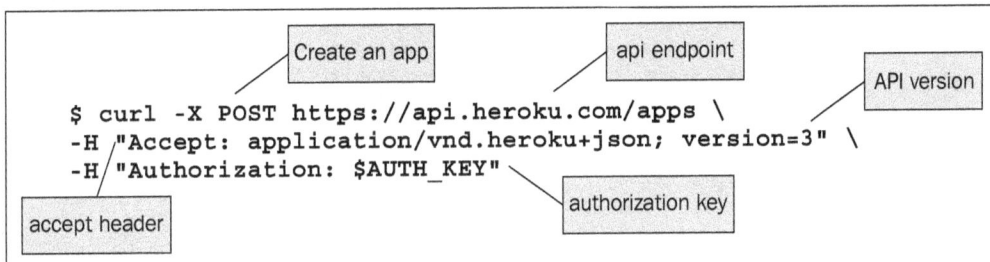

Create an application API response

On successful completion of an action, the platform API returns a JSON response with the details of the newly created Heroku app as follows:

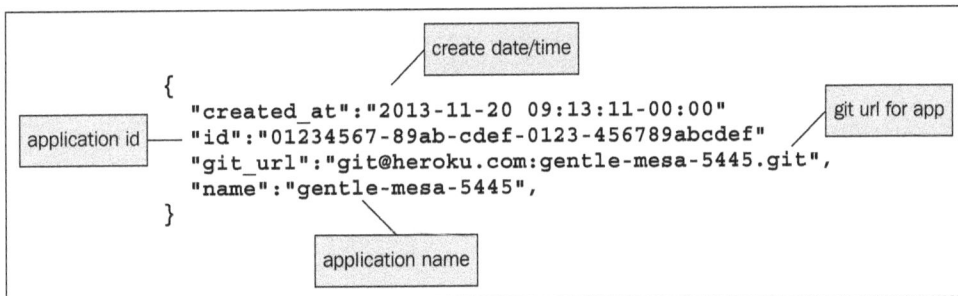

Retrieving application information

The API request passes the application ID to the API endpoint along with the GET command to retrieve further details about the application:

```
                           ┌──────────────┐                    ┌────────────────┐
                           │ API Command  │                    │ application id │
                           └──────────────┘                    └────────────────┘
$ curl -X GET https://api.heroku.com/apps/01234567-89ab-
cdef-0123-456789abcdef \
-H "Accept: application/vnd.heroku+json; version=3" \
-H "Authorization: $AUTH_KEY"
```

The API response includes all details of the application as follows:

```
HTTP/1.1 200 OK
ETag: "0123456789abcdef0123456789abcdef"
Last-Modified: Sun, 02 Dec 2012 12:00:00 GMT
RateLimit-Remaining: 1200

{
  "archived_at": "2012-12-02T12:00:00z",
  "buildpack_provided_description": "Ruby/Rack",     ┌────────────────┐
  "created_at": "2012-12-02T12:00:00z",              │ build pack used │
  "git_url": "git@heroku.com/someapp.git",           └────────────────┘
  "1d": "01234567-89ab-cdef-0123-456789abcdef",
  "maintenance": false,
  "name" : "someapp",
  "owner": {                                          ┌───────────────────┐
    "email": "username@someapp.com",                  │ app owner details │
    "id": "01234567-89ab-cdef-0123-456789abcdef"      └───────────────────┘
  },
  "region": {
    "id": "01234567-89ab-cdef-0123-456789abcdef",
    "name": "us"
  },
  "released_at": "2012-12-02T12:00:00Z",
  "repo_size": 0,
  "slug_size": 0,              ┌────────────┐
  "stack": {                   │ stack used │
    "id": "01234567-89ab-cdef-0123-45678
    "name": "cedar"
  },
  "updated_at": "2012-12-02T12:00:00z",
  "web_url": "http://someapp.herokuapp.com"
}
```

Labels pointing to the response:
- git url of the app
- region details for app
- web url of the app

Modifying application information

You can change the properties of an application, including the name, by using the `PATCH` command. Pass the application ID to the API endpoint and specify the new name, API version, and the content type.

You can issue the following `curl` command to update the Heroku app name:

```
$ curl -X PATCH https://api.heroku.com/apps/01234567-89ab-
cdef-0123-456789abcdef \
-H "Accept: application/vnd.heroku+json; version=3" \
-H "Authorization: $AUTH_KEY"
-H "Content-Type: application/json".\
-d "{\"name\":\"sampleapp-012014\"}"
```

Labels: API method for updating app; application id; API version; Specify content type; newapp name

The API response to the `update` command will be similar to the JSON response of the `GET` call as follows:

```
HTTP/1.1 200 OK
ETag: "0123456789abcdef0123456789abcdef"
Last-Modified: Sun, 02 Dec 2012 12:00:00 GMT
RateLimit-Remaining: 1200

{
    "archived_at": "2012-12-02T12:00:00z",
    "buildpack_provided_description": "Ruby/Rack",
    "created_at": "2012-12-02T12:00:00z",
    "git_url": "git@heroku.com/sampleapp-012014.git",
    "ld": "01234567-89ab-cdef-0123-456789abcdef",
    "maintenance": false,
    "name" : "sampleapp-01234",
    "owner": {
        "email": "username@sampleapp-012014.com",
        "id": "01234567-89ab-cdef-0123-456789abcdef"
    },
    "region": {
        "id": "01234567-89ab-cdef-0123-456789abcdef",
        "name": "us"
    },
    "released_at": "2012-12-02T12:00:00Z",
    "repo_size": 0,
    "slug_size": 0,
    "stack": {
        "id": "01234567-89ab-cdef-0123-456789abcdef",
        "name": "cedar"
    },
    "updated_at": "2012-12-02T12:00:00z",
    "web_url": "http://sampleapp-012014.herokuapp.com"
}
```

Labels: application new name; application owner details; region details; application's new URL

Deleting an application

You can delete a Heroku app using the `DELETE API` command, passing the application ID as a parameter.

The following figure shows the `curl` command to delete an app. You need to pass the application ID (or name) to the API endpoint besides using the `DELETE` command to delete the app:

```
┌────────────────────────┐                    ┌──────────────────┐
│ DELETE command for app │                    │ application id   │
└────────────────────────┘                    └──────────────────┘
            /                                          /

$ curl -X DELETE https://api.heroku.com/apps/01234567-89ab-cdef-0123-456789abcdef \
-H "Accept: application/vnd.heroku+json; version=3" \
-H "Authorization: $AUTH_KEY"
```

Interpreting an API response

Successful Heroku Platform API responses could be categorized based on their status as per the following table:

Status	Meaning
200 OK	API request is successful
201 Created	API request resulted in a resource getting created or a new resource getting added to the app (for add-on provisioning)
202 Accepted	API request is accepted by the platform but processing is not completed yet
206 Partial Content	API request is successful but the response received is only part of the entire response or part of a range of the overall response expected

The platform API could respond to the client with an error if something goes wrong during server processing; alternatively, the client request itself can be erroneous and should be corrected before sending the request again. Hence, the erroneous responses are classified on the basis of whether it is a client-related error or a server-related one.

Error operations

Client-related error responses are usually a result of malformed or inadequate client requests. It could be an invalid request or an unauthorized one. The client error response could occur as a result of some action needed related to the account involved or the requested resource being nonexistent. The parameters could be invalid, or the account might need verification before issuing the API call. The reasons could be many, but it helps to check a few things to make sure that errors are minimized:

- Ensure that billing information is entered for the account, so that Heroku can keep a record of API usage.
- Provide the correct form of the API request.

Server-related error responses are only of two types: either an internal error (HTTP 500) or a service unavailable error (HTTP 503).

Error format

When the platform API request for a particular resource fails and the response returns with a failed status, the returned JSON body contains more details about the error. The response contains a unique identifier or ID for the error and a corresponding message in the message field. The message field helps the calling entity or client understand the root cause of the failed request.

The format of the received error response is shown in the following table:

Name	Type	Description
ID	String	Unique identifier for the error
Message	String	Detailed error message text for the end user

An example error response

Whenever a client issues more than its limit of API requests, the platform API returns a response indicating that the client has exceeded the API rate limit. This might require the client to wait for some time to reissue a request or modify the billing plan to buy a larger API limit. Whatever the client chooses, the client can issue a request only when either the API limit is restored or increased.

For example, the following response is issued from the platform API for exceeding API access limit:

```
{
  "id":        "rate_limit",
  "message":   "Your account reached the API rate limit\nPlease
    wait a few minutes before making new requests"
}
```

Warnings

When the platform API call results in warnings, the API response add header contains the detailed description of the warning to help the client take appropriate action when sending further requests. The add header contains the ID field and the corresponding description of the unique warning identifier.

Sharing your app on Heroku

One of the driving factors for the popularity and success of many technologies today is the concept of social or collaborative development. This spans not just the ability to cowrite applications, but also the opportunity to co-maintain and upgrade them. Heroku believes in the philosophy of social collaboration to build really bug free and maintainable web applications. Heroku provides the facility to collaborate and share your applications with other users who can do pretty much everything that the owner of the application can.

Prerequisites for collaboration

You can add other users as collaborators for your application in the following two ways:

- Heroku dashboard
- The Heroku CLI

The prerequisites for sharing your app include having a Heroku account and the Heroku toolbelt (`http://toolbelt.heroku.com`). Installing the Heroku toolbelt provides you with access to the Heroku CLI and Git revision control system.

Adding app collaborators to the Heroku dashboard

Perform the following steps to add app collaborators to the Heroku dashboard:

1. To add collaborators using the Heroku dashboard, you need to first log in to your Heroku account. Once you're logged in, you will see the listing of your Heroku apps, as shown in the following screenshot:

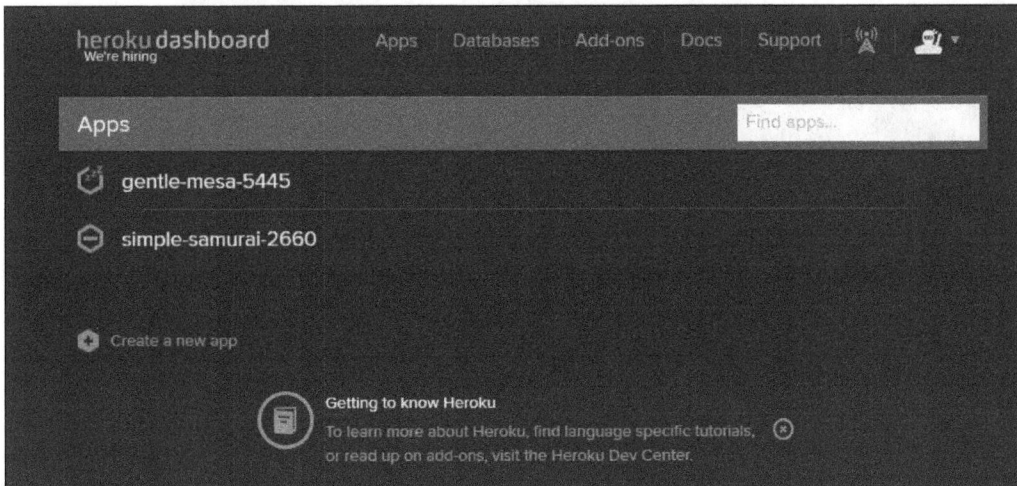

2. For each app that is displayed in the list, you will see a set of icons for various operations that can be done on the app. Click on the **Access** icon as shown in the following screenshot:

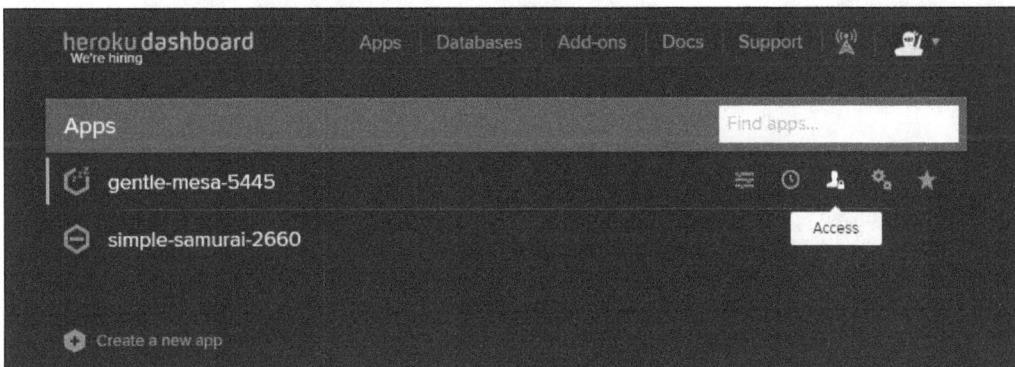

3. The following screen will display a list of users (owner and collaborators for this application). Additionally, you can add a new collaborator by sending an invitation via an e-mail:

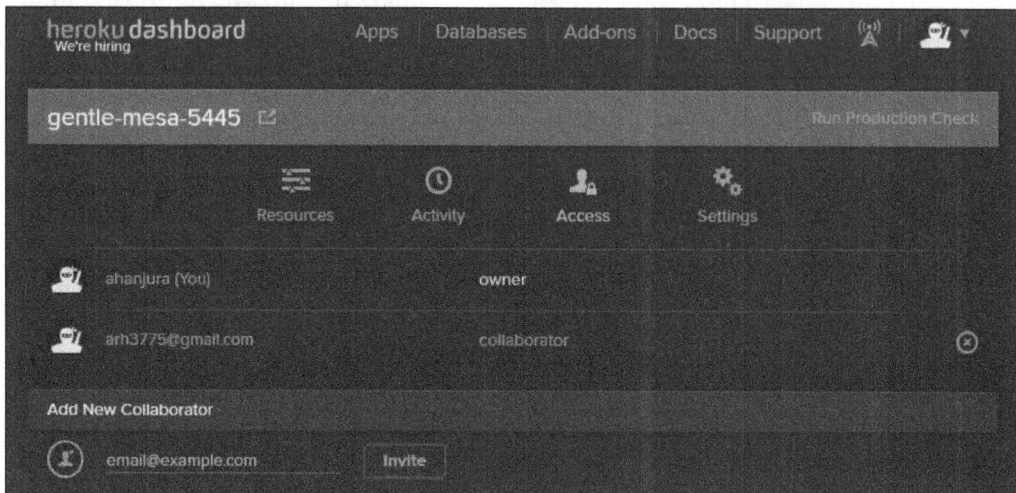

4. Add a collaborator by entering a valid e-mail address and clicking on **Invite**:

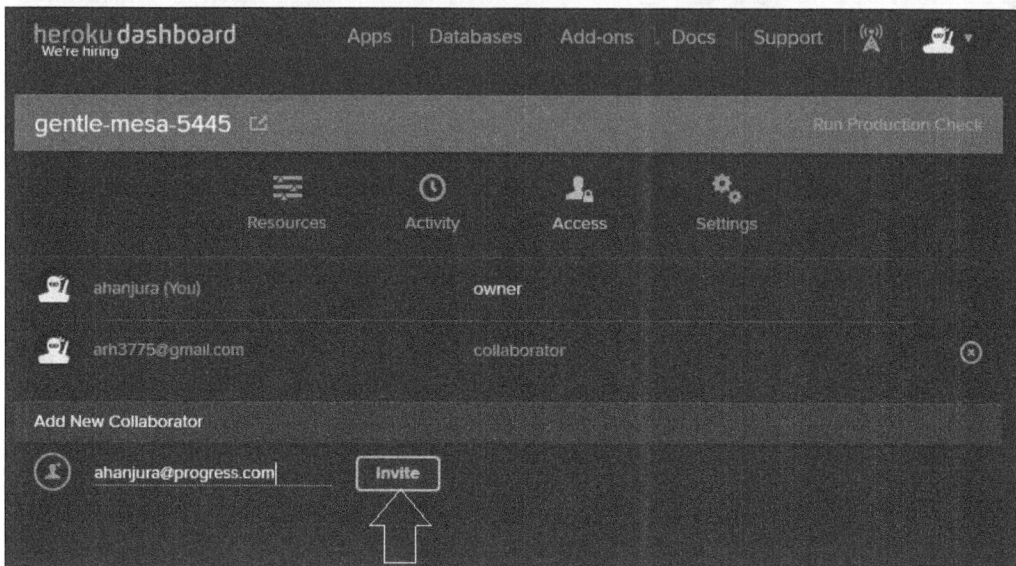

5. An e-mail is sent to the user who is added as a collaborator, informing the new user that he/she has been granted access to the app. If there is no existing Heroku account that matches the e-mail specified, an invitation e-mail is sent as shown in the following screenshot:

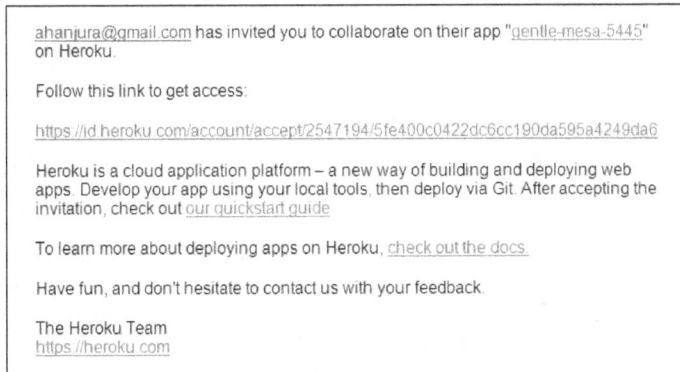

> ahanjura@gmail.com has invited you to collaborate on their app "gentle-mesa-5445" on Heroku.
>
> Follow this link to get access:
>
> https://id.heroku.com/account/accept/2547194/5fe400c0422dc6cc190da595a4249da6
>
> Heroku is a cloud application platform – a new way of building and deploying web apps. Develop your app using your local tools, then deploy via Git. After accepting the invitation, check out our quickstart guide.
>
> To learn more about deploying apps on Heroku, check out the docs.
>
> Have fun, and don't hesitate to contact us with your feedback.
>
> The Heroku Team
> https://heroku.com

The collaborator can click on the link sent via the e-mail and register for Heroku if the user does not already have a Heroku account.

6. The user is added to the collaborators list as shown in the following screenshot:

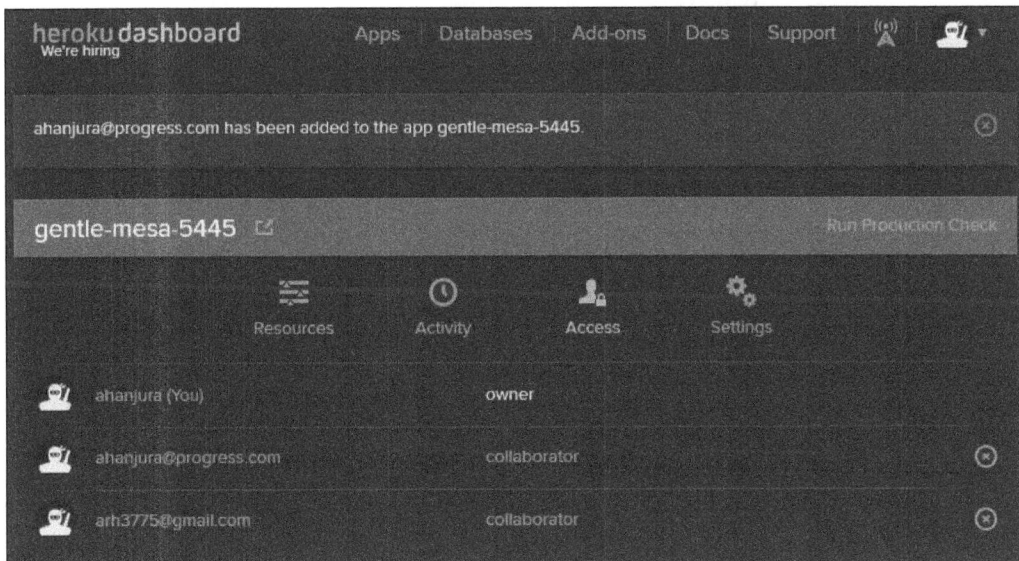

Deleting a collaborator

Deleting a collaborator can be done through the following steps:

1. Click on the cross mark to the extreme right of the collaborator's name as shown in the following screenshot:

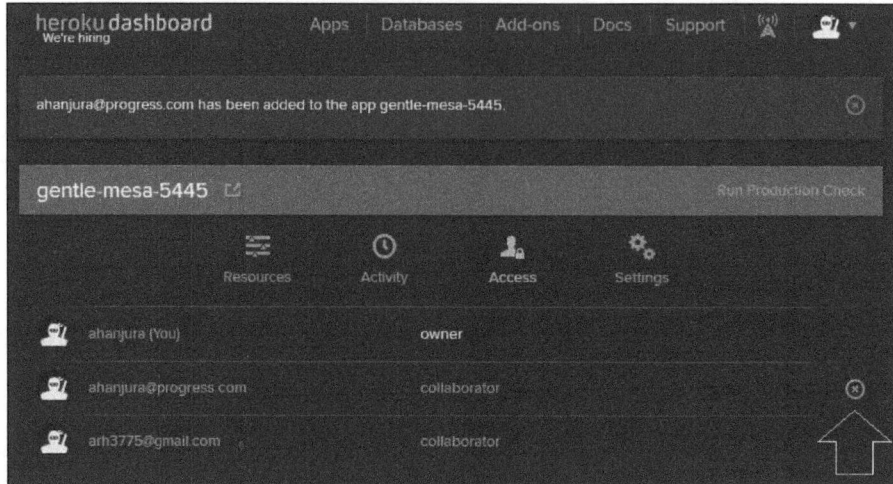

2. Click on the confirmation dialog box to remove the collaborator to complete the deletion operation:

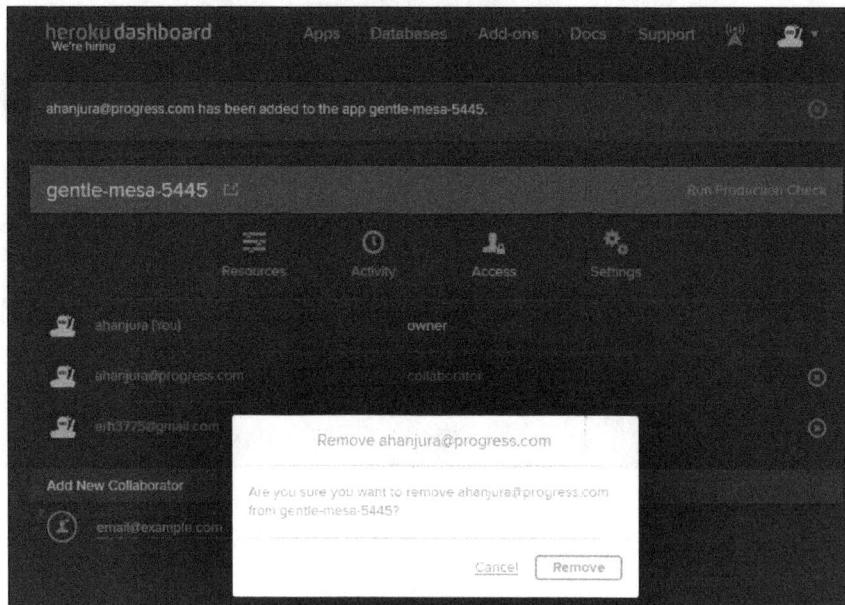

Adding collaborators via the Heroku CLI

You can add other developers to collaborate on your application using the
`sharing:add` command as follows:

```
$ heroku sharing:add johndoe@sampleapp.com
```

```
Adding johndoe@sampleapp.com to gentle-mesa-5445 collaborators...
done
```

The collaborator added in this process can perform all operations that a owner can,
except for a few that include adding or removing paid add-ons, deleting or renaming
an application, or viewing account invoices.

Listing collaborators

To list all the collaborators for an app, use the following `heroku sharing` command:

```
$ heroku sharing
```

```
=== sampleapp Collaborators
```

```
madana@sampleapp.com
```

```
johndoe@sampleapp.com
```

Removing a collaborator

To revoke a collaborator's access, use the following `heroku sharing:remove`
command:

```
$ heroku sharing:remove johndoe@sampleapp.com
```

```
Removing johndoe@sampleapp.com from gentle-mesa-5445 collaborators...
done
```

On successful revoking of the collaborator's access, the collaborator can no longer
deploy any code changes or change the application's configuration.

Collaborator actions

Once a collaborator is added to the app, the collaborator can perform multiple
operations on the app, including modifying the app itself and viewing the app
details. In this section, we look at the specific steps a collaborator can take to
modify the app and view its details.

Working on the app

Now that the collaborator has received access to the app, it is time to use the application. To use the application and modify it, the collaborator needs to perform the following:

1. Clone the app locally. Use the `heroku git:clone --app sampleapp` command to clone the app.

2. Alternatively, you can get access to the app owner's canonical repository and then use `heroku git:remote` to add a Git remote to your checkout.

3. Edit the source code.

4. Use `git push heroku` to deploy local commits. Make sure changes are updated to the app's canonical repository (using the `git push origin master` command) as well as to the remote created earlier. This is to avoid code synchronization issues with fellow collaborators.

5. If you get an error similar to the following one, there would be potential conflicts between the remote and your local repository outside of the changes you have done:

   ```
   $ git push heroku
   ```

   ```
   error: remote 'refs/heads/master' is not a strict subset of local
   ref 'refs/heads/master'.
   ```

   ```
   maybe you are not up-to-date and need to pull first?
   ```

6. Pull down the latest changes using the `git pull -rebase` command from the remote master, merge them with your code, and then try to push the code again.

Viewing the app

On gaining access to your app, a collaborator can verify the details of the app using the familiar `heroku info` command as follows:

```
$ heroku info --app sampleapp
=== sampleapp
Web URL:        http://sampleapp.herokuapp.com/
Git Repo:       git@heroku.com:sampleapp.git
Repo Size:      1024k
Slug Size:      512k
Owner Email:    owner@sampleapp.com
Collaborators:  madana@sampleapp.com
                johndoe@sampleapp.com
```

Summary

In this concluding chapter, we learned about some experimental features of the Heroku platform that help us build, deploy, and monitor our apps better. We explored Heroku's experimental support for a powerful, bidirectional communication protocol called Websockets—a natural choice for developing real-time web apps. We got an introduction to the use of Heroku Platform API to build Heroku apps programmatically. We also discussed the workings of collaboration on the Heroku platform, that is, how you can use the Heroku dashboard and/or the Heroku CLI to add your collaborators and share your app with them instantly.

This does not end our journey of Heroku. This is just the beginning. The demand for robust, scalable, and highly performant platforms as a service is bigger than ever. More and more providers are enabling developers to build faster apps using the latest cloud development tools. The fact that the developer platforms for the cloud are growing rapidly tells us that more innovation is on the way. New open source platforms such as Flynn (`www.flynn.io`) and an open source version of Heroku, Openruko (`https://github.com/openruko`), are also drawing a lot of contribution and developer attention. This book has attempted to familiarize the reader with how as a developer, you can leverage the capabilities of the Heroku platform and build robust, scalable, and performant web apps. Hopefully, it has met that need to a fair extent.

Index

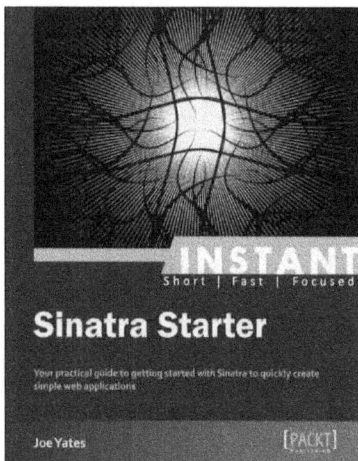

Instant Sinatra Starter

ISBN: 978-1-78216-821-8   Paperback: 70 pages

Your practical guide to getting started with Sinatra to quickly create simple web applications

1. Learn something new in an Instant! A short, fast, focused guide delivering immediate results.

2. Set up a Sinatra project.

3. Deploy your project to the Web.

4. Learn about the advanced features of Sinatra.

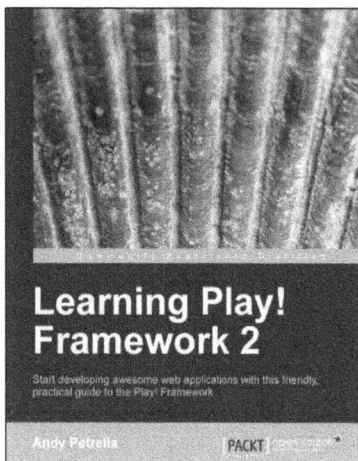

Learning Play! Framework 2

ISBN: 978-1-78216-012-0   Paperback: 290 pages

Start developing awesome web applications with this friendly, practical guide to the Play! Framework

1. While driving in Java, tasks are also presented in Scala – a great way to be introduced to this amazing language.

2. Create a fully-fledged, collaborative web application – starting from ground zero; all layers are presented in a pragmatic way.

3. Gain the advantages associated with developing a fully integrated web framework.

Please check **www.PacktPub.com** for information on our titles

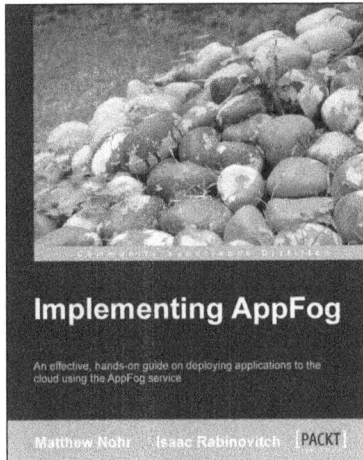

Implementing AppFog

ISBN: 978-1-84969-818-4   Paperback: 86 pages

An effective, hands-on guide on deploying applications to the cloud using the AppFog service

1. Create applications from scratch using the AppFog web console.

2. Learn the knack of deploying applications to the Cloud using AppFog.

3. Know the steps to avoid compatibility issues using the node module function of AppFog.

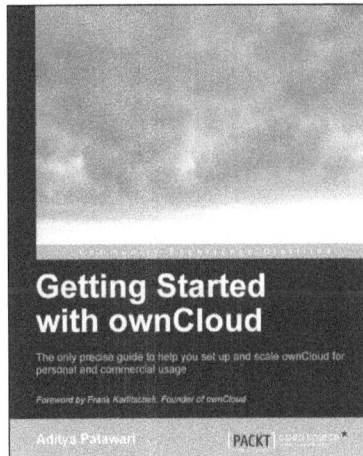

Getting Started with ownCloud

ISBN: 978-1-78216-825-6   Paperback: 134 pages

The only precise guide to help you set up and scale ownCloud for personal and commercial usage

1. Learn ownCloud User Management.

2. Scale ownCloud to support thousands of users.

3. Integrate user management systems such as LDAP.

Please check **www.PacktPub.com** for information on our titles